SMASHING
HTML5

PUBLISHER'S ACKNOWLEDGMENTS

Some of the people who helped bring this book to market include the following:

Editorial and Production
VP Consumer and Technology Publishing Director: Michelle Leete
Associate Director–Book Content Management: Martin Tribe
Associate Publisher: Chris Webb
Publishing Assistant: Ellie Scott
Development Editor: Elizabeth Kuball
Copy Editor: Elizabeth Kuball
Technical Editor: Harvey Chute
Editorial Manager: Jodi Jensen
Senior Project Editor: Sara Shlaer
Editorial Assistant: Leslie Saxman

Marketing
Senior Marketing Manager: Louise Breinholt
Marketing Executive: Kate Parrett

Composition Services
Compositor: Wiley Composition Services
Proofreader: Susan Hobbs
Indexer: Potomac Indexing, LLC

SMASHING
HTML5

Bill Sanders

A John Wiley and Sons, Ltd, Publication

This edition first published 2011
© 2011 William B. Sanders.

Registered office
John Wiley & Sons Ltd, The Atrium, Southern Gate, Chichester, West Sussex, PO19 8SQ,
United Kingdom

For details of our global editorial offices, for customer services and for information about
how to apply for permission to reuse the copyright material in this book please see our
website at www.wiley.com.

Wiley also publishes its books in a variety of electronic formats. Some content that
appears in print may not be available in electronic books.

Designations used by companies to distinguish their products are often claimed as
trademarks. All brand names and product names used in this book are trade names,
service marks, trademarks or registered trademarks of their respective owners. The
publisher is not associated with any product or vendor mentioned in this book. This
publication is designed to provide accurate and authoritative information in regard to
the subject matter covered. It is sold on the understanding that the publisher is not
engaged in rendering professional services. If professional advice or other expert
assistance is required, the services of a competent professional should be sought.

A catalogue record for this book is available from the British Library.

978-0-470-97727-9

Set in 10/12 Minion Pro by Wiley Composition Services
Printed in the United States by Krehbiel

This book is dedicated to Jacob Sanders.

Author's Acknowledgments

I became aware of the immediate importance of HTML5 thanks to Michael Wilson, Zach Dunn, and Nick Greenfield, who brought it to my attention. They also introduced me to *Smashing Magazine* and a number of other emerging new trends. Chris Webb of Wiley guided the direction of the book and, in concert with Margot Hutchinson of Waterside Productions, was able to clear a path for the book to move ahead. Ellie Scott of Wiley helped take care of the many details necessary in forging the book's inception. Elizabeth Kuball worked as an able editor to clarify and smoothen everything I wrote, and Harvey Chute, the technical editor, worked to make sure that all the code was done correctly and offered suggestions for improvement. Finally, my colleagues at the University of Hartford's Multimedia Web Design and Development program, John Gray and Brian Dorn, helped when asked, including one terrible moment when a missing semicolon wrecked havoc on a program.

About the Author

Bill Sanders is one of the founding faulty members of the University of Hartford's Multimedia Web Design and Development program where he teaches courses covering HTML5, information and interface design, CSS3, Flash, ActionScript 3.0, ASP.NET, C#, PHP, and streaming video. He has written numerous books on Internet computing, on topics ranging from JavaScript to ActionScript 3.0 Design Patterns. He lives in rural Connecticut with his wife, Delia, and one and a half dogs.

Contents

IX

X

Introduction

In 1992, I was stumbling the Internet (we used to stumble prior to surfing) with a program using the Gopher protocol. From El Paso, Texas, I was able to look up the train schedule between London and Cambridge in England. At the time, it was like a miracle. Here I was in West Texas with a London-Cambridge train schedule. Unbelievable!

Shortly after that time when I didn't think it could get any better than Gopher on the Internet, up popped the Mosaic browser and the World Wide Web. Netscape Navigator soon supplanted Mosaic, and I discovered HTML. Now I was able to see graphics and text plus I could link to other Web pages. In short order, I worked out how to create my own Web pages using a text editor and the new markup language, HTML. Some of the guys in computer services set up a host for me, and I was in business.

For a while, it seemed that a new version of HTML was coming out every year or so. CSS and JavaScript were introduced and more and more browsers became available. It just kept getting better and better, but after HTML4 (in its many forms, including XHTML), things seemed to stagnate. This HTML Dark Ages lasted from about 2000 to 2008. Then the World Wide Web Consortium (W3C) published the HTML5 Working Draft in 2008. However, after publication of the HTML5 standards in a draft format, everything was back to a crawl as far as getting my hands on an HTML5 browser. The team developing the standards has been methodical in the development process and was planning on implementing the final draft of the standards in browsers in 2012!

Then one day in 2009 or 2010, I read about a beta version of a browser that supported HTML5, or at least some of its features. By 2010, several browsers were supporting HTML5, including browsers made for mobile devices. Online blogs like `www.smashingmagazine.com` were publishing posts about HTML5 and so, ready or not, HTML5 was here! Somehow HTML5 has escaped from the zoo, and the race was on to produce HTML5 browsers. We have officially entered the HTML Renaissance Period. The excitement is back!

HTML5 is so big that I had to select a focus that would encompass the essence of the markup language without devolving into a mere reference or encyclopedia attempting to touch on everything and explain nothing. Naturally, the new features were going to be a major focal point, but they exist in the context of a host of other tags, and readers learning HTML for the first time need foundational elements. Also, I had to drop the discontinued elements like a bad habit and show how the continued and new elements work in concert. Further, CSS3 and JavaScript play an important role, but they're only introduced insofar as they relate to HTML5. (Smashing JavaScript and Smashing CSS cover these important features in detail.) So I've divided Smashing HTML5 into four parts that bring together the heart and soul of HTML5.

PART I: THE LANGUAGE OF THE WEB

The first part of the book starts off looking at the different browsers available for HTML5—including mobile browsers—and gives you a handle on where to start working with this newest version of HTML. It also deals with the details of working with different file types and getting organized so that creating Web pages and sites is an orderly process. It explains how to use HTML5 tags (elements) and the different attributes and values that can be assigned to tags. Also, you learn how to get going with CSS3. At the end of the first part, you learn about using color and different color codes with HTML5 and how to put together color schemes to enhance any site.

PART II: PAGES, SITES, AND DESIGNS

The second part looks at the bigger picture of creating Web page and Web sites. At one time, designers and developers just needed to concern themselves with how a page appeared on a computer screen—as screen real estate expanded to monitors reminiscent of drive-in theater screens. Suddenly, users with mobile devices were looking at Web pages, and design strategies had to be reformulated to include mobile users. Throughout the book, you'll see Web pages presented in mobile configurations for devices like the iPhone and Droid. So, expect to see screenshots of Windows 7 and Macintosh OS X browsers interspersed with screenshots taken on mobile devices displayed in Mini Opera and mobile Safari browsers—as well as other new mobile browsers you didn't even know existed. It's not your father's Web! (It's not even your older sister's Web anymore.)

PART III: MEDIA IN HTML5

Only one of the three chapters in this part deals with media that was available in earlier versions of HTML—Chapter 9, on images. The other two chapters deal with audio and video, both new to HTML5. In addition to the general types of media, HTML5 brings with it different decisions about media formats. Several of the video formats are relatively new and were developed for use on the Web in a number of versions. Not all HTML5 browsers use the same video formats, but, fortunately, HTML5 has structures whereby it can check the video formats until it finds one that will run on a given browser. In addition to the new elements for audio and video come several new attributes and values available to optimize media on the Web, and I cover these attributes and values in this part.

PART IV: DYNAMIC HTML5 TAGS PLUS A LITTLE JAVASCRIPT AND PHP

One of the most anticipated features of HTML5 has been the `canvas` element. However, in order to get the most out of `canvas`, you need both JavaScript and CSS3. So, in this part, you learn enough JavaScript with the HTML5 Document Object Model (DOM) to work effectively with canvas and CSS3. Likewise, HTML5 brought with it several new form attributes, but as with most forms, they need help for processing the information. Using JavaScript, you'll learn how form data can be saved with the new storage objects in HTML5. Also, you'll learn how to use PHP to process information entered in HTML5 forms so that you can automatically send and receive e-mails via the Web. Also, I take a look at the new `geolocation` objects and their properties and show you how you can have your Web page automatically load a map based on your current latitude and longitude coordinates. You'll find Part IV full of new materials that will add many new features to your site.

THE LANGUAGE OF THE WEB

1

INTRODUCING HTML5

THIS CHAPTER IS a general overview of what's new, what's the same and what's been removed from HTML that makes HTML5. At this time, one of the most important tasks is to find out which browsers work with HTML5, which ones are in development that promise HTML5 compatibility and how each has started to implement HTML5. Also, you'll want to learn about some of the new browsers that are specifically developed for mobile devices, so you can test HTML5 pages on your mobile device, too. To get started, download all the HTML5 browsers (covered in this chapter) so that you can learn what users will see when they encounter an HTML5 Web page that you've created.

CREATING WITH TAGS: AN OVERVIEW

Most of the content on the Internet is created with HyperText Markup Language (HTML). You may be surprised to learn that several applications you use every day — for example, your word processor — also were created with markup languages. However, like all computer languages, with HTML, all you see is the content, not the underlying language. The language works like the frame of a building — you know it's there underneath all that paint and drywall, but you can't see it. In this book, I make the language of HTML very visible and show you how to use it to build your own structures.

If you're familiar with previous versions of HTML and XHTML, you'll be able to transfer the bulk of your knowledge to HTML5. And if you're brand-new to working with HTML, you'll find HTML5 quite simple. Essentially, all you have to do is place your content between an opening tag and a closing tag, called a container, and the container will style your text or display your graphics and media on the Web page. Figure 1-1 illustrates containers:

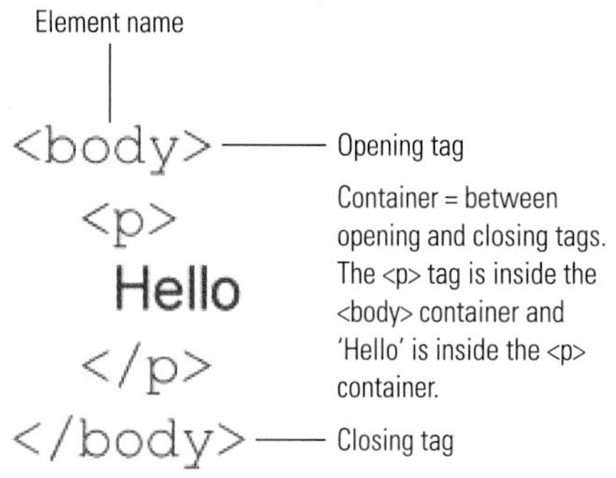

```
Element name
    |

<body> ———— Opening tag

    <p>            Container = between
                   opening and closing tags.
    Hello          The <p> tag is inside the
                   <body> container and
    </p>           'Hello' is inside the <p>
                   container.
</body> ———— Closing tag
```

Figure 1-1: Containers in HTML5.

For example, the following line,

```
<h1>This is big text.</h1>
```

tells the interpreter in your browser to create big text that looks like this:

This is big text.

The text inside the arrow brackets < > is the code. In this case, h1 is the code for big text. The arrow brackets tell where to begin the container (<h1>) and where to end the container (</h1>). Everything inside the container is configured to the size and style of the tag, which is either built into the tag or created using CSS3.

While we're getting started here, you can have a little fun creating and viewing some HTML5 with little examples. All you have to do is type any of the code provided in this chapter in a text editor such as Notepad if you're running Windows or TextEdit if you're on a Mac. Save the file with the extension .html, and then open it in an HTML5 browser. To open a Web page, just start your browser and then, from the menu bar, select File → Open File (or Open), and locate the filename. (You can just double-click the file icon on the desktop to open most HTML files.)

INCORPORATING THE NEW HTML5 ELEMENTS

A tag is made up of an element and attributes. The tag is identified by its element, such as `<h1>` — h1 is the element. When we speak of a tag, we're usually referring to its element, but actually a tag is its element and attributes. Attributes are the different characteristics or properties of an element that you can code to change features of the content in the tag's container. For now, I'm just going to deal with the element, so I'll use the terms *tag* and *element* interchangeably.

To give you a sense of the new elements in HTML5, Table 1.1 shows all the new elements, along with a brief description of each. Later in this book, I give lots of examples and explain how to use these elements.

Table 1.1   New Elements in HTML5

New Element	Description
`<article>`	Self-contained composition in document
`<aside>`	Content tangentially related to content of the article
`<audio>`	Sound content container
`<canvas>`	Graphic development container
`<command>`	A command that the user can invoke
`<datalist>`	List generator when used with the `<input>` element and its new list attribute
`<details>`	Discloses details of an element
`<embed>`	External interactive plug-in or content
`<figcaption>`	Caption tag for the figure element
`<figure>`	Contains a group of media content and their caption
`<footer>`	Container for a footer for a section or page
`<header>`	Container for header for a section or page
`<hgroup>`	A heading of a section with multiple h1 to h6 elements in a document
`<keygen>`	The key pair generator control representation.
`<mark>`	A string of text in one document, marked or highlighted for reference in another document

continued

Table 1.1   (continued)

New Element	Description
<meter>	Container for a known range of values (for example, disk use)
<nav>	Representation of a section of a document intended for navigation
<output>	Defines the progress of a task of any kind
<progress>	Representation of the progress made in a task (such as percentage complete in a download operation)
<rp>	Indicator in Ruby (a programming language) annotations to define what to show browsers that don't support the <ruby> element
<rt>	Marks the ruby text component of a ruby annotation
<ruby>	Element for spans with ruby annotations
<section>	Theme identifier for content grouping
<source>	Container for multiple specification of media resources
<summary>	Information on a <details> element
<time>	Container for a date/time
<video>	Element for linking to a video file
<wbr>	Representation of a line break opportunity to guide the hyphenation of long words or text strings

Some of the new elements, like <video> and <audio> add multimedia to HTML and represent a major new capacity to HTML. Others, like <ruby>, are quite specialized, and unless you need certain East Asian characters, you're unlikely to use that element.

One characteristic of many of the new tags is that they work in conjunction with CSS3 or JavaScript. However, most of the new elements still work on their own, without any added help. When adding a style or some of the cooler features, you may find yourself using a bit of CSS3 or JavaScript, but you don't have to learn the entire JavaScript language or even CSS3 to have some fun with it.

For example, the following script uses the new <datalist> element that has not been available in earlier versions of HTML. Enter the following code in a text editor, save it as Datalist.html, open it in your Web browser, and you'll see how it assists users in entering data. (You can find Datalist.html in this chapter's folder at www.wiley.com/go/smashinghtml5.)

```
<!DOCTYPE HTML>
<html>
<head>
```

```
<meta http-equiv="Content-Type" content="text/html; charset=UTF-8">
<title>Datalist</title>
</head>
<body>
<p>
  <label> Which of the following would you like to learn?<br />
    <input type="text" name="web" list="lang">
    <datalist id="lang">
      <option value="HTML5">
      <option value="JavaScript">
      <option value="jQuery">
      <option value="ActionScript 3.0">
      <option value="Java">
    </datalist>
  </label>
  <br />
</p>
</body>
</html>
```

When you open the file in an Opera browser, you'll be given a list of input options, as shown in Figure 1-2.

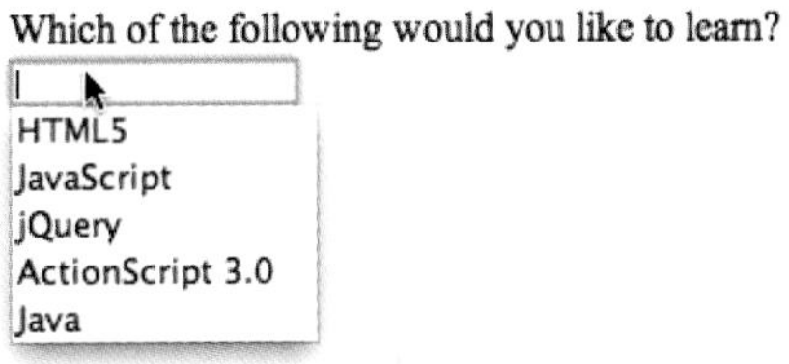

Figure 1-2: Using the `<datalist>` tag in an Opera browser.

Unlike earlier versions of HTML, in which text input didn't show the user an options list, this one does.

USING CONTINUED TAGS FROM HTML4

Even if you're familiar with HTML4 (or earlier versions of HTML), you'll be surprised by the number of HTML elements you may not know how to use or may not have even heard of before. For example, what's the <q> tag? When is it used? If you're new to HTML, don't try to remember all of the elements in Table 1.2, but go over them to get a general sense of the available tags and a little about their description.

Table 1.2   Continued Tags from Previous HTML Versions

Continued Tags	Description
`<!--...-->`	A comment
`<!DOCTYPE>`	The document type (only one in HTML5)
`<a>`	Hyperlink to a page or page area
`<abbr>`	An abbreviation
`<address>`	Container for an address
`<area>`	An area inside an image map
`<b>`	Bold text
`<base>`	A base URL for all the links in a page
`<bdo>`	Direction of text display
`<blockquote>`	A block of text
`<body>`	Beginning a body element
` `	A single line break
`<button>`	A clickable button
`<caption>`	A table caption
`<cite>`	Container for a citation
`<code>`	Format for computer code text
`<col>`	Defines attributes for table columns
`<colgroup>`	Container for groups of table columns
`<dd>`	Container for a value for the `<dt>` element
`<del>`	Container for deleted text
`<dfn>`	Representation of the defining instance of term
`<div>`	Demarcation of division in a document
`<dl>`	Head for an association list
`<dt>`	Specification for a name in name-value group (description list)
`<em>`	Emphasized text
`<fieldset>`	Container for a set of form controls
`<form>`	Container for a form typically with input elements
`<h1>` to `<h6>`	Text header 1 to header 6
`<head>`	Container for the first code to be interpreted by browser
`<hr>`	Horizontal rule (line)

Continued Tags	Description
`<html>`	Container for an HTML document
`<i>`	Italic text
`<iframe>`	Frame an inline sub window
`<img>`	Image container
`<input>`	User-input field within a form container
`<ins>`	Container for inserted text within implied paragraph boundaries
`<kbd>`	Container for user keyboard input
`<label>`	Representation of a caption in a user interface
`<legend>`	Title in a fieldset border
`<li>`	List item indicator
`<link>`	A resource reference (for example, CSS)
`<map>`	Image map container
`<mark>`	Text in one context marked for text in different context
`<menu>`	Container for a list of commands
`<meta>`	Container for meta information
`<object>`	Container for embedded object (for example, a SWF file)
`<ol>`	A numbered (ordered) list
`<optgroup>`	An option grouping header in an options list
`<option>`	Container for individual options in a drop-down list
`<p>`	A paragraph block
`<param>`	Plug-in parameters
`<pre>`	Preformatted text format
`<q>`	Enclosed text with quotation marks
`<samp>`	Computer code output or snippet
`<script>`	Container for script for CSS, JavaScript, or another recognized script
`<select>`	A selectable list
`<small>`	Small text
`<span>`	Inline section in a document
`<strong>`	Strong text that looks like bold
`<style>`	Container for a style definition

13

continued

Table 1.2   (continued)

Continued Tags	Description
<sub>	Subscripted text
<sup>	Superscripted text
<table>	A table definition
<tbody>	Demarcation for a block of rows for a table's body
<td>	A table cell
<textarea>	A text area container
<tfoot>	Representation for a block of rows of column summaries for a table
<th>	Table header format
<thead>	Representation of a block of rows of column summaries for a table header
<title>	The document title
<tr>	Demarcation of a table row
<ul>	An unordered list (a bullet list)
<var>	Variable style in formula

Most of the elements with the same names from HTML4 are the same in every way in HTML5, but some have slightly modified meanings. Also, rules for some tags have changed. For example, in creating tables, the tag for specifying a row <tr> no longer requires a closing </tr> tag. Some attributes for elements have changed as well. As you continue to learn about the new features of HTML5, you'll find that many of the "old" elements have lots of new characteristics. The following HTML table script provides a new example with old elements. Enter this text into your text editor, save it as NewOldTable.html, and open it in an Opera browser.

```
<!DOCTYPE HTML>
<html>
<head>
<meta http-equiv="Content-Type" content="text/html; charset=UTF-8">
<title>Table</title>
</head>
<body>
<table>
  <caption>
  =Element Types=
  </caption>
  <thead>
```

```
    <tr>
      <th> Type
      <th> Text
      <th> Graphics
  <tbody>
    <tr>
      <th> UI
      <td> text input
      <td> button
    <tr>
      <th> Links
      <td> underlined
      <td> icon
</table>
</body>
</html>
```

Figure 1-3 shows what your table looks like.

=Element Types=

Type   Text   Graphics

UI text input button

Links underlined icon

Figure 1-3: A table created with HTML5.

Generally, you don't use tables for formatting text. Instead, tables are used for formatting data — such as data that's loaded from a database or created dynamically by another program like JavaScript. In HTML5, though, tables used in conjunction with CSS3 do a bit more formatting than in previous versions of HTML and CSS.

FORGETTING OR REPLACING DISCONTINUED TAGS

This final set of tags (see Table 1.3) is for anyone familiar with HTML4 and earlier versions of HTML. The following tags have been discontinued, either because they posed certain problems or were replaced by other structures that better handled what they used to do.

If you're new to HTML, you can look at these to get an idea of what to avoid. In working with HTML, you find many samples on the Web, and you're likely to incorporate them into your own code. However, because HTML5 is so new, you'll find that most of the HTML was created with earlier versions that may have obsolete tags, and you'll want to replace them with the newer structures.

Table 1.3   Discontinued Tags

Deleted Tags	Removed or Replaced
`<acronym>`	Replaced by `<abbr>`
`<applet>`	Replaced by `<object>`
`<basefont>`	Better handled by CSS
`<bgsound>`	Replaced by `<audio>`
`<big>`	Better handled by CSS
`<blink>`	Removed in HTML5
`<center>`	Better handled by CSS
`<dir>`	Replaced by `<ul>`
`<font>`	Removed in HTML5
`<frame>`	Removed in HTML5
`<frameset>`	Removed in HTML5
`<isindex>`	Replaced by explicit `<form>`
`<marquee>`	Removed in HTML5
`<multicol>`	Removed in HTML5
`<nobr>`	Removed in HTML5
`<noframes>`	Removed in HTML5
`<noscript>`	Only conforming to HTML syntax
`<s>`	Better handled by CSS
`<spacer>`	Removed in HTML5
`<strike>`	Better handled by CSS
`<tt>`	Better handled by CSS
`<u>`	Better handled by CSS

One of the most common discontinued tags is `<center>`, but you can easily center text using a little CSS, as shown in the following example. Type this text into your text editor, save it as `CenterMe.html`, and open it in your Web browser.

```
<!DOCTYPE HTML>
<html>
<head>
<style type="text/css">
h1 {
    text-align:center;
}
```

```
</style>
<meta http-equiv="Content-Type" content="text/html; charset=UTF-8">
<title>Center with CSS</title>
</head>
<body>
<h1>Headers Can Be Centered</h1>
</body>
</html>
```

All you're going to see when you test the code in your browser is:

Headers Can Be Centered

It may look like a lot of work to get a simple centered header, but pages are generally short, and you can center any header with an <h1> tag because you've changed the behavior of the tag. You can change any tag you want with CSS. (You'll learn about CSS3 in Chapter 3, but you've already used it if you see the header in the middle of your page.)

CHOOSING A BROWSER TO INTERPRET HTML5

If you want to start a lively discussion with other HTML5 developers, just ask, "What's the best browser?" You should be most concerned with what browser those who will be viewing your Web site use — not which browser other developers use. In general, developers use the best browser until another best browser comes along, so they may actually use more advanced and better browsers than the average Web user. If you want the people who visit your site to have the best experience possible, try to find out what browser they're most likely to use. An even better idea when developing software for yourself or a client is to test your Web pages on all major browsers and on at least the two major platforms — Macintosh and Windows. The major browser developers also make browsers for the Linux OS, but very few people use their Linux box for browsing the Web.

In looking at the major browsers that support HTML5, most can be used either by Windows or by Macintosh operating systems, but sometimes a browser will require a newer OS. So if you have an older system, be sure that the requirements for the browser you use work with your OS.

Several years ago, Microsoft quit making Internet Explorer (IE) for the Macintosh. However, Apple does make a version of its browser, Safari, for Windows. Three browser developers — Google, Mozilla, and Opera — do not make operating systems for computers but make browsers. In this section, I review Firefox, Chrome, Opera, Safari, and IE9.

Keep in mind that browsers' features change all the time. What's here is current as of this writing, but it may have changed by the time you read it.

MOZILLA FIREFOX

Mozilla has its roots in the original browser by Netscape called Netscape Navigator, which was introduced in the early 1990s. It featured a mascot resembling the movie creature Godzilla. Mosaic was a browser developed at the University of Illinois; it later became Netscape Navigator. The combination of Mosaic and Godzilla resulted in Mozilla, which is currently a nonprofit company, the Mozilla Foundation. Firefox is Mozilla's primary browser that supports HTML5.

Besides supporting both Windows and Macintosh operating systems, Firefox also supports the Linux operating system. Linux is not considered a primary OS for home computers, but it is for servers. Firefox is available free for all the supported operating systems. Figure 1-4 shows a screenshot of an HTML5 application in Firefox.

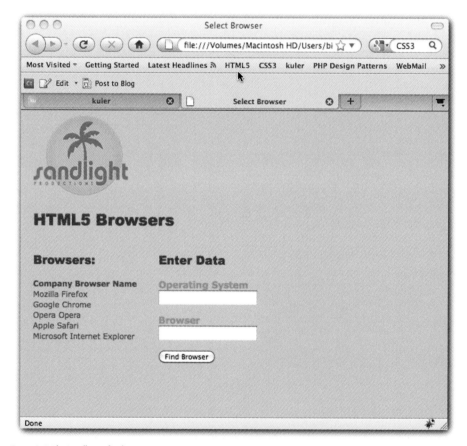

Figure 1-4: The Mozilla Firefox browser.

Notice that in the URL window (the window where you put the HTML address) the reference is to `file:///Volumes/Macintosh HD/` instead of an `http://` address. That's because the page is sitting on the computer's desktop. Also, you'll find that things looks differently if displayed in a Windows environment than they do in a Macintosh one — even for the same browser. (The example page is just for illustration and does not select browsers for you.)

GOOGLE CHROME

Google, famous for its search engine and maps, created its browser, Chrome, from the ground up with HTML5 in mind. It has browsers for Apple, Windows, and Linux operating systems — all available for free. Figure 1-5 shows the same exact Web page on the same computer as Figure 1-4 — see if you can detect the differences.

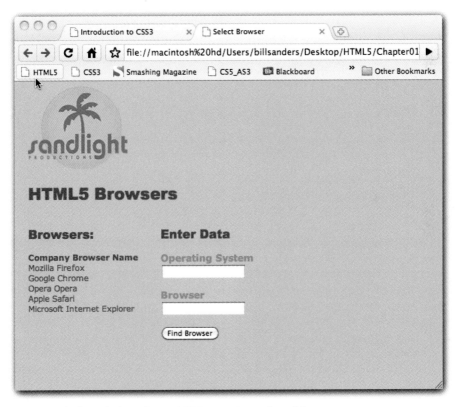

Figure 1-5: Google Chrome displaying the same HTML5 page as shown in Figure 1-4.

Other than the different styles of the two browsers, it can be difficult to see the differences in the page. With a simple page, subtle differences won't affect how your Web page looks. However, as your pages get bigger and more complex, small differences can grow.

One Web page development tool, Adobe Browserlab (`https://browserlab.adobe.com`) lets you see how a Web page looks in different browsers at the same time. Browserlab can be run directly from Adobe Dreamweaver CS5, or you can visit the Adobe Browserlab Web page. To get a little more dramatic difference, let's compare the sample Web page in Firefox on a Macintosh with one in Windows 7 running Google Chrome. Figure 1-6 shows what the side-by-side comparison looks like. (Graphics are not displayed.)

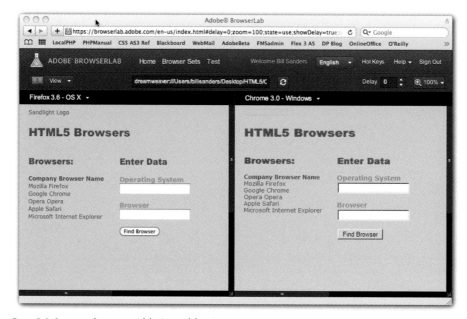

Figure 1-6: Comparing browsers in Adobe Browserlab.

Part of the difference is due to the ways in which Windows and the Macintosh operating systems display text and user interfaces (UIs). Another view that Browserlab provides is called an onionskin; it superimposes one over the other and you can see more precisely where text and UIs appear. Figure 1-7 shows this difference.

The blurrier an onionskin appears, the greater the differences in the way the Web page materials are rendered. In Figure 1-6, you can see that the view is very blurry, indicating that some key differences exist between the browsers and operating systems.

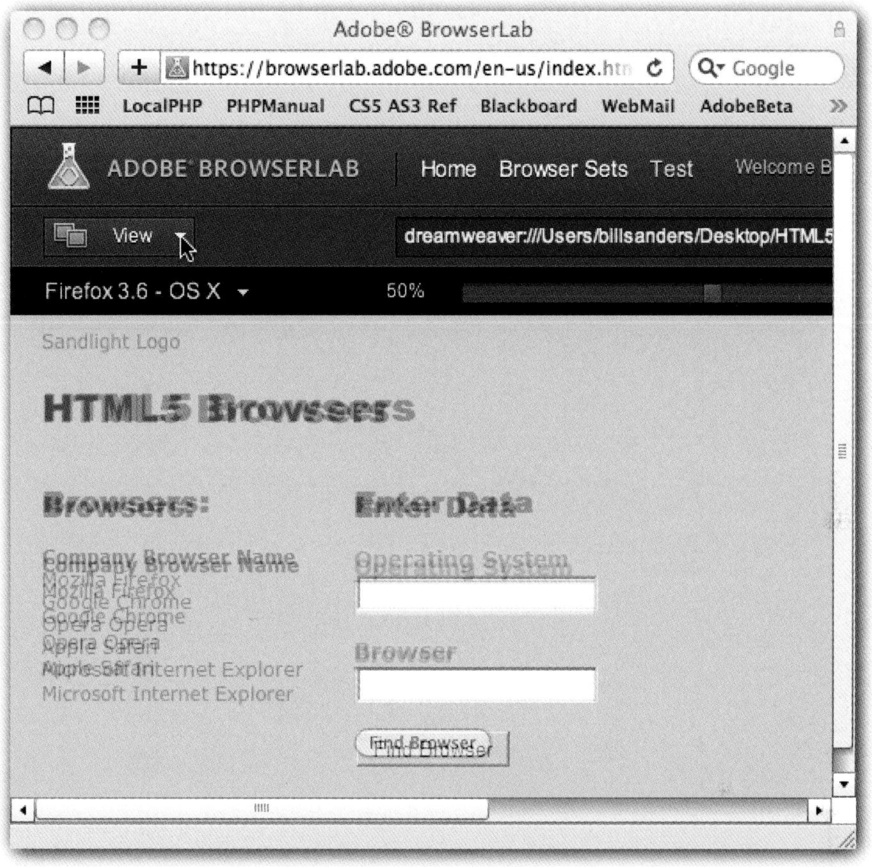

Figure 1-7: An onionskin view of superimposed browsers.

OPERA

When I was examining the Opera browser at the time of initially testing the different browsers, it seemed to have the best HTML5 features actually working. Plus, Opera has a special browser, Opera Mini 5, that you can download free for your mobile devices. HTML5 works fine on mobile devices, as you can see in Figure 1-8, which displays the sample Web page on an iPhone using Opera's mobile browser.

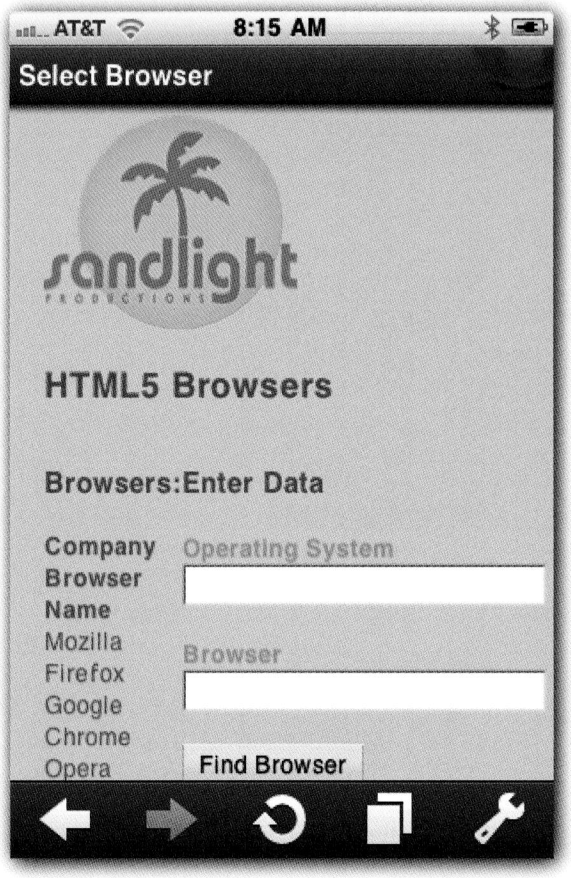

Figure 1-8: Opera Mini 5 browser.

Full-size Opera browsers are available for Windows, Macintosh, and Linux operating systems as well. When creating Web pages, you should plan for different size devices. As you can see, the sample application we've been using can fully fit in a mobile device as well as on large screens.

APPLE SAFARI

Apple makes Safari browsers for Macintosh and Windows as well as for mobile devices. For comparative purposes, Figure 1-9 shows how the sample application looks on Apple's Mobile Safari, developed for the iPhone. Compare this with Opera Mini 5 in Figure 1-8.

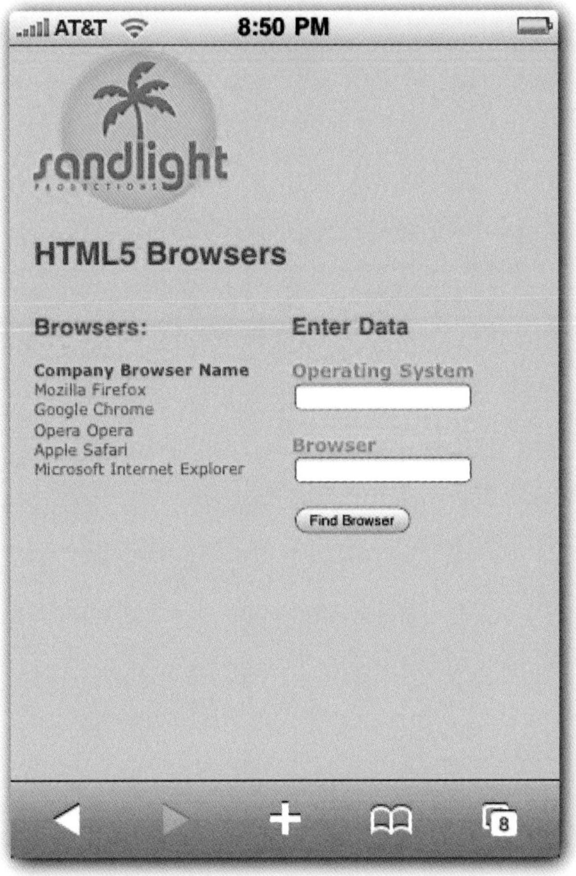

Figure 1-9: The Mobile Safari browser.

Just as there are few differences between the appearances of the Web pages as viewed on a desktop or laptop computer, you shouldn't see many differences between what different browsers show on mobile devices. That's a good thing! Web developers waste a good deal of time trying to make sure that all their pages look the same on different browsers and platforms. With a common implementation of HTML5, that shouldn't be a problem. Other unique features on browsers, such as having tabs, or other characteristics that make Web browsing easier, are fine as long as the browser's implementation of HTML5 is implemented according to the specifications defined by the World Wide Web Consortium (W3C).

MICROSOFT INTERNET EXPLORER 9

At the time of this writing, Internet Explorer 9 (IE9) was still in beta stage. According to Microsoft, its IE9 browser will be fully compliant with HTML5 standards. Where possible, throughout this book, I've included examples showing the IE9 at work with HTML5 Web pages using the IE9 beta browser. Figure 1-10 shows the test page in the IE9 beta browser.

Figure 1-10: Internet Explorer 9.

PREVIEWING DIFFERENT DISPLAYS

As you've seen, Web pages can be viewed on a number of different browsers and operating systems. Web developers need to consider the characteristics of the devices that their pages are to be viewed on, such as a desktop computer or a mobile phone. Suppose you develop for an iPhone and iPad (or some other mobile device and tablet); if you can preview your work side by side, you're better able to make comparisons. Adobe Dreamweaver, a Web page development tool, allows the developer to view multiple dimensions simultaneously, as shown in Figure 1-11.

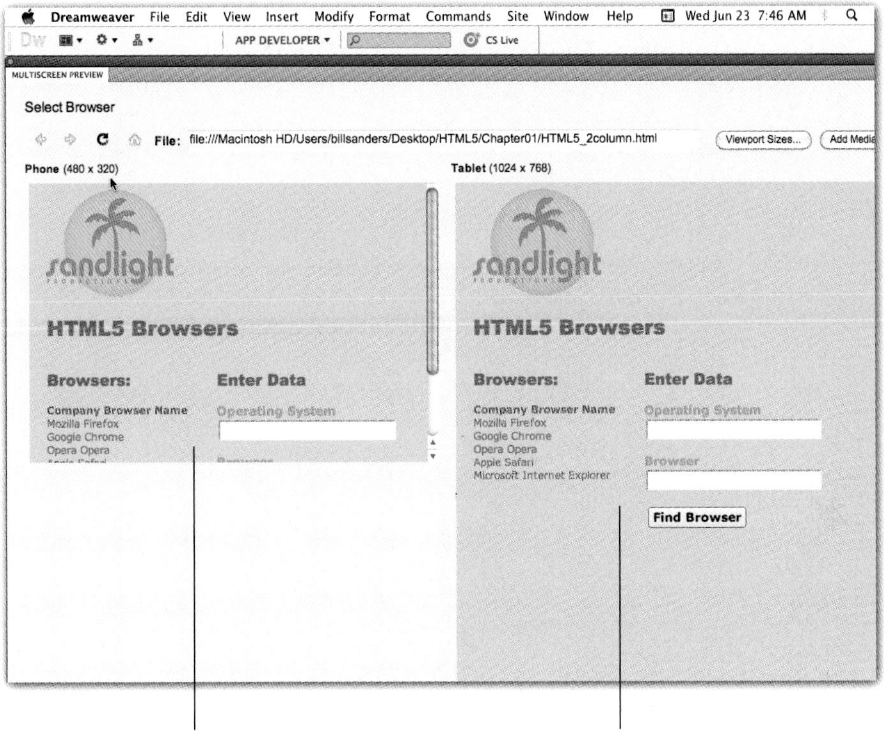

Phone set for iPhone: 480 x 320   Table set for iPad: 1024 x 768

Figure 1-11: Multiscreen preview in Adobe Dreamweaver.

You can change the device dimensions. For example, a Motorola Droid displays an 854 x 480 screen and a Sony VAIO UX displays a 1024 x 600 screen. The multiscreen preview helps you decide how to set up your page to optimize it for your viewers. Finding the best compromise is an art and one that can be made less onerous by knowing as much as possible about your audience and the devices they're likely to use to view your materials.

TAKE THE WHEEL

To get started, this first example lets you add some information about yourself. Don't worry about understanding everything (or anything!) unless you have some background in HTML. Just substitute things about yourself in the areas marked with double equal signs. Save the page to your computer using the name `wheel1.html`. (You can find `wheel1.html` in this chapter's folder at `www.wiley.com/go/smashinghtml5`.)

```
<!DOCTYPE HTML>
<html>
<meta http-equiv="Content-Type" content="text/html; charset=UTF-8">
```

```
<head>
<style type="text/css">
body {
     background-color:blanchedAlmond;
     color:saddleBrown;
     font-family:Verdana, Geneva, sans-serif;
     font-size:12px;
     margin-left:20px;
}
h1, h2 {
     font-family:"Arial Black", Gadget, sans-serif;
     color:midnightBlue;
}
h1 {
     text-align:center;
}
h3 {
     background-color:goldenrod;
     color:ghostwhite;
     font-size:11px;
     font-family:"Arial";
}
</style>
<title>The Wheel</title>
</head>
<body>
<h1> ==Your Name== : The Mighty HTML5 Web Developer</h1>
<h2> ==Your Company Name== provides full Web services</h2>
<ul>
  <li>==Service 1==</li>
  <li>==Service 2== </li>
  <li>==Service 3== </li>
  <li>==Service 4== </li>
  <li>==Service 5== </li>
</ul>
<h3>  All services guaranteed. Our complaint department is located at: ==URL
  where complains can be sent==  . </h3>
</body>
</html>
```

When you test it in a browser, see if it looks like what you expected. Also, you might want to see what it looks like in different browsers and on your mobile device. (*Remember:* Web browsers are free.) If you want to make some more changes, go to www.w3.org/TR/ css3-color/#svg-color. There you'll find a list of all the color names you can use with HTML5. See if you can change the color names in the code to ones you like.

2 UNDERSTANDING HTML5 TAGS

PROGRAMMERS CHARACTERIZE COMPUTER languages as ranging from low-level languages that virtually mimic the native language of the computer to high-level languages that are close to how people talk. HyperText Markup Language Version 5 (HTML5) is a very high-level language. However, the original HTML had very few "words" with which to describe what the developer and designer wanted. As the Web grew, the demands on HTML grew. With help from Cascading Style Sheets (CSS) and JavaScript, designers could do more with Web pages, but still, a lot was lacking.

More help was available for creating Web pages in the form of plug-ins that were able to run languages like Java and applications made with Flash. In fact, most browsers were bundled with the latest plug-ins for Flash so that users could view pages created with Flash and Flash Builder (Flex).

However, Web developers still wanted more from HTML and CSS to run natively with browsers. Browser makers quietly were adding functionality to JavaScript required to work with the new elements in HTML5. With new versions of each browser, not only was HTML5 being fully implemented, so too was JavaScript and CSS3. This chapter explains how the different HTML5 elements work and how they work in conjunction with CSS3 and JavaScript.

PARSING CODE

Sooner or later, you'll hear the phrase *parsing code* in reference to browsers and HTML5, CSS3, and JavaScript. All that means is that the browser is reading the code and interpreting it to do what it's told to do. It's just like an international interpreter who speaks English and Russian — the interpreter parses Russian so that the English speaker understands it and English so that Russian speaker understands it. Strictly speaking, the parser is part of the interpreter in the browser, but for all practical purposes, just think of parsing as involved in getting the Web page to do what you told it to do in the tags you used in your Web file.

In order to correctly parse HTML5, two things have to happen: You have to write the code correctly, and your browser has to interpret it correctly. That's why standards are important. Basically, standards insure that when you write HTML5 code according to the rules set down, your code does what you expect it to do in all browsers and on all computers. Using HTML5, CSS3, and JavaScript with the browsers discussed in Chapter 1, you shouldn't have any surprises when they're all fully HTML5 compliant.

Ironically, the standards allow for the most designer and developer creativity. If you want to have the page look or act in a certain way, following the standards used by the browsers that interpret your creations, they'll look the way you want them to look and behave as expected. If either you or the browser fails to follow the standards, your creativity is ruined. (We don't want that now, do we?)

UNDERSTANDING HTML5 AND RELATED FILES

As you saw in Chapter 1, to create an HTML5 file, all you have to do is save the code using a text editor like Notepad (Windows) or TextEdit (Mac) and use the extension `.html` at the end of the file name. (`MyCoolPage.html` is an example.) The `.html` extension is important because it is recognized as a Web page and not something else that your browser can't parse. You'll also find that only certain kinds of other files are recognized by the browser's interpreter and need certain extensions. Here are the most common file types you'll encounter:

- `.jpg` (JPEG graphic file)
- `.gif` (GIF graphic file)
- `.png` (PNG graphic file)
- `.svg` (SVG graphic file)
- `.css` (Cascading Style Sheet)
- `.js` (JavaScript file)

The most important of these are the graphic files because the tools you use for your graphics may automatically save them with different filenames than those that can be used for the Web. For example, Adobe Photoshop automatically saves files as `.psd` files, and Adobe Illustrator saves its files in `.ai` format. Neither graphic file format can be used with Web pages. However, most graphic creation tools will save the files as `.jpg`, `.gif`, or `.png` if you use Save As instead of just plain Save. When you use Save As, you can select from an available list of file types on most tools, including text editors, word processors, and graphic drawing tools.

Fixing Windows default file extension settings

The default settings for Windows 7 (and earlier versions) is to hide file extensions. That will give your files a cleaner appearance, but if you have to decide between selecting a graphic file with a `.psd` extension or a `.png` extension, you need to see what the extension is. Here's what to do:

1. Open the Control Panel.
2. Choose Appearance and Personalization → Folder Options → Show Hidden Files and Folders.
3. Uncheck Hide Extensions for Known File Types (see the figure).

Uncheck this box

Unchecking the Hide Extensions for Known File Types check box in Windows.

Now you'll be able to see all your file extensions. So, when you want to load a graphic file, you'll know whether it's a `.png`, `.jpg`, or `.gif` file just by looking at the filename displayed on your computer screen.

29

Fixing TextEdit on your Mac

If TextEdit on your Mac has its default settings, you may have had problems saving plain HTML files. That's because the default file type that TextEdit saves files as is Rich Text Format (`.rtf`) and not plain text (`.txt`). With `.rtf`, your text is saved with other code that you don't want in your Web pages. Here's what you need to do to fix it for writing Web pages:

1. Open TextEdit.
2. In the TextEdit menu at the top of the screen, choose Preferences.

   The Preferences dialog box appears.
3. Select the Plain Text radio button (see the figure).

Changing TextEdit from Rich Text to Plain Text.

Now when you create an HTML5 page in TextEdit, when you save the file, it defaults to `.txt` and you can just change that to `.html` using Save As.

LEARNING WHICH FILES WORK WITH THE WEB

If you're new to writing Web pages, the first thing to learn is what files work with Web pages. Directly, HTML5 recognizes, the .html extension and the three graphic file extensions discussed earlier (.jpg, .png, and .gif). However, you'll see a reference to .css files. These are external CSS files, whether CSS3 or older versions. Likewise, JavaScript files are saved with a .js extension, and they, too, may have a link reference.

The browsers that parse HTML also parse CSS and JavaScript. In fact, you can have HTML files with CSS and JavaScript code written right in with the HTML tags. Whenever you see the <script> tag, you'll find either a JavaScript or CSS script in the script container (between the opening <script> and closing </script> tags). At other times, the developer chooses to put all the CSS and JavaScript code in external files and load them using the <link> tag for CSS and the <script> tag for JavaScript.

For example, the following code loads the external .css file lookingGood.css:

```
<link rel="stylesheet" type="text/css" href="lookingGood.css" />
```

With JavaScript, the external .js file is called from within the <script> container rather than inside of a <link> tag. The following loads a JavaScript file named doMagic.js:

```
<script language="JavaScript" src="doMagic.js" />
```

This book concentrates on HTML5, but you definitely need CSS3 for formatting, so you'll see it here a good deal, too. For the most part, you'll see CSS embedded in the HTML code. In Chapter 3, you learn more about using CSS3 with HTML5. Chapter 12 provides you with a little JavaScript to use with HTML5 tags, and there you'll see exactly how to create and use JavaScript with HTML5.

KNOWING HOW TAGS WORK

When you write code in HTML5, you're going to need to know which elements to use to get what you want. As we saw in Chapter 1, you can change the size and appearance of a font using the <h1> tag. To get started, you won't be modifying the tags with CSS. When you use <h1>, you can expect to get the same big black bold text every time. (You can modify it to be a small green font with CSS if you want, but you'll have to wait for Chapter 3 to see how to use CSS to do that.)

In a nutshell, your tags work by dividing up your page into sections that begin with an opening tag <element> and end with a closing </element> tag. You can write all the HTML5 pages you want using that method and not much else, and your page will work just fine. Naturally, you're going to want to create pages with a bit of flair and help the browser know right off the bat what you're up to, but for the most part, you just write tags. So, let's start with the basic HTML5 container.

STARTING OFF WITH THE BASIC HTML TAG

If you're familiar with HTML4 and describing the document type, you know that you can add a great deal of detail to tell the browser what's up with your page. So, the first tag that you need to consider is not really an HTML tag but instead a tag that communicates with the browser to tell it that you're writing HTML5 and not one of the many versions of HTML4 or XHTML. Here it is:

```
<!DOCTYPE HTML>
```

That's it! Nothing fancy, it just announces to the browser, "You can expect an HTML5 document type." Every Web page you make should begin with that tag, and you do not need a closing tag. The exclamation mark (!) tells you it's not an HTML tag, but something a little different.

DESCRIBING YOUR PAGE WITH TAGS

Right after the first tag that tells the browser what it can expect, you begin your HTML container (everything between the opening and closing tags). This tag announces the beginning of HTML code and ends when the browser encounters the closing tag. The closing HTML tag is at the end of every HTML page.

Following the HTML element is the `<head>` container. Think of the head area as the housekeeping portion of a page. Whatever is in the head will be loaded first, no matter where it's used in the rest of the HTML page. To get started, all that's going into the head is the page's title. The title appears at the top of the Web page when you run it. For example, consider the following title:

```
<title>Seriously Sweet Page</title>
```

That title appears on the page's Windows and tabs. If you don't put it in, you'll end up with a blank or default title. Figure 2-1 shows how the title appears in different browsers.

As you can see, the title Seriously Sweet Page appears in different places on the four main browsers. On some, it appears at the top of the window and the tab, only at the top of the page, and only on the tab. This helps the user find your page when multiple pages are open simultaneously — or simply reminds the user which page he's viewing. Lots of other content goes in the `<head>` container, such as CSS and JavaScript, but for now, just remember to include a title.

Moving right along, the `<body>` tag demarcates the beginning of the page's content. As the name implies, the body is the main part of any Web page, and only content inside the `<body>` container is visible on the page. Between the opening and closing body elements, you put everything you want on your page. The following set of tags should go on every page you create — in fact, you might as well use it as a template and save it somewhere so you don't have to start off with an empty page to code.

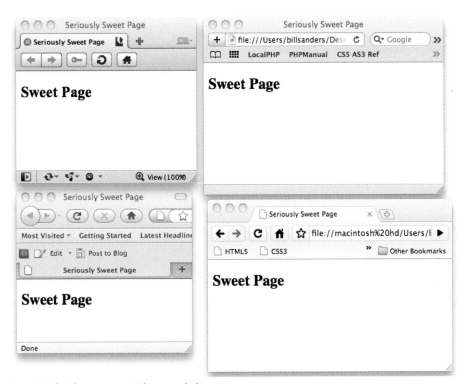

Figure 2-1: The title appearing on Web pages and tabs.

```
<!DOCTYPE HTML>
<html>
<head>
<title>Title goes here</title>
</head>
<body>
Content goes here: A Really Swell Page
</body>
</html>
```

As you proceed in this book, you'll find more and more structural elements to include. However, the preceding few lines will get you off and running with your Web pages.

IDENTIFYING THE PARTS OF A TAG

Up to this point, I've used the terms tag and element more or less interchangeably. However, the element is just one part of a tag. Each tag has attributes and the attributes have values. So, tags are better conceived of in the following terms:

- **Element:** The name
- **Attribute:** Some characteristic of the element
- **Values:** A state or condition of the attribute

33

Figure 2-2 shows all three parts of a tag.

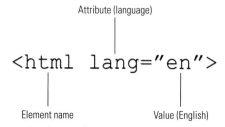

Figure 2-2: The parts of a tag.

The number of attributes is different for different elements.

Depending on the element, different kinds of attributes will be available, and depending on the attribute, different types of values can be applied. As a general rule of thumb, use quotation marks around values, including around numbers. Here are some different examples:

```
<form action="http://localhost/php/phpversion.php" method="post">
<input type="text" width="120" hidden="false">
<input type="submit" value="Sick 'em">
```

You have to be careful about what you put in between the double quotes. For example, `value="Sick 'em"` is permissible because `'em` has a single quote mark. However, the value `""Sick 'em," he said"` would not work because two pairs of double quotes are included.

The language attribute

The language (`lang`) attribute in the HTML tag is not used unless you're creating a page for something other than English. For example, the following are a list of other languages in which you may develop Web pages and their corresponding language attribute values:

- Arabic: `"ar"`
- Chinese (Mandarin): `"cmn"`
- German (Deutsch): `"de"`
- Hebrew: `"he"`
- Hindi: `"hi"`
- Japanese: `"ja"`
- Portuguese: `"pt"`
- Russian: `"ru"`
- Spanish: `"es"`

Unlike some attributes, the `lang` attribute has a wide range of values. Go to `www.iana.org/assignments/language-subtag-registry` for the full list.

A typical situation that may arise is one in which your page has a quoted reference in two different parts of the page. Within a paragraph, you can put in as many quotation marks as you want and they'll show up on the page. However, only a single set of double quotes can be assigned as a value to an attribute's value. Consider the following script (`quotes.html` in this chapter's folder at www.wiley.com/go/smashinghtml5):

```
<!DOCTYPE HTML>
<html>
<head>
<title>Be careful with quotation marks</title>
</head>
<body>
<p>We read Emily Dickinson's "Wild nights! Wild nights!"<p/>
<input type="text" size="50" value="Emily Dickinson's 'Wild nights! Wild nights!'">
</body>
</html>
```

In the <p> container, the double quotes identify the name of a poem. If the same text is to be set off as a poem in a value for an attribute, you can use only single quotes for the name of the poem, as shown in the value assigned to the value attribute. Figure 2-3 shows what the page looks like in a browser.

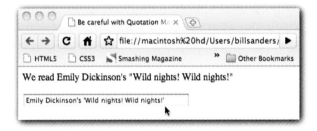

Figure 2-3: Using quotation marks in HTML5 pages and attributes.

When assigning values to attributes, remember to stick with double quotes for the entire value and use single quotes for highlighting sections within the value. By and large, life will be easier if you avoid using single quote marks when assigning values to attributes.

UNDERSTANDING THE ROLE OF THE COMMENT TAG

The role of the comment tag is to help the developer communicate with other developers, as well as to serve as a self-reminder of what the page is doing. A well-organized page contains information about what the page is doing, what may be added or changed, and any other information that aids developers in looking at a Web page script and quickly seeing what's taking place.

The comment tag is really two tags — a beginning tag and an ending tag. Unlike other tags, the comment tag has no text in it to help identify it. The following script (`comments.html` in this chapter's folder at www.wiley.com/go/smashinghtml5) shows where the comment tag goes and explains what it's doing.

```
<!DOCTYPE HTML>
<html>
<head>
<title>Use Comments in Your Code</title>
</head>
<body>
<h2>Comments Are Important</h2>
<!--Notice that the header uses an h2 element instead of an h1 element.-->
Comments help you remember and show others your page design plan.<br/>
Here are some different uses:
<h5>1. Explain to others what you are doing.</h5>
<!--This page is explaining comments.-->
<h5>2. Provide specific directions for tags to use.</h5>
<!--Don't use bullet points (<ul>). We haven't learned how to do that yet.-->
<h5>3. List the hexadecimal values for your color scheme.</h5>
<!-- Only use the following color values on this page: 69675C, 69623D, ECE8CF,
  E8D986, B5AA69.-->
<h5>4. Remember to recharge your portable computer.</h5>
<!--After working for two hours on coding, don't forget to recharge your battery!
  Otherwise, you may lose everything.-->
<h5>5. Remind yourself that you have a life away from computers.</h5>
<!--Don't forget your date with Lola on Friday night!-->
</body>
</html>
```

As you can see when you load the page none of the comments is visible in the browser, but as soon as you go back to work coding the Web page, they'll be there. You can put any kind of text in a comment container and it won't get in the way of what you see.

One of the many uses of comment tags is what's called commenting out (using your comment tags to temporarily remove tags that you may want to keep around for later use). So, instead of deleting the tags, all you do is to put comment tags around them, and test your page to see if you like it better without the tags in question. If you think that it looked better in the original, you just remove the comment tags. If the page looks better without the commented-out tags, just remove the tags permanently.

For example, suppose, you're wondering whether a page you're preparing for a client looks better or worse with a subheading and footnote. Here's the original code with the subheading:

```
<!DOCTYPE HTML>
<html>
<head>
<title>Commenting Out</title>
</head>
<body>
<header>
   <h1>Eat at Joe's Restaurant</h1>
   <h2>*Has passed most health inspections since 2005</h2>
</header>
```

```
<section>
Joe's has the best food on the block! The food is good, cheap, and tastes great!
</section>
<footer>
<h6>*Little boo-boo in 2010</h6>
</footer>
</body>
</html>
```

Figure 2-4 shows what the page looks like.

Figure 2-4: The original design.

After thinking about the design, you suggest to the restaurant owner, who is quite proud of his restaurant's record, that maybe the message might be better received if the subheading and footnote were removed. However, instead of removing the tags completely, you just comment them out, as the following code (CommentOutCode.html in this chapter's folder at www. wiley.com/go/smashinghtml5) shows:

```
<!DOCTYPE HTML>
<html>
<head>
<title>Commenting Out</title>
</head>
<body>
<header>
   <h1>Eat at Joe's Restaurant</h1>
   <!-- <h2>*Has passed most health inspections since 2005</h2> -->
</header>
<section>
Joe's has the best food on the block! The food is good, cheap, and tastes great!
</section>
<footer>
<!-- <h6>*Little boo-boo in 2010</h6> -->
</footer>
</body>
</html>
```

When to use (and not use) comment tags

A general problem with comment tags is that they're not used sufficiently in a Web page. Sometimes a few comments suffice — and if a page only needs a few, you shouldn't add more. Other times, a page needs a good deal more comments than it has. The number of comments required depends completely on the size and scope of the Web project and whether you're working by yourself or with other developers.

However, sometimes developers get carried away and have so many comment tags that you can't see the flow of the HTML code. A page with a long comment after every tag can act like barbed wire in a field — you keep tripping over it and can't reach your destination. If a large number of comments are required for a complex page, put them together in a single container, and then the other developers can see the HTML code and understand how it's used.

Once you've made the changes by commenting out the unwanted tags, you display it to your client again, as shown in Figure 2-5.

Figure 2-5: The page with the commented-out code.

If the client likes the original better, all you have to do is remove the comment tags, and the page will look like it did before. You may want to experiment with several different appearances; by using the comment tag, you can quickly change it while keeping the original tags — they're just commented out.

NESTING TAGS

When you create an HTML page, you may nest tags —you can place one HTML5 container within another container. In fact, I've been doing that all along. The rule is: Add an end tag inside of a container before the container's end tag. So, if you're writing a tag within another tag's container, be sure to close the inside container before closing the outside container. Look at the following examples to see what I mean.

In the following example, the `<h1>` tag closes outside the `<section>` container:

```
<section>
<h1>Smash this!
</section>
</h1>
```

Instead, it should look like this:

```
<section>
<h1>Smash this!</h1>
</section>
```

Here, the `<body>` tag closes outside the `<html>` container. The `<h3>` container is correct.

```
<html>
<body>Really interesting stuff
<h3>Don't forget to vote!</h3>
</html>
</body>
```

Instead, it should look like this:

```
<html>
    <body>Really interesting stuff
        <h3>Don't forget to vote!</h3>
    </body>
</html>
```

Here, the `<header>` tag closes before the `<nav>` tag does:

```
<header>
<nav>
<a href="html5.org">HTML5</a>  |  
<a href="css3.org">CSS3</a>>  |  
<a href="php.net">PHP</a>
</header>
<footer>
<a href="html5.org">HTML5</a>  |  
<a href="css3.org">CSS3</a>>  |  
<a href="php.net">PHP</a>
</nav>
</footer>
```

Instead, use two `<nav>` container sets — one for the header and one for the footer:

```
<header>
<nav>
<a href="html5.org">HTML5</a>  |  
```

```
<a href="css3.org">CSS3</a>   |   
<a href="php.net">PHP</a>
</nav>
</header>
<footer>
<nav>
<a href="html5.org">HTML5</a>   |   
<a href="css3.org">CSS3</a>   |   
<a href="php.net">PHP</a>
</nav>
</footer>
```

Sometimes, when you test your HTML5 page, you won't see what you expect — or even anything at all. The first thing you need to check is your tag nesting.

In case you're wondering about the   code, it's a non-breaking space. (The semicolon is part of the tag.) Simply think of it as a space around the vertical bar character (|) used to separate the links. In your browser, you'll see:

> HTML5 | CSS3 | PHP

When you place your navigation code inside of <nav> tags, you can easily spot it as navigation. However, like all other tags, you have to pay attention to the nesting conventions used in HTML5.

TAKE THE WHEEL

The HTML for the following Web page (TakeTheWheel.html in this chapter's folder at www.wiley.com/go/smashinghtml5) has errors that need correcting. It starts off with several tags that are empty or partially completed. You'll be responsible for making sure that the correct tags and text are added where they need to be. Sometimes, you'll need to close a container that has been opened (<tag>) or open one that has been closed (</tag>). And be sure that your tags are correctly nested. (**Hint:** The very first tag is not an HTML tag but that special one that begins with an exclamation point!)

```
<!      >
<html lang=   >
<head>
<!-- Color Combination
0B0B0D,29272A,A99A93,E27107,F8AC00 -->
<style type="text/css">
body
{
background-color:#F8AC00;
color:#29272a;
font-family:Verdana, Geneva, sans-serif;
font-size:12px;
margin-left:20px;
```

```
}
h1
{
color:#29272A;
font-family:"Arial Black", Gadget, sans-serif;
}
h2
{
text-indent:10px;
color:#0B0B0D;
background-color:#E27107;
font-family:"Trebuchet MS", Arial, Helvetica, sans-serif;
}
header
{
text-align:center;
}
</style>
<title>==???===</title>
<      >
<body>
<header>
<   >My Favorite Things</h1>
</header>
<section>
<h2>My Favorite Music</h2>
   ==????==<br/>
   ==????==<br/>
   ==????==<br/>
< >My Favorite Movies</h2>
   ==????==<br/>
   ==????==<br/>
   ==????==<br/>
   <h2>My Favorite Computers</h2>
   ==????==<br/>
   ==????==<br/>
   ==????==<br/>
   <h2>My Favorite TV</h2>
   ==????==<br/>
   ==????==<br/>
   ==????== <br/>
<      >
<      >
<h5>Not responsible for my tastes.<br/>
Take it or leave it.<   >
</footer>
</body>
</html>
```

This exercise should help you pay attention to the little details. Of all of the gotchas, it's the little things that slip under the radar.

3

TEXT TAGS AND A LITTLE CSS3

A WEB PAGE is unlike the kind of page you put in your word processor and start typing. Web pages are designed for computer screens of some sort — whether it's a big desktop, a laptop, or even a mobile device. You're not dealing with an 8½-by-11-inch sheet of paper — you're dealing with a far more dynamic viewing platform. So, the first thing you want to think about is how your page is going to look on a digital screen.

THE FUNDAMENTALS

Before we get going on dealing with text on a Web page, we need to consider the fundamental elements of a Web page. They include three types of actions:

- Displaying text
- Loading and displaying graphics
- Linking to other pages

To display text, all you need to do is type it on the page in the `<body>` container. You can style it with the `<h>` tag as you know from previous chapters, but basic text requires only that it be in the body of a page.

Loading and displaying graphics uses the `<img>` tag with the following format:

```
<img src="imageName.png">
```

You can use only `.jpg`, `.png`, or `.gif` files with the `img` element. The `src` attribute refers to the source of the graphic. The `img` element has other attributes, but all you need to get an image on the page is the `src` attribute so that the file can be located.

Throughout the book, the term URL is often used to refer to a file's location — no matter what type of file is involved. URL stands for Uniform Resource Locator and refers to a standard protocol for finding and using different types of files.

Finally, a link to another page uses the following format:

```
<a href="anotherPage.html">Link abel</a>
```

The `href` refers to the linked page's hypertext reference, or more simply put, its address. Like an image's source locations, you'll see the term url used for a linked page's address as well.

One more thing you need to know before continuing. The document type declaration (`<!DOCTYPE HTML>`) in the very first line is important — don't ever leave it out. However, an equally important line is declaring the character encoding. This is used to tell the Web browser which character set of letters to use, such as the A to Z alphabet, Hebrew characters, Japanese, Cryllic, or some other set. You can do it in several ways, but this book uses the following code:

```
<meta http-equiv="Content-Type" content="text/html; charset=UTF-8">
```

You always should specify character encoding. Although using the `<meta>` tag is a bit long, you can just cut and paste it in all your Web pages. If you don't, you can run into security vulnerabilities, and nobody wants that.

Throwing a Web page together works fine but may leave much to be desired in terms of what the user sees and whether she wants to visit the site again. Let's look at a Web page with no structure but with the fundamental elements of a Web page:

```
<!DOCTYPE HTML>
<html>
    <head>
<meta http-equiv="Content-Type" content="text/html; charset=UTF-8">
        <title>Fundamentals</title>
    </head>
    <body>
    This is text. You don't need a tag for Plain Old Text (POT).
    <a href="anotherPage.html"> Click here for another page </a>
    <img src="logo.png">
    </body>
</html>
```

As you can see in Figure 3-1, everything is jumbled. The image appears right in the middle of the link (blue underlined text), the image appears right in the middle of the page, and generally it doesn't make much sense.

Figure 3-1: The most basic Web elements.

When you're organizing a Web page, the links should be organized into a navigation system that's easy for those looking at your Web page to use. In the page shown in Figure 3-1, the link is broken up by the graphic and seems to be part of the text rather than part of a navigation system.

A LITTLE MORE ORGANIZATION

One of the basic conventions in Web design is placing the logo in the upper-left corner of the page. Likewise, Web pages place links organized into a coherent system of navigation. By adding two more tags, you can go a long way toward organizing your page:

-
: Generates a single-space line break
- <wbr>: Generates a line break opportunity

A line break (`<br>`) forces a break in the lines of text. You can think of it as a single space between lines, or if you're old school, a carriage return. HTML5 has added something new called a line break opportunity. Sometimes you'll have a very long word, especially in URLs and e-mail addresses. The `wbr` element doesn't force a line break, but you can place the `<wbr>` tag where you would like a word to break in case the page is compressed. This consideration is especially important for mobile devices because they have small screens. For example, suppose you have a very long URL that is being shown as a non-linking description like,

```
www.eatatjoesfinerestaurant.com
```

If the link name is not broken up, and if the page is compressed, you'll see a big gap in the text or the word broken where you don't want it to be. The `<wbr>` tag helps you keep your text broken where you want it. Consider the following script (`BasicBreaks.html` in this chapter's folder at `www.wiley.com/go/smashinghtml5`), which uses both of the line-breaking tags:

```
<!DOCTYPE HTML>
<html>
     <head>
<meta http-equiv="Content-Type" content="text/html; charset=UTF-8">
     <title>Adding ine Breaks and ine Break Opportunities</title>
     </head>
     <body>
<img src="logo.png"><br>
     This is text. You don't need a tag for Plain Old Text (POT).<br>
     <br>
He said, "Sometimes you have extremely long words, and you want to make sure that
  they break at appropriate places. For example, you have a long name for a URL like
  www.eat<wbr>at<wbr>joes<wbr>fine<wbr>restaurant<wbr>.com, and if it has to break,
  you want the break to appear in a particular place."<br><br>
He said, "Sometimes you have extremely long words, and you want to make sure that
  they break at appropriate places. For example, you have a long name for a URL like
  www.eatatjoesfinerestaurant.com, and if it has to break, you want the break to
  appear in a particular place."<br><br>
   <a href="anotherPage.html"> Click here for another page </a>
     </body>
</html>
```

By adding the two line-break tags, the page looks much better. The paragraph that does not use the `<wbr>` tag has a big gap in it where the long URL was not divided up into sensible break points. Figure 3-2 shows how the page now appears.

Although it's still not perfect, it's a lot better than the original, even though two more paragraphs were added. The graphic is in the upper-left corner (as most logos are), the paragraphs are separated by line breaks, and in the first paragraph using the long URL, the breaks are where the `<wbr>` tag specified.

46

Figure 3-2: Adding line breaks.

THINKING ABOUT STRUCTURE

At this point, more thought should go into structure. With the ability to add text, graphics, and links, the page can have far more features and much more content. So, you should begin thinking about things like headings, navigation, and positioning beyond the logo in the upper-left-hand corner. Start with a simple sketch. Use a scrap of paper to jot down an idea of a Web page. (Use paper, not your graphic tools just yet.) Figure 3-3 shows an example:

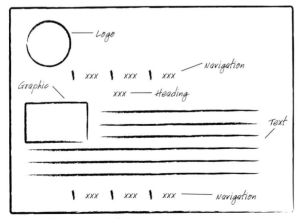

Figure 3-3: Sketch a structure for your site.

Given the tags discussed so far, will you be able to create a page based on the sketch? The only attribute lacking is one to wrap the text around the image. The `align` attribute of the `img` element will do that. In this case, the image will be to the left and the text to the right, so the following line will do the trick:

```
<img src="kid.png" alt="kid" align="left">
```

You may have noticed that the `alt` attribute was also included. That attribute lets users know what to expect if the image takes a while to load.

So, now, with just a few tags and an added attribute, this next script does a fair job of creating the page with the structure in the sketch in Figure 3-3.

As you'll see in the following code (`Sketch2Web.html` in this chapter's folder at www. wiley.com/go/smashinghtml5), I've used a pound sign (#) instead of an actual URL in the navigation links. The pound sign acts as a placeholder while we're working on the structure; it works just like a real URL except that it doesn't go anywhere or cause an error message.

```
<!DOCTYPE HTML>
<html>
<head>
<meta http-equiv="Content-Type" content="text/html; charset=UTF-8">
<title>Sketch to Web</title>
</head>
<body>
<img src="logo.png" alt="logo"><br>
<a href="#">Toys</a>  | <a href="#">Clothes</a> | <a
 href="#">Sports</a> <br>
<br>
A Good Place for Kids <br>
<br>
<img src="kid.png" alt="kid" align="left"> Kids are serious business. They need toys
 that are both safe and educational. Toys need to be fun and allow children's minds
 to create beyond any functionality the toy has. There is no reason that they cannot
 be both safe and fun. Children need lots of clothes because they grow so fast. And
 they need sports to offset childhood obesity and the illnesses associated with
 obesity. <br>
<br>
<a href="#">Toys</a>  | <a href="#">Clothes</a> | <a
 href="#">Sports</a>
</body>
</html>
```

Notice that we didn't use any of the H elements introduced in the previous two chapters. That's because I cover them in the next section and give you a better sense of their value. Figure 3-4 shows how close the page came to the sketch in Figure 3-3.

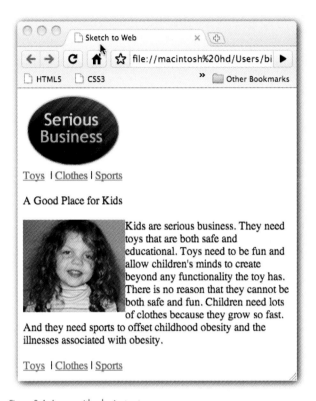

Figure 3-4: A page with a basic structure.

© David Sanders

Now the Web page shown in Figure 3-4 has more structure than any of the previous examples. The navigation bars at the top and bottom are helpful to the user, but perhaps they'd look better centered on the page. Maybe the top navigation bar should be at the very top of the page in the center, right next to the logo. Also, the text is jammed right next to the image and could use some space. Of course, the heading should be in a different style, weight, size, and font. Also, it's pretty boring — especially since it's for kids. However, because the structure is coming along, you can address those other details when you learn to use more styling tools.

ADDING MORE HTML5 STRUCTURE

In the previous section you learned about the `wbr` element that is new to HTML5, and this section takes a closer look at using the familiar `<h..>` tag and some related tags for structuring text. Also, you saw how to start with a hand-drawn sketch of what you want and implement it in a HTML5 script. Moving from a fairly concrete sketch to a more general block outline helps understand how HTML5 is organized into blocks. The first kind of block examined is the text block — in fact we've already begun, in Chapters 1 and 2, discussing `<h1>`, `<h2>`, and other `h` elements. Figure 3-5 illustrates the block organization.

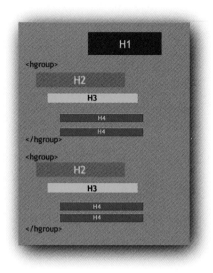

Figure 3-5: Text block organization.

In terms of organizing your page, the layout for different levels of h elements is the HTML5 <hgroup> tag. For example, take a look at the following Web page (HelementOrg.html in this chapter's folder from www.wiley.com/go/smashinghtml5) from Wittgenstein (who seemed to write using h tags in 1918 when he completed writing Tractatus Logico-Philosophicus):

```
<!DOCTYPE HTML>
<html>
<head>
<meta http-equiv="Content-Type" content="text/html; charset=UTF-8">
<title>Tractatus logico-Philosophicus</title>
</head>
<body>

<h1>Tractatus logico-Philosophicus</h1>
<h1>by Ludwig Wittgenstein</h1>
<hgroup>
<h2>1 The world is all that is the case.</h2>
<h3>1.1 The world is the totality of facts, not of things.</h3>
<h4>1.11 The world is determined by the facts, and by their being all the facts.</h4>
<h4>1.12 For the totality of facts determines what is the case, and also whatever is not the case.</h4>
<h4>1.13 The facts in logical space are the world.</h4>
<h3>1.2 The world divides into facts.</h3>
<h4>1.21 Each item can be the case or not the case while everything else remains the same.</h4>
</hgroup>
</body>
</html>
```

If we look at the Web page, we can see where the different h elements give the parts different sizes, but we don't see the indentations Wittgenstein used in his original writings. Figure 3-6 shows the Web page on a mobile phone — whatever else you think of Wittenstein, his style sure works well for mobile screens.

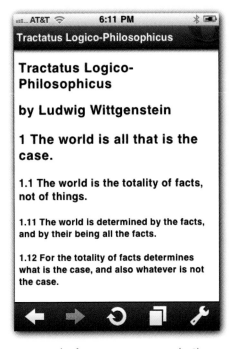

Figure 3-6: Outline format using <h> tags on the iPhone.

If you look at the original Wittgenstein, you'll find that his style of writing used an indented outline that appeared as the following:

    1 The world is all that is the case.

        1.1 The world is the totality of facts, not of things.

            1.11 The world is determined by the facts, and by their being all the facts.

            1.12 For the totality of facts determines what is the case, and also whatever is not the case.

We can fix that if we want by adding indents to the <h..> tags. We could do this by adding margins using CSS3 as you'll see in the next section. However, the purpose of the h element and the <hgroup> is not to set indents but to help with more general outlines. The <hgroup> tag sets the highest level <h..> tag in the hgroup container as the outline element. For example, since Wittenstein wrote Tractatus Logico-Philosophicus wholly in outline, his entire work using the hgroup element would look exactly like the outline in his actual Abstract to the work.

1 The world is all that is the case.

2 What is the case — a fact — is the existence of states of affairs.

3 A logical picture of facts is a thought.

4 A thought is a proposition with a sense.

5 A proposition is a truth-function of elementary propositions. (An elementary proposition is a truth-function of itself.)

6 The general form of a truth-function is [p, E, N(E)]. This is the general form of a proposition.

7 What we cannot speak about we must pass over in silence.

The `hgroup` element is tied into the outline algorithm in HTML5, and although it's unlikely that you'll be using it for writers like Wittenstein, it is useful for helping you think about your page in terms of the structure within an HTML5 page. One way to think about the `<hgroup>` tag is as a mask (or even a Romulan cloaking device) over other h elements below the highest-level element in the `hgroup` container. In our example, the `h3` and `h4` are masked and only the `h2` element is recognized as part of the outline.

ADDING STYLE TO TEXT WITH CSS3

Throughout the book, the reference to Cascading Style Sheets will be to CSS3. That's because HTML5 and CSS3 are paired in many aspects, but like other elements I discuss in this book, those continued from earlier versions have been incorporated in the newest version of HTML and CSS. We really have a mix of new and old in CSS3, just as in HTML5. So, if you're familiar with older versions of CSS and you see the same properties in CSS3 references, just treat it as a continued feature.

STYLING HTML5 ELEMENTS WITH CSS3 PROPERTIES

In Chapters 1 and 2, you saw examples of CSS3 but were given no explanation of what was going on to add a new style to an existing element. Here, the focus is on adding style to h elements. In the next three chapters, you'll see far more aspects of using CSS3. Here, I focus on the basics of incorporating CSS3 into your HTML5.

All style sheets can be added in three ways:

- You can use the `<style>` tag to define the properties of elements in the HTML5 page.
- You can use external style sheets, which are text files where you store a style you may want to reuse.

Most professional developers and designers prefer the CSS3 external style sheets because perfecting the desired style takes a lot of work. When you want to make a change to the design of a Web site, you can make changes to many pages that use an external style sheet, just by changing the one style sheet. It's just more efficient than having to change the `<style>` attributes in each individual Web page.

52

You also can add styles without style sheets by using inline styles. An inline style is like a "Break Glass in Case of Emergency!" technique. A good-looking page has a plan developed in a style sheet. However, sometimes, you run into a case where you need some feature added, and instead of changing the style sheet, you just pop it in with a tag.

Embedded style sheets

An embedded style sheet is simply adding the style sheet directly into the HTML5 script. In the <head> of the program, add the style sheet using the <style> container. Place the element you want to style in the style container, and then add values to the property to be styled. Figure 3-7 shows the general format.

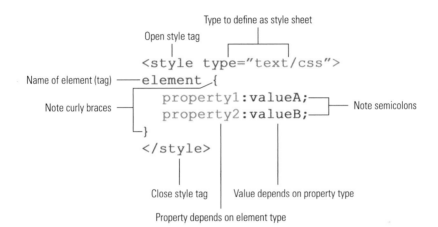

Figure 3-7: An embedded style sheet.

Each element has a unique set of properties, and each property has values that can be assigned to it. When you change the value of the property, that value appears in the text inside the element's container. So, if you change the text color to red, all the text inside the element's container will be red. The following script (CSS3fonts.html in this chapter's folder at www.wiley.com/go/smashinghtml5) provides an example.

```
<!DOCTYPE HTML>
<html>
<head>
<meta http-equiv="Content-Type" content="text/html; charset=UTF-8">
<style type="text/css">
body {
    background-color:#fbf7e4;
    font-family:Verdana, Geneva, sans-serif;
    margin-left:20px;
    color:#8e001c;
}
h1 {
    background-color:#8E001C;
    color:#e7e8d1;
```

53

```
        font-family:"Arial Black", Gadget, sans-serif;
        text-align:center;
}
h2 {
        background-color:#424242;
        color:#d3ceaa;
        font-family:"Trebuchet MS", Arial, Helvetica, sans-serif;
        margin-left:5px;
}
</style>
<title>CSS3-Embedded Stylesheet</title>
</head>
<body>
<h1>This Is the Big Head</h1>
<h2> Here Is the Second Head</h2>
The body text is styled for a bit of a eft margin and picks up the color of the body
  along with its font. Notice that the background of the heads extends all the way
  across the page. Also notice that a space (& nbsp;) gives the h2 text a ittle
  indent so that it stays "within" the background. That's not a problem with the h1
  head because it's centered.
</body>
</html>
```

Figure 3-8 shows how the styled page looks.

Figure 3-8: Text styled with CSS3.

You should be aware that when you use style sheets, you have to pay attention to the little details — like adding both curly braces, separating the property from the values by colons, and ending each property value with a semicolon. If your CSS3 style sheet doesn't work as you think it should, check those little gotchas!

When using background colors, the background often extends across the entire page. Certain inline elements such as <span> can be used to contain the background to the affected text. With background colors in headers that are left- or right-justified, you'll want to add a space ( ) so that it doesn't bleed into the background color of the page.

External style sheets

With all the different kinds of style combinations you may have to consider — including different formats for desktops, laptops, and small mobile screens — the work involved in creating a good style sheet or set of style sheets can be considerable. By saving your CSS3 work to a text file, you can reuse your style sheet as often as you want. Plus, you can copy your embedded CSS and easily paste it into a text file and save it as a `.css` file.

For example, let's take a color scheme with a set of colors that a corporate client, Mighty Smite Web Development, has described as the corporate palette. (That means you can use only the set of colors provided.) You start with the following company colors:

```
#3C371E, #8C5F26, #BCA55F, #F2CC6E, #F26205
```

The background color must be `#F2CC6E`. You don't have to know what the color is — you just have to know that the company has decided that it's going to be the background color. You're told that the designers can figure out the rest.

Further, you're told that they'd like a version that looks good on a phone and a different one that looks good on a desktop. So, that means you're going to need two different CSS3 style sheets. Later on, you'll worry about how the browser is going to know whether the user is viewing from a desktop with a screen the size of a drive-in theater or viewing from a Droid phone.

All that's required is the following tag:

```
<link rel="stylesheet" type="text/css" href="mightySmiteSmall.css" />
```

This tag goes in the `<head>` container where the `<style>` tag had gone along with the CSS3 code. Now the CSS3 code goes into a separate file. Notice that the `<link>` tag contains an `href` attribute assigned the value `mightySmiteSmall.css`. That's the name of the CSS3 file in this chapter's folder at www.wiley.com/go/smashinghtml5. The `Small` indicates that it's designed for mobile devices. Another CSS3 file will be created called `mightySmiteLarge.css` for non-mobile devices.

To create a CSS3 file, all you have to do is enter the CSS3 code in a text editor or Web development application minus the `<style>` tags. The following shows the example to be used here:

```css
@charset "UTF-8";
/* CSS Document */
/*3C371E,8C5F26,BCA55F,F2CC6E,F26205 */
body
    {
        background-color:#F2CC6E;
        font-family:"Lucida Sans Unicode", "Lucida Grande", sans-serif;
        color:#8C5F26;
        font-size:11px;
        max-width:480px;
```

```
        }
h1
    {
        color:#BCA55F;
        background-color:#3C371E;
        font-family:"Arial Black", Gadget, sans-serif;
        text-align:center;
    }
h2
    {
        color:#F26205;
        font-family:"Lucida Sans Unicode", "Lucida Grande", sans-serif
    }
h3
    {
        color:#3C371E;
        font-family:Tahoma, Geneva, sans-serif;
    }
```

The top line lets the browser know that it's a UTF-8 character set, and the second two lines are comment lines. They're different from the comment lines in HTML5, but they work the same. The second comment line is a handy way to keep track of the color palette and can save time in setting up the style sheet.

To test this mobile version of the CSS3 code, the following HTML5 file (`ExternalSmall. html` in this chapter's folder at www.wiley.com/go/smashinghtml5) is used:

```
<!DOCTYPE HTML>
<html>
<head>
<link rel="stylesheet" type="text/css" href="mightySmiteSmall.css" />
<meta http-equiv="Content-Type" content="text/html; charset=UTF-8">
<title>Mighty Smite Sofware Test Sheet</title>
</head>
<body>
<h1>Mighty Smite Software Conglomorate</h1>
<h2>This is an h2 head</h2>
<h3>Here's an h3 head</h3>
Lorem ipsum dolor sit amet, consectetur adipisicing elit, sed do eiusmod tempor
  incididunt ut abore et dolore magna aliqua. Ut enim ad minim veniam, quis nostrud
  exercitation ullamco aboris nisi ut aliquip ex ea commodo consequat. Duis aute
  irure dolor in reprehenderit in voluptate velit esse cillum dolore eu fugiat nulla
  pariatur. Excepteur sint occaecat cupidatat non proident, sunt in culpa qui officia
  deserunt mollit anim id est aborum.
</body>
</html>
```

All the styles in the CSS3 file are used to test their appearance, and the body text beginning with Lorem ipsum is filler text, used to get an idea of what a text block looks like. (It's been used since the 16th century, so it must be good.)

In setting up the CSS3 file, the only setting that specifically targeted mobile devices is the `width` setting in the `body` element. It's set to 480px because that's the width of the iPhone used in testing. However, depending on how users hold their mobile devices, they'll get different results. Figures 3-9 and 3-10 show what the page looks like when the phone is held at different angles.

Figure 3-9: Style set for mobile device vertical.

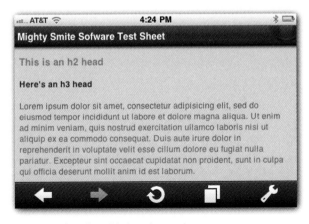

Figure 3-10: Style set for mobile device horizontal.

Different pixel density

When you're creating Web pages for output ranging from large desktops to mobile devices, you have to consider more than just the number of pixels on the vertical and horizontal planes. In the example CSS3 external style sheet, the width is set to 480 with the code `max-width:480px;` for an iPhone with 480-pixel horizontal resolution. However, when you run the application on your mobile device, the text may be way too big or way too small. What's going on?

We tend to think of screen resolution in terms of the number of pixels — the more pixels, the higher the resolution. So, if you set your screen to 1680 x 1050, it has a higher resolution than if I set it to 1024 x 768. However, the resolution actually depends on the number of pixels relative to the size of the display area. More important than the number of pixels is the number of pixels stuffed into your viewing area or pixels per inch (PPI) — pixel density. If you develop your Web page on a typical computer screen, the pixel density is around 100. However, your mobile device is likely to have a much higher pixel density. For example, my iPhone 3GS has a pixel density of 132 and a resolution of 480 x 320. If I upgrade to an iPhone 4, my pixel density will be 326 and the resolution will be 960 x 640. However, the phones both have a 3½-inch viewing area. The iPhone 4's resolution is double that of the iPhone 3GS, and its ppi is about 2½ times greater. For my Web page, that means a width setting of 480 will show up as coming only about halfway on an iPhone 4 even though it fills the width of iPhone 3GS models.

However, because I do my development on a computer with a ppi of 99 on a 20-inch screen, the best I can get is an estimation of what it will look like on any mobile device. I can estimate what a Web page will look like on different mobile devices by changing the size of the browser window, but ultimately, you need to actually see what your HTML5 Web page looks like on the target mobile device.

A unique feature of many mobile devices is that they allow Web pages to be viewed from different aspects — vertical or horizontal. So, when I'm preparing a CSS3 file for a mobile device, I tend to set the width to the horizontal. However, you'll quickly find that different mobile browsers work differently. At the time of this writing, the Apple Safari browser on the iPhone displayed the page in a tiny, unreadable page that had to be expanded, but the Opera Mini browser (as shown in Figures 3-9 and 3-10) on the same iPhone using the same size screen displayed the page immediately in an optimum viewing size, whether viewed horizontally or vertically.

Inline style

A third way to add CSS3 to your document is to simply add a `style` attribute to an element that redefines the content in the element's container. For example, the following code (`InlineCSS3.html` in this chapter's folder at `www.wiley.com/go/smashinghtml5`) has style changes in the `<div>` container and the second `<p>` container:

```
<!DOCTYPE HTML>
<html>
<head>
<meta http-equiv="Content-Type" content="text/html; charset=UTF-8">
```

```
<title>Inline CSS3</title>
</head>
<body>
<div style="font-family:Verdana, Geneva, sans-serif;font-size:24px;background-
   color:yellow;color:navy;">This is important!</div>
<p>But this...not so much</p>
<p style="font-size:10px;font-family:sans-serif;">And this you can ignore
   altogether....
</body>
</html>
```

Figure 3-11 shows what you see when you test the Web page in a browser. Keep in mind that the second line has no styling at all added.

Figure 3-11: Inline CSS3.

The use of inline CSS3 can be invaluable when some feature of your CSS3 external file doesn't have a style for something on your Web page that needs to be there. Generally, inline is one of those tools you want to use both sparingly and judiciously. This is especially true when dealing with other developers and designers who are working from a common style sheet.

CREATING CSS3 CLASSES AND IDS

CSS3 classes and IDs are ways to extend a style to any element. For example, suppose you have a feature that you want to add to just some items such as a yellow highlight. If you define a div or a p element's background color as yellow, all the text in either of those containers will be bright yellow — not what you want. On the other hand, if you have a class that defines a yellow background, all you have to do is to assign that class to an element to lighten it up.

CSS3 classes

You create style classes in an almost identical way as you do element styles. The "dot" (.) definitions used to create a class in CSS3 are labels you make up instead of using element names. Figure 3-12 shows how to create a CSS3 class definition.

```
                        <style type="text/css">
Class name ————.highlight
                            {
     dot                       background-color:yellow;
                            }
                        </style>
```

Figure 3-12: Creating class definition.

As you can see, the dot definition goes where the element name goes. The rest is identical to CSS3 definitions for elements. However, implementing a class style is a bit different because it can be used in almost any element tag.

In order to see how we might want to use a bit of highlighted text, a very handy inline element is span. The <span> tag can be added in the middle of a block element and only change that part of the content in the span container without changing the rest of the block. To add a class to an element, you use the following format:

```
<element class="myClass">
```

Notice that the name of the class does not include the "dot" from the dot definition. The dot is used only in the style definition to let the parser know that the word is a class and not an element. The following program (SpanClass.html in this chapter's folder at www.wiley. com/go/smashinghtml5) gives you an example of how you might use the class with the <span> tag.

```
<!DOCTYPE HTML>
<html>
<head>
<style type="text/css">
body {
     background-color:#F93;
}
.highlight {
     background-color:yellow;
}
div {
     font-family:"Comic Sans MS", cursive;
     font-size:18px;
}
h1 {
     font-family:"Arial Black", Gadget, sans-serif;
     color:#930;
     text-align:center;
     font-size:20px;
}
</style>
```

```
<meta http-equiv="Content-Type" content="text/html; charset=UTF-8">
<title>Halloween Highlight</title>
</head>
<body>
<h1>Halloween Party!</h1>
<div>You are invited to a Halloween Party on <span class="highlight">Saturday,
 October 29</span>. Costumes are <span class="highlight"><i>de rigueur</i></span>.</
 div>
</body>
</html>
```

When you test the program, you'll see that the two portions of the text within the `<span>` containers are affected. Figure 3-13 shows how they're displayed in a Chrome browser on a Mac (top) and an Opera Mini browser on an iPhone (bottom).

Figure 3-13: Class defined style in `<span>` container on desktop computer (top) and mobile device (bottom).

Both displays clearly show that the CSS3 class named `highlight` is working fine. However, the Opera Mini browser displays neither the defined fonts nor the italicized words. (The Safari browser does display the italicized words, but not the defined fonts.)

CSS3 IDs

A CSS3 ID is set up almost exactly like a class except that it uses a pound sign (#) instead of a dot (.) in the definition. Further, in assigning an ID, you use ID instead of class to specify which ID to use with an element. You even can use IDs and classes with the same element. The following tag is perfectly correct:

```
<p ID="this" class="that">
```

Both can select styles, and the ID provides a unique ID for the paragraph.

The ID has some major differences from a class. Both a class and an ID can be used as style sheet selectors. However, an ID has some other limitations and features:

- An ID can be used only once in a document.
- An ID can serve as an anchor (see Chapter 7).
- An ID can act as a script reference. That's important for JavaScript.
- An ID can be used as a name in a declared object element — more stuff from JavaScript.
- An ID can be used by agents for processing information in translating an HTML document.

Of these features, you'll be using only the first two until you decide to incorporate JavaScript and other languages into your résumé. Nevertheless, if you pay attention to these differences, your Web pages won't run into problems later on (and others will think you're a pro). The following example (IDwork.html in this chapter's folder at www.wiley.com/go/smashinghtml5) shows a use of the ID with CSS3:

```
<!DOCTYPE HTML>
<html>
<head>
<style type="text/css">
#littleHead {
    font-family:Verdana, Geneva, sans-serif;
     background-color:#9FC;
    font-size:16px;
}
#javascript {
    /* red */
        color:#cc0000;
}
#php {
    /* blue */
        color:#009;
}
#actionscript {
    /* green */
        color:#063;
}
```

```
</style>
<meta http-equiv="Content-Type" content="text/html; charset=UTF-8">
<title>Using IDs</title>
</head>
<body>
<div id="littleHead">Everything you always wanted<br>
  to know about variables:</div>
<p id="javascript"> JavaScript variables do not have to be given a data type.</p>
<p id="php"> PHP variables can be nudged toward a data type with type hinting.</p>
<p id="actionscript"> ActionScript variables must be assigned a data type.</p>
</body>
</html>
```

In looking at that code, you may have wondered what the slash-asterisk (/* ... */) marks are. Quite simply, they're comment code for CSS3. Within a `<style>` container and in external style sheets, they work just like the `<!-- -->` comment marks in HTML5. Figure 3-14 shows what you'll see when you test it.

Figure 3-14: IDs in a Web page.

If you have a long Web page with discussions about JavaScript, PHP, and ActionScript, the user may have to scroll down to find the topic he wants. Using IDs, you can write the URL to include the exact paragraph the user is trying to find. For example, the following URL will go directly to the paragraph covering PHP: www.smashingHTML5.com/myIDs#php. The added #php calls the specific paragraph with the php ID.

TAKE THE WHEEL

This chapter has covered a lot of material, and you'll want to see what you can do with it. Here are two challenges:

- **You can design better than that!** After starting a Web page using different h elements, the page that resulted in what you see in Figure 3-4 still needs help. For a kid's page, it's not too colorful and the font is boring. Besides, the text is right next to the image. Using CSS3, see if you can make it better.

63

- **Help poor Wittenstein!** After ducking bullets in World War I while preparing Tractatus Logico-Philosophicus, our Web page in Figure 3-6 shows Wittenstein's work without the indents! However, using CSS3 and the `margin-left` property, see if you can fix those `h` elements so that all the elements are there. By the way, if you want all 29 pages of Tractatus Logico-Philosophicus, you can download it for free at `http://filepedia.org/ tractatus-logico-philosophicus`.

Have some fun with this and see the flexibility that CSS3 gives you.

4 WORKING WITH COLOR VALUES

UPTOTHIS point, you've seen several examples of using color codes, but unless you understand what you're looking at, you may as well be looking at the enigma code. In some examples, color names are used, but other than the basic colors, you need to understand how colors are constructed in CSS3. By doing so, you have access to millions of colors rather than a handful.

UNDERSTANDING RGB COLOR

If you've ever mixed colors in anything from finger paints to a watercolor set, you have a sense of what happens when you mix colors. For computer screens, red, green and blue lights are mixed to generate different colors. For example, if you mix equal amounts of red and green, you get yellow.

To mix colors for Web pages, different values are mixed using integers, percentages, and hexadecimal numbers. CSS3 also has a limited number of named colors available that can help while figuring out the other color-mixing methods. HTML5 and CSS3 have some very sophisticated elements such as canvas that can do more with color and drawings than has been possible in previous versions of HTML. These advanced elements require a bit of JavaScript, and you'll find them discussed in detail in Chapter 13. For now, we'll get started with the basics.

USING NAMES

One of the stranger experiences in working with HTML5 and CSS3 is the name set used with colors. At the root are the 16 standard colors shown in Table 4.1.

Table 4.1 **Standard Color Names**

Aqua	Black	Blue	Fuchsia
Gray	Green	Lime	Maroon
Navy	Olive	Purple	Red
Silver	Teal	White	Yellow

Using the HTML5 that you've learned so far, you can easily create a chart showing all the colors. (In the "Take the Wheel" section at the end of this chapter, you'll work out how to re-create the table.) Figure 4-1 shows what they look like on a Web page on a mobile device.

Figure 4-1: The standard CSS3 colors in a Web page.

From this root base, you can include another 131 names that seem to have no rhyme or reason in terms of why they were selected. They're all part of a set created back in the 1980s called X11. They were adopted in the early browsers and have been with us ever since. In the official W3C documentation, they're listed under Scalable Vector Graphics (SVG), and all the names were adopted from the original X11. (See `www.w3.org/TR/SVG/types.html#ColorKeywords`.)

The reason that all the names haven't been listed here is because designers and developers generally don't use them. For designers, not only do the 131 names severely limit their palette, but the ones selected are nuts! Colors like papayawhip and mistyrose are hardly standard names for artists. Likewise, for developers, the values used don't conform to any mathematical set such as the old Web-safe colors that follow a logical numeric standard. (Of course, if you want to have some fun, go ahead and include darkkhaki and ghostwhite in your Web page's color palette.) In the next sections, you'll see how to create the exact color you want from over a million possible combinations.

RGB AND HSL PERCENTAGES

In mixing paint colors, the amount of paint is sometimes listed in percentages. A certain percent of red, green, and blue will give different colors. In setting colors in CSS3, you can use percentages in two different ways. First, you can assign a color value using the following format:

```
rgb(r%,g%,b%);
```

The first value is the percent red; the second, green; and the third, blue. For example, the setting, `rgb(43.9%,50.2%,56.5%)` generates the color that the Los Angeles Dodgers use. The three percentage values add up to more than 100 percent, so you know that the percentage is a percent of the color itself and not the total. As you can see, you can be very precise for values, including fractions of percentages. The following script (`RGBpercent.html` in this chapter's folder at `www.wiley.com/go/smashinghtml5`) shows how to use this color assignment in an HTML5 page:

```
<!DOCTYPE HTML>
<html>
<head>
<style type="text/css">
body {
    background-color:rgb(43.9%,50.2%,56.5%);
}
h1 {
    background-color:rgb(11.8%,56.5%,100%);
    color:rgb(100%,100%,100%);
    font-family:"Arial Black", Gadget, sans-serif;
    font-style:italic;
    text-align:center;
}
</style>
<meta http-equiv="Content-Type" content="text/html; charset=UTF-8">
<title>Dodger Blue</title>
</head>
<body>
```

67

```
<h1>Los Angeles Dodgers<br>
(Formerly of Brooklyn)</h1>
</body>
</html>
```

When you launch the page, the colors come out precisely as you instructed, as shown in Figure 4-2.

Figure 4-2: Setting colors with RGB percentages.

A second way to assign colors using percentages is to use a hue-saturation-light (HSL) model. The big advantage of HSL is that lightness is symmetrical. That makes it easier to tweak a color to what you'd like it to be.

By thinking of a color circle arranged around 360 degrees like a compass, you select a hue. At the top, or 0 percent, you find the reds. Moving clockwise, at 30 percent the hues turn red-yellow. At 60 percent, they're yellow. And so on around the color spectrum until you're at 360 percent (0 percent) where you're back to the red hues. For designers who understand the color spectrum, this makes choosing colors much easier. To create a lighter color, increase the light value; decrease the light value to make the color darker. For example, suppose you're trying to get just the right shade of red. You start with the following color assignment:

```
hsl(0,100%,50%);
```

Notice that the first value is not a percentage. That's because it has values between 0 and 359 — the 360 degrees of a circle. (**Remember:** 0 and 360 are the same point on the circle.) By raising and lowering the light (the third parameter), you can make your color lighter or darker — which is far more intuitive than changing RGB percentages. The following HTML5/CSS3 script (HSLColor.html in this chapter's folder at www.wiley.com/go/ smashinghtml5) shows how easy it is to lower and raise the light value to get just the right shade of red.

```
<!DOCTYPE HTML>
<html>
<head>
```

```
<style type="text/css">
.redBase {
    color:hsl(0, 100%, 50%);
}
.redDarker {
    color:hsl(0, 100%, 25%);
}
.redLighter {
    color:hsl(0, 100%, 75%);
}
</style>
<meta http-equiv="Content-Type" content="text/html; charset=UTF-8">
<title>HSL Color Assignment</title>
</head>
<body>
<h1 class="redBase">Red Base</h1>
<h1 class="redDarker">Red Darker</h1>
<h1 class="redLighter">Red Lighter</h1>
</body>
</html>
```

When first using HSL, it helps to think of adding light by going higher to the sun or making it darker by going lower into a well. The tweaking process is easier for designers to get just what they want. Figure 4-3 shows what the different red tints look like.

Figure 4-3: HSL makes tweaking tints easy.

Hue and light are fairly intuitive to understand, but saturation can be a little murky. Essentially, saturation is the amount of colorfulness in a given color. A 100 percent saturation is the full colorfulness of a hue in a given light, while a lower percent subtracts from a hue — something like a color fading. For all colors, a midpoint light is going to be gray when saturation is 0 percent. Sometimes a faded or muted color is preferred, like blue jeans that have been washed many times.

RGB DECIMAL INTEGER SETTINGS

A second way of mixing your colors using the rgb() value assignment is to insert values from 0 to 255 (a total of 256 values because you count the 0), instead of the percentages used in the earlier example. The value 256 represents the number of possible combinations on two 8-bit bytes. In other words, it's based on how a computer stores and processes information. With a set of three values from 0 to 255, you can generate 16,777,216 combinations. However, color technology is far more complex than we can possibly discuss here, and modern color process-ing keeps generating better color processors. Suffice it to say, you can generate lots of colors with those combinations of red, green, and blue. Here's the format to assign a color value:

```
rgb(integerR, integerG, integerB);
```

For example, yellow, which mixes red and green would be

```
rgb(255,255,0);
```

It's not as intuitive as HSL, but after a while, you start getting a sense of mixes based on 256 values rather than percentages. The following example (DecColor.html in this chapter's folder at www.wiley.com/go/smashinghtml5) shows a simple implementation.

```
<!DOCTYPE HTML>
<html>
<head>
<style type="text/css">
body {
    /* Red background */
        background-color:rgb(255,0,0);
}
h1 {
    /* Big Yellow Text */
        color:rgb(255,255,0);
    font-family:"Arial Black", Gadget, sans-serif;
}
h2 {
    /*Blue Text + Gray Background */
        color:rgb(0,0,255);
    background-color:rgb(150,150,150);
}
</style>
<meta http-equiv="Content-Type" content="text/html; charset=UTF-8">
<title>Decimal Colors</title>
</head>
<body>
<h1>  Big Yellow Header</h1>
<h2>  Blue header with a gray background</h2>
</body>
</html>
```

The only difference between using RGB with values from 0 to 255 and 0 percent to 100 percent is in perception. You may be thinking that you can be more precise with your colors using the 256 values instead of the 0-to-100 range of percentages, but that isn't the case because you can use fractions in percentage assignments. Whether you use the percentage notation or the 0-to-255 notation really comes down to a matter of personal preference. Figure 4-4 shows the outcome using the Opera Mini browser on an iPhone.

Figure 4-4: Colors mixed using integer values, shown on a mobile device.

As you can see in Figure 4-4, the mobile device is not picking up the Arial Black font, but it has no problems with the colors. Be sure to check your mobile device for fonts and other effects if they're essential to how your page looks. *Remember:* Most computers have a far more complete set of fonts and styles than mobile devices do. In time, though, they should be very similar.

HEXADECIMAL SETTINGS: THINKING LIKE YOUR COMPUTER

In previous chapters, you've seen color assignment made using values made up of alphanumeric values. (An alphanumeric value is any value that contains both numbers and letters.) For example, the value 6F001C generates a rich mocha red. If we break it down, we can see that it, too, is simply a mixture of red, green, and blue. But to understand what's going on, we need to understand a little about computer numbering systems.

We're used to counting using a decimal system. We use the values 0 through 9 (ten digits), and once those ten digits are used up we start over with two digits — 1 and 0 — which we call "ten." As you may know, computers are based on switches being in an On state or an Off state. By substituting a "1" for On and a "0" for Off, we can write a code based on a binary system using 1s and 0s; so instead of having ten digits to work with, we have only two. Table 4.2 shows what it takes to count up to 16 using the binary system. It also includes a third column that shows a base-16 numbering system called hexadecimal.

Table 4.2   Numbering Systems

Binary	Decimal	Hexadecimal
0	0	0
1	1	1
10	2	2
11	3	3
100	4	4
101	5	5
110	6	6
111	7	7
1000	8	8
1001	9	9
1010	10	A
1011	11	B
1100	12	C
1101	13	D
1110	14	E
1111	15	F

Each of the binary values is called a bit. A group of bits is called a byte. In Table 4.2, the largest binary value is a 4-bit byte. Computers are arranged in different types of bytes, and the 8-bit byte is commonly used as a general reference to a byte. However, modern computers are actually organized into 8-, 16-, 32-, 64-, and even 128-bit bytes. (They just keep getting bigger, so don't expect 128-bit bytes to be the top limit.)

The highest value for a binary counting system in an 8-bit byte is 11111111. When you look at that compared with decimal and hexadecimal numbers, you see a very interesting pattern, as shown in Table 4.3.

Table 4.3   Byte Values

Binary	Decimal	Hexidecimal
11111111	255	FF

As you can see in Table 4-3, the hexadecimal value FF is the highest possible value for two digits; similarly, the binary value 11111111 is the highest possible value for eight digits (a byte). However, the decimal number is three digits and does not represent a limit for those digits. In other words, the decimal system isn't very symmetrical with the binary counting system, but the hexadecimal system is.

As you know, the RGB system of assigning integers to color values uses values from 0 to 255. Using hexadecimal values, you need only two digits (actually, hexadecimal integers) to represent all 256 values in an 8-bit byte. It's neater.

This leads to using hexadecimal integers in assigning color values. Using six values — two each for red, green, and blue — all the color values can be assigned using six hex integers. So returning to the value 6F001C, we can see the following:

Red: 6F

Blue: 00

Green: 1C

Getting used to hexadecimal can take some time, but once you do, it's easy to add color values with them. Also, you can understand them in the same way as RGB decimal integers, but instead of values of 0 to 255, you use 00 to FF. The following example (HexPalette.html in this chapter's folder at www.wiley.com/go/smashinghtml5) shows some color using hexadecimals.

```
<!DOCTYPE HTML>
<html>
<head>
<style type="text/css">
/* Palette -- only use these colors!
69675C, 69623D, ECE8CF, E8D986, B5AA69
gray, olive, cream, dark cream, khaki */
body {
     font-family:"Comic Sans MS", cursive;
      background-color:#ECE8CF;
     color:#69675C;
}
h1 {
      font-family:"Arial Black", Gadget, sans-serif;
      color:#B5aa60;
     background-color:#E8D986;
     text-align:center;
}
h2 {
     font-family:"Lucida Sans Unicode", "Lucida Grande", sans-serif;
     color:#b5aa69;
}
</style>
<meta http-equiv="Content-Type" content="text/html; charset=UTF-8">
<title>Hexadecimal with Palette</title>
</head>
<body>
<h1> Style with a Color Palette</h1>
<h2> Desert in the Fall</h2>
In the fall, when the air cools a bit, the desert begins to settle down and cloak
```

```
   itself in a warmer set of hues.
</body>
</html>
```

This example uses a color palette and simply places the color values in a comment within the `<style>` container so that it can be viewed while putting the Web page together. Figure 4-5 shows what you can expect to see.

Figure 4-5: A hexadecimal color palette.

The colors belong to a set of colors that create a certain mood or feeling. This one, "Desert in the Fall" was based on what the designer believed to be a palette representing that time of year in the desert.

ADDING TRANSPARENCY TO COLOR

One of the new features you can see on an HTML5-compliant browser is transparency, or variable opacity. A fully opaque object on the screen blocks whatever is beneath it, while a fully transparent object allows anything beneath it to be fully seen — like glass. The value used to describe the level of opacity is expressed in an alpha property set between 0 and 1. Using either the RGB or HSL color formatting, the alpha is the fourth parameter. (Unfortunately, there is no hexadecimal alpha parameter in CSS3.) For example, `rgba(255,0,0, 0.5)` generates red with 50 percent opacity. Likewise, `hsla(120, 100%, 50%, 0.3)` creates green with 30 percent opacity (or 70 percent transparency).

In Part IV of this book, I discuss ways to add depth to your page with the `<canvas>` tag so that when you stack objects on top of one another, you can better see why having some transparency in your creations is important. For now, though, you need something that you can place beneath text blocks that can be viewed through a transparent text block. The easiest method is to place a background object using the `background-image` property. The following code snippet shows how:

```
body { background-image:url(imageFile.png); }
```

You can use any `.jpg`, `.gif`, or `.png` file for a background image. For this example, three circles in the colors red, green, and blue are used as a background and on top are `<h1>` text with 50 percent opacity to show the effect that different colors have when viewed through a transparent object. The following code (`Transparent.html` in this chapter's folder at www. wiley.com/go/smashinghtml5) uses both `rgba()` and `hsla()` formats.

```
<!DOCTYPE HTML>
<html>
<head>
<style type="text/css">
body {
     background-image:url(rgbBalls.png);
}
.transRed {
     color:rgba(255, 0, 0, .5);
}
.transGreen {
     color:rgba(0, 255, 0, .5);
}
.transBlue {
     color:hsla(240, 100%, 50%, .5);
}
.transBackground
{
     background-color:hsla(120, 100%, 50%, .5);
}
</style>
<meta http-equiv="Content-Type" content="text/html; charset=UTF-8">
<title>Transparency/Opacity</title>
</head>
<body>
<h1 class="transRed">Testing 123, Testing 123, Testing 123</h1>
<h1 class="transGreen">Testing 123, Testing 123, Testing 123</h1>
<h1 class="transBlue">Testing 123, Testing 123, Testing 123</h1>
<h1 class="transBackground">Testing 123, Testing 123, Testing 123</h1>
</body>
</html>
```

The results shown in Figure 4-6 are shown on an iPhone and they look no different than what you'll see on your a computer screen.

As you can see, the transparent text and background allow the background object to show through. When a color is transparent, it picks up some of the underlying color; so, when you use it, bear in mind what the combination of the underlying and overlying colors look like together. (By the way, Figure 4-6 shows why you rarely want to use background images — they have a way of cluttering the screen and destroying any sensibility in the text.)

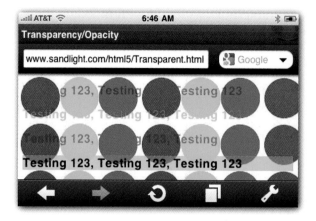

Figure 4-6: Transparent text over solid graphics.

CREATING A COLOR SCHEME

If you're a designer, you may be thinking, "How on earth am I ever going to get the colors I want with all these numbers?" If you're a developer, you may wonder, "How can I know if the colors I use go together?" Both of these questions have the same answer: Kuler. Kuler is a site where you can enter a key color (base color) and, using different algorithms, Kuler works out which colors are compatible and presents the information for decimal and hexadecimal color values. Designers can put in any colors they want to use in creating their own color schemes and Kuler generates all the math; developers can put in the math, and Kuler generates color schemes.

You can find Kuler at `http://kuler.adobe.com`. It requires a Flash plug-in (which is already built into most browsers), but if your browser doesn't have one you can get it for free at `www.adobe.com/products/flashplayer`. You can also download a Kuler widget that works on your desktop.

FROM A BASE COLOR

To create a color scheme with Kuler, you begin with a base color and try it out with different algorithms to generate color schemes. Then you select an algorithm to show different ways that colors look good together. Based on color theory, you choose from analogous, mono-chromatic, triad, complementary, compound, shades, or custom. The custom category is for designers who use their artistic skills to generate a palette. (Developers are well served by one of the automatic algorithms.) Figure 4-7 shows a typical example of a color scheme centered on a base color using the triad algorithm.

FROM AN IMAGE

In addition to creating a color palette from a base color, you also can load an image, and Kuler automatically generates a color scheme based on the image's color. For example, Figure 4-8 shows two different images — a logo and a painting — with their respective color palettes.

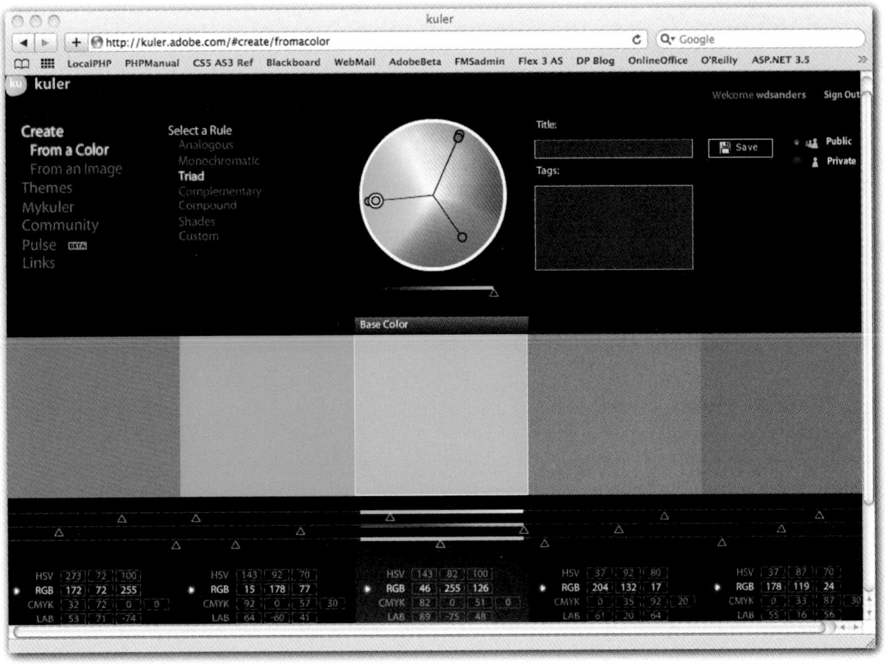

Figure 4-7: A color scheme with base color.

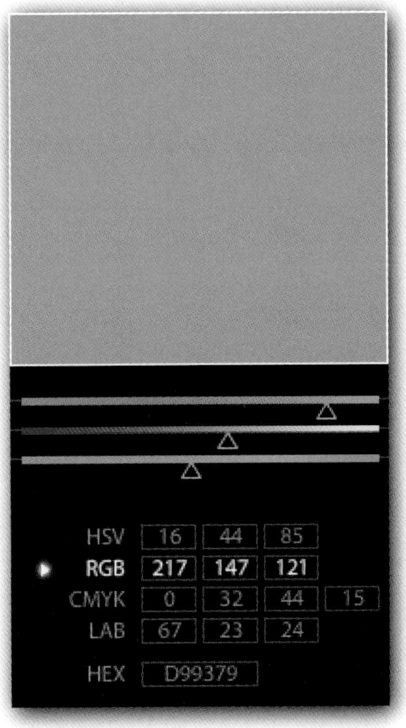

Figure 4-8: Color schemes based on imported images.

Bad color combinations

In order to see the difference between using a good color scheme and a bad one, we'll look at an example. Leslie Cabarga's book *The Designer's Guide to Color Combinations* contains a chapter on bad color. The following figure shows what two identical Web pages shown in a mobile device look like with a color scheme based on a photo and one using an example of bad color from Cabarga's book.

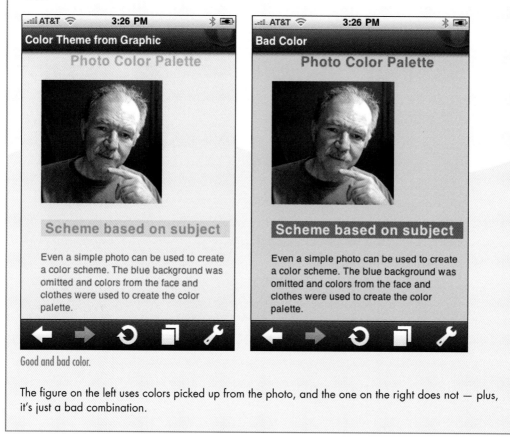

Good and bad color.

The figure on the left uses colors picked up from the photo, and the one on the right does not — plus, it's just a bad combination.

When using an image, you can further modify the color scheme by selecting from several moods — colorful, bright, muted, deep, and dark. All color schemes can be saved and when loaded, they maintain all the information you need for entering color data into an HTML5 Web page.

INTEGRATING YOUR COLOR PALETTE WITH YOUR WEB PAGE

Having a color palette doesn't mean that your page will look good — even color-wise. Within the same palette, some colors go together better than others. For example, a midtone background may not provide the contrast you need for other midtone colors, so a dark or light color in the palette may be a better choice. Figure 4-9 shows the color palette developed around a logo that will be used as the page's palette.

Figure 4-9: A logo-based color palette.

The hexadecimal integer values for the four colors are pasted right in with the CSS3 at the top of the HTML5 page for reference. The following script (`ColorsPhoto.html` in this chapter's folder at www.wiley.com/go/smashinghtml5) employs the colors so that they work with the logo and rest of the page.

```
<!DOCTYPE HTML>
<html>
<head>
<style type="text/css">
/* 027333,7FA646,D9B448,F2DFA7 */
body {
    margin-left:1em;
    background-color:#F2DFA7;
    color:#027333;
    font-family:Verdana, Geneva, sans-serif;
    font-size:11px;
}
h1 {
    font-family:Tahoma, Geneva, sans-serif;
    color:#7FA646;
}
h2 {
    font-family:"Lucida Sans Unicode", "Lucida Grande", sans-serif;
    color:#7FA646;
    background-color:#D9B448;
}
div
    {
        text-align:center;
    }
a {
    font-family:Arial, Helvetica, sans-serif;
    text-align:center;
    font-size:10px;
    text-decoration:none;
    background-color:#027333;
    color:#F2DFA7;
}
a:hover {
    color:#D9B448;
```

```
        }
    </style>
    <meta http-equiv="Content-Type" content="text/html; charset=UTF-8">
    <title>Arranging Colors</title>
    </head>
    <body>
    <div><nav>
        <a href="#">  Link 1 | </a>
        <a href="#">  Link 2 | </a>
        <a href="#">  Link 3  </a>
    </nav> </div>
    <img src="Sandlightlogo.gif" alt="Logo" align="left">

    <header><h1>    Welcome</h1></header>
    <br><br>
    <article>
    <h2> We are all about...</h2>
    Sandlight Productions is an international development company that specializes in
        HTML5/CSS3, streaming video, mobile device development, online education, Action-
        Script 3.0 architecture, Flash, and PHP.
    </article>
    <br>
    <footer><div>
    <nav>
        <a href="#">  Link 1 | </a>
        <a href="#">  Link 2 | </a>
        <a href="#">  Link 3  </a>
    </nav>
    </div></footer>
    </body>
    </html>
```

The CSS3 script uses the property `a:hover` to change the property when the mouse is over the link. In the `<a>` tag CSS3 definition, the `text-decoration` is set to `none`, which means that the text link will not be underlined. Without the underline, you want to do something to alert the user to the presence of a link; you do that using the hover property. Changing the color of the link text subtly yet effectively shows the user that the mouse is over the link. Both the initial color and the hover color are part of the palette. So, in setting up the page, remember that more than just the `<body>` and `<h>` tags use the color palette.

This particular design is focused on mobile devices (see the right side of Figure 4-10), but it should work with computer and table screen as well (see the left side of Figure 4-10).

Of course, your page is always going to look better if you have a Web designer do the page design. However, even developers can make it look better by paying attention to the color combinations.

Figure 4-10: A color scheme applied to a page.

TAKE THE WHEEL

The following two challenges should be fun, and you'll learn a lot from doing them both:

- **Reproducing the standard color chart:** In Figure 4-1 is an image with the standard colors. Your first challenge is to see if you can reproduce the Web page that displays those colors. Here are a couple hints to get started:

  - Define each named color as a class in your `<style>` container with the same color for the text and background colors.

    ```
    .aqua { color:aqua; background-color:aqua; }
    ```

  - One way to do this is to use the `<span>` tag to assign classes to the content of the `<span>` container.

    ```
    <h3> <span class=aqua>COLORNAME</span><span class=black>COLORNAME
    </span><span class=blue>COLORNAME</span><span class=fuchsia>COLORNAME
    </span> <h3>
    ```

- **Your picture belongs on a Web page!** This is a three-part task:

  1. Make a digital image of yourself using the built-in camera on your computer or upload one from a digital camera.
  2. Load the image into Kuler and create a color palette.
  3. Create a Web page with your picture using the color palette you created in Kuler.

II

PAGES, SITES, AND DESIGNS

5

ORGANIZING A PAGE

MANY OF THE new tags in HTML5 are organizational tags. In previous chapters some have been used but not really explained. This chapter looks closely at organizing HTML5 pages with the help of CSS3 and a way of understanding this organizational process. Some of the organizational elements become clear only once you start using JavaScript, but if you set up your page according to HTML5 guidelines, your page will be good to go when you start adding a little JavaScript.

THE TOP OF THE HTML5 DOCUMENT

The first four chapters of this book explain much of how the information above the <body> tag is put to use. The code above the <body> tag adds no content to the Web page, but it influences how the page appears and informs the browser that it's a Web page and what kind of Web page it is. Figure 5-1 shows the general organization of the first part of the Web page.

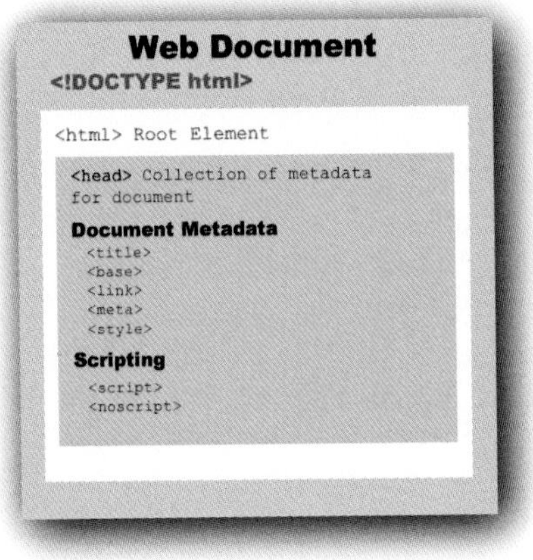

```
Web Document
<!DOCTYPE html>

<html> Root Element

    <head> Collection of metadata
    for document
    Document Metadata
        <title>
        <base>
        <link>
        <meta>
        <style>

    Scripting
        <script>
        <noscript>
```

Figure 5-1: Organizing the top of a Web page.

The <html> tag is the root element, and within that element, you can include a language attribute. Then within the <head> container are metadata elements. Also in the <head> container are the scripting elements; they, too, are briefly covered in this section and expanded upon in Part IV of this book.

Other than the CSS3 scripts, the examples so far have not put a lot of tags into the head of the HTML5 document. The <meta> tag has many uses, but so far, we've used it only to specify the character set. This chapter shows more uses for the <meta> tag.

SETTING YOUR HOME BASE

Within the typical Web site, you're likely to have several different pages to which your page will link. In fact, the typical Web site is arranged as a navigation system that links different pages. If you set a <base> tag in the head of your page with a link to a URL, you can reference other pages relative to the base page. For example, the following two scripts (Base.html and FirstBase.html in this chapter's folder at www.wiley.com/go/smashinghtml5) have links to one another, but they're relative to the base that is set in the head container.

```
<!DOCTYPE HTML>
<html><head>
<base href="http://www.sandlight.com/html5/smashing/ ">
<style type="text/css">
body {
```

86

```
        background-color:#FCC;
}
</style>
<meta http-equiv="Content-Type" content="text/html; charset=UTF-8">
<title>Home Base</title></head>
<body>
<h1>This Is the Home Base</h1>
<a href="FirstBase.html">First Base</a>
</body></html>
<!DOCTYPE HTML>
<html><head>
<base href="http://www.sandlight.com/html5/smashing/ ">
<style type="text/css">
body {
        background-color:#FC0;
}
</style>
<meta http-equiv="Content-Type" content="text/html; charset=UTF-8">
<title>First Base</title>
</head>
<body>
<h1>This Is First Base</h1>
<a href="Base.html">Home Base</a>
</body>
</html>
```

What is happening here? The <base> tag is telling your browser how to resolve any references to other documents in your HTML — such as the <a href="Base.html"> anchor tag. Your browser will know to look for the Base.html document in the location specified in the <base> tag; namely, http://www.sandlight.com/html5/smashing/.

ADDING CHARACTER TO YOUR SITE WITH METADATA

To this point, we've used the <meta> tag to establish that your site uses the UTF-8 character set, but the meta element can do much more. Think of the meta element as the one that performs multitasks. One of the most important attributes of the meta element is the name and contents pair. With the name attribute set to keywords, you can specify the contents on your site. In this way, the search engines can find your site when people are trying to find your products or services — or just the topics you'd like to include on your Web pages. For example, suppose your site has links to blogs and other sites on topics about dog kennels. Your meta tag would look something like this:

```
<meta name="keywords" content="kennels, dog fences, pet containment">
```

Each of the content values must be separated by a comma. These tokens can be directly related to your content or what someone might look for. Content meta tags are easy to set and you can help users find their way to your site.

One other `<meta>` tag attribute that's very cool is `http-equiv` set in the `Refresh` state. Using this attribute, you can automatically refresh a page or even change HTML pages. For example, you could have part of your site have an automatic slide show to display photos of a party or friends in a club. The tag format for using the `Refresh` state is:

```
<meta http-equiv="Refresh" content="[secs]">
```

For example, the following tag refreshes (reloads) the page every 30 seconds:

```
<meta http-equiv="Refresh" content="30">
```

Not only can you reload the same page, but you can reload different pages. If you want to load a sequence of pages, you can set the initial meta tag set as follows, to set the page assigned as a URL value after ½ second:

```
<meta http-equiv="Refresh" content=".5; URL=pg2.html">
```

Notice how the content value of both the number of seconds and the URL are in the same set of quotation marks. The following HTML5 code launches a series of pages that keep refreshing until a home page is loaded:

```
<!DOCTYPE HTML>
<html>
<head>
<meta http-equiv="Content-Type" content="text/html; charset=UTF-8">
<meta http-equiv="Refresh" content=".5; URL=pg2.html">
<title>Image 1</title>
</head>
<body>
<img src="one.png" alt="one">
</body>
</html>
```

After the initial page, you would have the following sequence — only one per page:

- **Page 2:** `<meta http-equiv="Refresh" content=".5; URL=pg3.html">`
- **Page 3:** `<meta http-equiv="Refresh" content=".5; URL=pg4.html">`
- **Page 4:** `<meta http-equiv="Refresh" content=".5; URL=pg5.html">`
- **Page 5:** `<meta http-equiv="Refresh" content=".5; URL=homeNow.html">`

The home page, `homeNow.html`, would have no `Refresh` state in the `<meta>` tag. In fact, other than the meta element with the `Content-Type`, it would have no other meta tag. (This thing would go on forever if you looped the home page back to the first page!)

KNOWING WHEN YOU NEED A SCRIPT

The more you use HTML5, the more you need a script to get the most out of your Web pages. The most common scripting language used with HTML5 is JavaScript. Your browser has an interpreter for JavaScript just as it does for HTML5. Fortunately, JavaScript is easy to learn and can work in small snippets — even non-developers can do it.

To include JavaScript, all you need to do is to add a little script to the head of your page. Here's the tag format:

```
<script type="text/javascript">
```

The JavaScript program goes into the remainder of the `<script>` container. The following HTML5 code (`ScriptTag.html` in this chapter's folder at www.wiley.com/go/smashinghtml5) shows how easy JavaScript is to learn.

```
<!DOCTYPE HTML>
<html>
<head>
<script type="text/javascript">
    alert("I can do JavaScript!");
</script>
<meta http-equiv="Content-Type" content="text/html; charset=UTF-8">
<title>A Taste of JavaScript</title>
</head>
<body>
A regular Web page....
</body>
</html>
```

When you test that little program, you'll see an alert box pop up (shown in Figure 5-2).

Figure 5-2: A JavaScript alert window.

As a side note, you'll see that the JavaScript alert window is loaded before your Web page loads. That's because everything in the head container loads first. If you have a more elaborate JavaScript program that will be used in your HTML5 page, you'll want to test it on different browsers and also put it in an external JavaScript file. Figure 5-3 shows the same alert window in Safari on an iPhone; you can clearly see that the Web page associated with the HTML5 code has not loaded.

89

As soon as the user clicks OK, the Web page loads. In the meantime, you can see the files from the directory in the background on your mobile device. Additionally, notice that the alert window shows the domain where the JavaScript resides. Some browsers, such as Google's Chrome, first check to see if the user wants to accept the JavaScript from the named site before it shows the actual alert (a double alert!).

Figure 5-3: Alert window loading before Web page.

As with style sheets, JavaScript programs can be loaded from external files. However, instead of using the link element, the JavaScript files are loaded using the script element, as the following example shows:

```
<script type="text/javascript" src="smashingJS.js"></script>
```

The JavaScript file is saved using the .js extension, just as CSS3 files are saved using the .css extension.

You'll see JavaScript is employed a good deal when using the <canvas> tag and several other HTML5 tags in Part IV of this book. Further, <script> tags and the JavaScript code in them can be added right in the middle of an HTML5 script. The advantage of placing your JavaScript in the head container, though, is that it's loaded first, before the Web page.

A DESIGN IN SECTIONS

One of the major changes in HTML5 compared with older HTML versions is in the sections. Prior to HTML5, you could pretty well think of sections in terms of the body element and some <h> tags. In HTML5, a page can be envisioned in terms of a number of sections with subsections. A larger context in a Web page is an article, and just like an article in a magazine, you can find different sections that constitute the building blocks of the article. Figure 5-4 provides an overview of the sections in an HTML5 page.

Figure 5-4: Some sections that make up a page.

In looking at Figure 5-4, you can see different blocks of information, but the tags used generally don't have any inherent capacity to structure the information visually. The <h> tags, which are section elements, certainly configure text to different sizes. However, the other section tags are as much for helping to organize a page as they are for specifying the visual display of the page.

The section elements include the following:

- Body
- Section
- Nav
- Article
- Aside
- H1 . . . H6
- Hgroup

- Header
- Footer
- Address

The `body` element is the sectioning root just as the `html` element is the page root. Throughout the previous chapters, you've seen several of the section elements, so you're familiar with them. However, a script helps to see how they're used in conjunction and consider their uses (`ArticleStructure.html` in this chapter's folder at `www.wiley.com/go/smashinghtml5`).

```
<!DOCTYPE HTML>
<html>
<head>
<meta http-equiv="Content-Type" content="text/html; charset=UTF-8">
<title>Sections</title>
</head>
<body>
<article>
  <header>
    <h1>Pilots and Planes</h1>
    <p><q>I never left one up there. </q><i>Ace Davis</i></p>
  </header>
  <nav><a href="#"> Safety</a> | <a href="#">Check Lists</a> | <a
href="#">Landings</a></nav>
  <section>
    <h2>Flying Stories by Real Pilots</h2>
    <h3>...and other cures for insomnia.</h3>
    <section>
      <h4>Short Final</h4>
      <p>As we were on short final, control cleared the Maule for immediate takeoff,
which it did in about 15 feet of runway at an airspeed of 20 mph. It filled my
windshield as I approached stall speed. After realizing its mistake, the tower
instructed the Maule to loop, and we were able to land without incident.</p>
    </section>
    <section>
      <h4>Thermal on Takeoff</h4>
      <p>Taking off from Gila Bend, Arizona, with the ambient temperature of 130 F,
we encountered a strong thermal at the end of the runway, which took our Cessna
177b to 15,000 feet in 12 seconds flat, at which time we leveled off and proceeded
to New Mexico via the jet stream, setting a new speed record.</p>
    </section>
  </section>
  <aside>
    <h2>Truthful Pilot Found!</h2>
    <p>Emily Rudders, a pilot in Moose Bite, Vermont, was recently found to be the
only truthful pilot in existence. When asked to relate her most exciting flying
adventure, Emily replied, <q>I ain't never flew no airplane. I jus' shoot at 'em
when they fly over and bother the moose.</q></p>
  </aside>
  <footer>
    <address>
```

```
      Contact us at:<a href="www.aopa.org">AOPA</a>
      </address>
   </footer>
</article>
</body>
</html>
```

The purpose of sections is to divide the page into coherent parts. They're an organizational set of elements, and while they can be used for formatting, that isn't their main purpose. For adding formatting to a paragraph or group of paragraphs, the W3C Standards encourage the use of the <div> tag.

Figure 5-5 shows what the page looks like. Although it isn't an attractive design, it is a functional one. The article is about pilots and flying. The article's header announces the topic (pilots and planes) and provides a quote from a pilot using a <q> tag. After the header, the first section is about flying stories. Nested within the first section are two other <section> tags that separate out the two stories.

A somewhat related section about the veracity of pilot stories is placed in a separate aside element container. In Figure 5-4, you may have noticed that the aside was placed in a separate column, but in and of itself, an aside element is a reference to the sense of the page. It is not a formatting element as such.

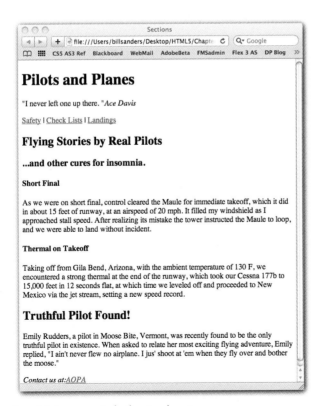

Figure 5-5: A page organized with section elements.

Why you really should pay attention to the section organization

You may be thinking that you can get a page up and running without the hassle of the section tags. That's true. However, under the hood of your mild-mannered Web page is a rumbling engine that can reference different parts of your page. Known as the Document Object Model (DOM), the different groupings you have set up using the section elements can be addressed as different objects and children of objects in a well-ordered stream of data coursing over the Internet. By paying attention to the organizational model used in HTML5, your Web page will be happy, the Internet will be happy, and the galaxy will be happy.

Finally, at the bottom of the article is a footer. Footer elements can go anywhere, including inside individual `section` and `aside` element containers. Footers act as a closing organizational element for the section elements. Within the footer is an `address` element with a link to a URL related to the article.

In looking at the page in Figure 5-5 and the code, you can see the sense of the page described in the section tags. As noted, they're really not for formatting but for organizing the sense of the page.

GETTING YOUR STUFF ORGANIZED

Once you have a general organizational plan, you want to arrange your content within the different sections. In Figure 5-4, you saw that several of the section elements contained grouping elements, such as the <p> tags. Grouping elements are a preferred place for adding your CSS3 styles; section elements are not. In this section, you'll find the major elements to help you organize your materials.

PARAGRAPHS, DIVISIONS, AND LISTS

The <p> and <div> tags used to be the workhorses of HTML pages for both grouping and styling. Both are still important, but you must remember that their job is no longer one of sectioning material on your page. Instead, think of both of these tags as grouping parts of a section. For example, the following code snippet shows the old way of using these two tags:

```
<div>
  <h1>All About Important Stuff</h1>
  <p>
  <h2>Finding True Love</h2>
  </p>
  <p>
  <h2>Choosing the Right Career</h2>
  </p>
  <p>
```

```
    <h2>Getting a Parking Place</h2>
    </p>
</div>
```

That code works perfectly well in HTML5, but it's better organized using the most specific element for the job. A better code would look like the following:

```
<header>
    <h1>All About Important Stuff</h1>
</header>
<section>
    <h2>Finding True Love</h2>
    <h2>Choosing the Right Career</h2>
    <h2>Getting a Parking Place</h2>
</section>
```

On your Web page, they look the same, but with HTML5 you'll find your pages more sensible using the new section elements.

So the question is, "Where can the p and div elements be used?" Actually, you don't want to rely on either very much. However, when you want to add a style element or some other attribute in the middle of an <article> or <section>, they can be handy. Consider the following (UseDiv.html in this chapter's folder at www.wiley.com/go/smashinghtml5).

```
<!DOCTYPE HTML>
<html>
<head>
<style type="text/css">
body {
        font-family:"Comic Sans MS", cursive;
        color:#0C6;
      background-color:#FFC;
}
.girls {
        background-color:pink;
}
.boys {
        background-color:powderblue;
}
</style>
<meta http-equiv="Content-Type" content="text/html; charset=UTF-8">
<title>Baby Names</title>
</head>
<body>
<article>
<header>
    <h1>Baby Names</h1>
</header>
<section>
```

```
      <div class="girls">
        <h2> Girls</h2>
        <ul>
          <li>Olivia</li>
          <li>Tess</li>
          <li>Emily</li>
        </ul>
      </div>
    </section>
    <section>
      <div class="boys">
        <h2> Boys</h2>
        <ul>
          <li>Jacob</li>
          <li>Ricky</li>
          <li>John</li>
        </ul>
      </div>
    </section>
  </body>
</html>
```

Figure 5-6 shows the output, but the important point is that the `<div>` tag was employed only to provide the background colors for two different `<section>` elements.

Figure 5-6: Using the `<div>` tag for styling.

As you can see in the listing, the `div` element allowed two different background styles in the `section` containers without having to add classes to the `<section>` tag. Overall, though, keep in mind that both `<p>` and `<div>` are more generalized elements, and at all times, you should use elements that are the most descriptive of your object on the Web page.

Besides grouping and styling using the `<div>` tag, lists also serve to outline data. HTML5 still uses the `<ul>` tags to group baby names for boys and girls. However, a subtle yet important difference is built into ordered (`<ol>`) and unordered lists (`<ul>`).

The use of unordered or ordered lists depends on the context. For example, in the 2010 Fédération Internationale de Football Association (FIFA) World Cup in South Africa, four of the teams competing for the championship were Germany, Netherlands, Spain, and Uruguay. If you were listing them at the beginning of the competition, you might use an unordered list. At the end of the competition, you may want to use an ordered list to show the final results. The following Web page (`ol_ul.html` in this chapter's folder at www.wiley.com/go/smashinghtml5) reflects the different groupings depending on the context and the meaning that accompanies the context.

```
<!DOCTYPE HTML>
<html>
<head>
<style type="text/css">
/*20268C,0C080C,2F8C2B,F27507,F20505 */
body {
    background-color:#2F8C2B;
    color:#0C080C;
    font-family:Verdana, Geneva, sans-serif;
}
h2 {
    background-color:#F27507;
    color:#20268C;
    font-family:"Comic Sans MS", cursive;
}
h3 {
    font-family:"Comic Sans MS", cursive;
}
ol {
    background-color:#F27507;
}
ul {
    background-color:#F20505;
}
</style>
<meta http-equiv="Content-Type" content="text/html; charset=UTF-8">
<title>Ordered and Unordered</title>
</head>
<body>
<h2> World Cup 2010</h2>
<h3>Beginning</h3>
```

```
<ul>
  <li>Spain</li>
  <li>Netherlands</li>
  <li>Germany</li>
  <li>Uruguay</li>
</ul>
<h3>End</h3>
<ol>
  <li>Spain</li>
  <li>Netherlands</li>
  <li>Germany</li>
  <li>Uruguay</li>
</ol>
</body>
</html>
```

As you can see in Figure 5-7, the meaning of the group at the beginning of the World Cup has no hierarchy — the list is just four teams at the World Cup. However, at the end, the order means everything, so the ordered list element is more appropriate.

Figure 5-7: Ordered and unordered lists convey different meanings.

You may also note that the two different kinds of lists have different background colors added with CSS3. So when using grouping elements, you might also want to further group the content using color, as shown in both Figures 5-6 and 5-7.

GROUPING WITHOUT FRACTURING

One of the grouping elements that you probably shouldn't use for more than grouping the head from the rest of the page (if even that) is the `<hr>` tag. The hr element (horizontal rule) is simply a line, but it should be used judiciously and sparsely. Take for example, the following excerpt from the poem "Kubla Khan" by Samuel Taylor Coleridge:

> In Xanadu did Kubla Khan
> A stately pleasure-dome decree:
> Where Alph, the sacred river, ran
> Through caverns measureless to man
> Down to a sunless sea.
>
> So twice five miles of fertile ground
> With walls and towers were girdled round;
> And there were gardens bright with sinuous rills,
> Where blossomed many an incense-bearing tree;
> And here were forests ancient as the hills,
> Enfolding sunny spots of greenery.
>
> But oh! that deep romantic chasm which slanted
> Down the green hill athwart a cedarn cover!
> A savage place! as holy and enchanted
> As e'er beneath a waning moon was haunted
> By woman wailing for her demon-lover!

The three stanzas are divided by a simple double space, as is the title. However, if `<hr>` tags are inserted, as in the following listing (HR.html in this chapter's folder at www.wiley.com/go/smashinghtml5), you'll see a quite different result in terms of an integrated sense of the poem.

```
<!DOCTYPE HTML>
<html>
<head>
<style type="text/css">
/*A1A680,D9D7BA,D90404,8C0303,590202 */
body {
    background-color:#A1A680;
    color:#590202;
    font-family:"Palatino Linotype", "Book Antiqua", Palatino, serif;
    font-size:8px;
}
h4 {
```

```
    background-color:#D9D7BA;
    color:#8C0303;
    font-family:Tahoma, Geneva, sans-serif;
}
</style>
<meta http-equiv="Content-Type" content="text/html; charset=UTF-8">
<title>Too many HRs</title>
</head>
<body>
<header>
  <h4> Kubla Khan</h4>
</header>
<article>
  <hr>
  In Xanadu did Kubla Khan<br>
  A stately pleasure-dome decree:<br>
  Where Alph, the sacred river, ran<br>
  Through caverns measureless to man<br>
  Down to a sunless sea.<br>
  <hr>
  So twice five miles of fertile ground<br>
  With walls and towers were girdled round;<br>
  And there were gardens bright with sinuous rills,<br>
  Where blossomed many an incense-bearing tree;<br>
  And here were forests ancient as the hills,<br>
  Enfolding sunny spots of greenery.<br>
  <hr>
  But oh! that deep romantic chasm which slanted<br>
  Down the green hill athwart a cedarn cover!<br>
  A savage place! as holy and enchanted<br>
  As e'er beneath a waning moon was haunted<br>
  By woman wailing for her demon-lover! </article>
</body>
</html>
```

As you can see, the <hr> tags are all within the `article` element, while the title is part of the `header` element. However, in Figure 5-8, the page is shown in a mobile device, and the horizontal rules do nothing to clarify and everything to fragment.

Where your page has a major division, a horizontal rule may be appropriate. However, even then you should add CSS3 to lighten the `hr` element so that it's subtle — even adding transparency will help. Good designers know how to use horizontal rules sparingly and subtly, but non-designers can easily make a mess of their Web pages with overuse of <hr> tags.

FIGURES AND CAPTIONS

One of the more frustrating elements in HTML5 is the use of <figure> and <figcaption> together. By placing a `figcaption` element inside of a `figure` element container, you might assume that they form a single object for layout and design. The `figcaption` element is considered a child of the `figure` when the `figcaption` is nested inside of a `figure` element. However, that doesn't mean that they'll appear on the page together. In fact, aligning a figure with its caption can be tricky.

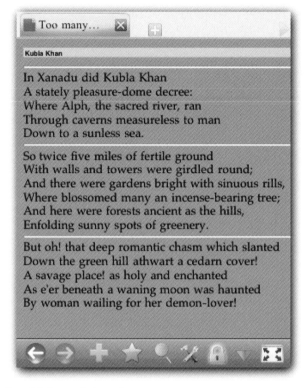

Figure 5-8: Horizontal rules can fragment meaning.

In more sophisticated CSS3 formatting, the figure and its caption can be treated as an object with a parent-child relationship. Just because `figure` and `figcaption` are part of HTML5's grouping elements that doesn't mean they're formatted on the page together; instead, it means that they can be referenced as a single flow in the main content of the page. In the meantime, you'll have to carefully work with the two elements together, as shown in the following HTML5 program (`Figure_n_caption.html` in this chapter's folder at www.wiley.com/go/smashinghtml5) where the caption references a stylized image.

```
<!DOCTYPE HTML>
<html>
<head>
<style type="text/css">
/* 732D3F,A66879,D9C3B0,260101,F2F2F2 */
body {
    background-color:#D9C3B0;
    color:#732D3F;
```

```
        font-family:Verdana, Geneva, sans-serif;
        font-size:11px;
}
aside {
     margin-left:260px;
}
h1 {
      font-family:"Trebuchet MS", Arial, Helvetica, sans-serif;
      background-color:#F2F2F2;
    color:#A66879;
    text-align:center;
}
figcaption {
      color:#A66879;
    background-color:#F2F2F2;
}
img {
     margin:5px;
}
</style>
<meta http-equiv="Content-Type" content="text/html; charset=UTF-8">
<title>Figure and Caption Grouping</title>
</head>
<body>
<header>
  <h1>Memories of Baja</h1>
</header>
<article>
  <figure> <img src="PuntaBufeo250.png" alt="Punta Bufeo"><br>
    <figcaption> Landing Strip on the Beach in Punta Bufeo </figcaption>
  </figure>
  <section>
    <p>Trips to the best places in Baja are accessible either by reinforced off-road
vehicles or small airplanes. The beaches are pristine, uncrowded, and uncluttered.
Fishing is most rewarding when the fish are cooked up in fish tacos—a delicacy not
to be missed. The <i>Sea of Cortez</i> (known also as the <i>Gulf of Baja</i> and
<i>Vermillion Sea</i>) is a bright and clear blue. Of course the beaches are
uncrowded and free of debris left by others.</p>
  </section>
</article>
</body>
</html>
```

You can begin to think about elements and their descendants. In this case, the figcaption element is a descendant of the figure element. Figure 5-9 shows the caption under the picture, both within the <figure> container.

As you can see clearly in Figure 5-9, the <figcaption> is differently styled, even though it's a descendant of the <figure> container. However, you can't assume that a figcaption element will be correctly positioned as in Figure 5-9 just because it's a child of the figure element that it captions.

Figure 5-9: Figure and figcaption used with a graphic.

ORGANIZING FILES

With a simple Web site, the organization of the files is simple. As the complexity of a site grows, especially if multiple designers and developers are involved, you need to get your site organized in separate directories and even servers sometimes. In this section, you'll learn about several organizational issues and how to deal with file organization and access.

IMAGE ORGANIZATION AND REFERENCE

A typical Web site will have one or more folders (directories) dedicated to image files or types of image files. In most of the examples so far in this book, the examples haven't used separate folders for images and the HTML5 pages that load them; instead all the image files are placed in the same directory as the HTML5 files. With a large number of Web pages and images to load into the pages, a more efficient ways to organize a site is to use separate folders for different groupings of media. How you actually organize your images depends on several different factors. The following are some possible directories and subdirectories that might be used:

- Formal Classifications (Animals > Mammals > Rodentia > Myomorpha > Mus musculus > Mickey)
- Topic (Vacations > Where to Go > Where to Stay > What to Pack)
- Processes (Baking > Making Dough > Preparing Dough > Setting Oven > Timing)

Whatever organizational plan is implemented, you need to understand how to access the images no matter how they're organized. All references are either to absolute or relative addresses.

ABSOLUTE REFERENCE

Any reference to an image is through a URL, whether it's a full listing of the address or one that references just the name of the file. An absolute address begins with `http://` and includes the full path to the HTML5 file. For example, the following is an absolute address to a file:

```
http://www.smashinghtml5.com/organization/graphics/faces.html
```

No matter where that URL is called from, it recognizes it as the named file at the end of the URL. The same is true with a source (`src`) reference to an image. If your code has the following link, no matter where the calling Web page is located, it will load `nose.png`.

```
<img src="http://www.smashinghtml5.com/organization/graphics/nose.png">
```

The calling Web page could be on an entirely different server, and it would go to the absolute address.

The advantage of using absolute addresses is that you don't have to worry about where a page is in your Web site. You don't even have to worry if it's on the same server. However, it leaves a good deal to be desired in terms of site organization, and then there are those long URL names you have to get just right.

RELATIVE REFERENCE

A relative reference is relative to the calling page's position on a Web site or its defined base. On your computer, your Web page has a `file` position rather than an `http` position. For example, the following is the absolute position on the file `somePage.html`:

```
"file:///Macintosh HD/Users/billsanders/Desktop/HTML5/somePage.html"
```

If I have a graphic in the folder `HTML5/`, I can use its relative address to call it from `somePage.html`. For example, if I have `anyGraphic.png` in the `HTML5` folder I just use the following relative reference:

```
<img src="anyGraphic.png">
```

However, if I want to organize my images into a separate folder called `images`, inside the `HTML5` folder, I would use the relative address:

```
<img src="images/anyGraphic.png">
```

You can drill down as many relative levels as you want with each level separated by a forward slash (/). For example, a more complex graphic set would look like the following:

```
<img src="images/animals/dogs/greaterSwissMtDogs/myDoggy.png">
```

Besides "drilling down" you may also want to "drill up." By drilling up, you access resources in folders your calling page is in. For example, suppose you have the following path and your HTML5 page is in the `baseFolder`.

```
topFolder/middleFolder/baseFolder
```

To access a graphic file in the `middleFolder`, you would use the following format:

```
<img src=".../anyGraphic.png">
```

If the graphic were in the `topFolder`, you would use the following format:

```
<img src="../../anyGraphic.png">
```

In drilling up, you don't name the target folder your calling Web page is in; instead, you use successive `../` characters until your call is at the level you want. This means, you can drill up to the level you want, and then drill down another branch. For example, the following drills up to the `topFolder`, and then inside the `topFolder` drills down through the image folder to the target graphic:

```
<img src="../../images/anyGraphic.png">
```

Figure 5-10 provides a general graphic illustration of accessing resources in higher- and lower-level folders.

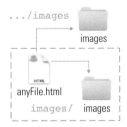

Figure 5-10: Relative paths.

As noted in the "Setting Your Home Base" section, earlier in this chapter, your relative position could be set to some location other than the one where the file itself is located. For example, consider the following two Web pages (`Earth.html` and `Alien.html` in this chapter's folder at `www.wiley.com/go/smashinghtml5`). The first calls the second on a different server; however, because the first page's base is set to the second server, the call is a relative one. The first file is named `Earth.html` and is located in the domain `smashingHTML5.com` in the `smashing` folder. However, its base is set to `smashingHTML5.net` in the `smashing` folder. So, it can use a relative URL to access the file `Alien.html` on a wholly different server.

Base Set to a Different Server

```
<!DOCTYPE HTML>
<html>
<head>
<base href="http://www.smashingHTML5.net/html5/smashing/">
<meta http-equiv="Content-Type" content="text/html; charset=UTF-8">
<title>Earth</title>
</head>
<body>
<h1>This is Earth</h1>
<a href="Alien.html">Blast off!</a>
</body>
</html>
```

Web Page on a Different Server

```
<!DOCTYPE HTML>
<html>
<head>
<meta http-equiv="Content-Type" content="text/html; charset=UTF-8">
<title>The Planet Smashing</title>
</head>
<body>
<h1>Page from an Alien Server</h1>
</body>
</html>
```

Even though the domain for the first page (`Earth.html`) is `smashingHTML5.com`, the base is set to `smashingHTML5.net`. As a result, a relative link to `Alien.html`, which resides on `smashingHTML5.net`, is made without having to use an absolute address.

TAKE THE WHEEL

In the first section of this chapter, you saw how to use the `Refresh` state to automatically change pages. To have a little fun with animation and the `Refresh` state, take a look at this link to the works of Eadweard Muybridge:

```
http://138.23.124.165/collections/permanent/object_genres/photographers/muybridge/
  contents.html#
```

What's interesting about Muybridge is that, in 1878, he was able to create movies using a series of photographs. So, well before Thomas Edison invented the motion picture, Muybridge was making short movies (about 12 frames) giving us an animated view to the past. The University of California, Riverside, has preserved and animated Muybridge's work using animated GIF files online. To see how you can make animations using refresh pages, download one of the animated GIF's from Muybridge's collection from the link above — locomotion studies — and extract the 12 individual photographs from the GIF file. You can extract animated GIF images with Adobe Photoshop, Adobe Fireworks, and several other programs. (Search on "extract images from animated GIF" in a search engine to find plenty of ways to get the individual images. If you have a Mac, you can use the Preview application, and just drag the individual images from Preview to a separate folder.)

Once you have extracted the individual GIF files, set up your animation using the Refresh state with the meta element in the <head> section of your program. To get started, use the following HTML5 script (an1.html in this chapter's folder at www.wiley.com/go/smashinghtml5).

```
<!DOCTYPE HTML>
<html>
<head>
<meta http-equiv="Content-Type" content="text/html; charset=UTF-8">
<meta http-equiv="Refresh" content="0.1; URL=an2.html">
<title>Image 1</title>
</head>
<body>
<img src="an1.png" alt="one">
</body>
</html>
```

The individual GIF files were saved as .png files and renamed an1.png through an12.png (the an is for animation). Likewise, the 12 HTML files were named using the an preface from an1.html through an12.html. Once you're finished, you'll have a walking horse. If you link the 12th page back to the first, the horse just keeps on truckin'.

6

DISPLAYING DATA WITH TABLES

WHEN HTML WAS in its infancy, the `table` element was used for the bulk of page formatting. The advent of CSS introduced a whole new set of rules for formatting and the table was abandoned as a formatting tool — and for good reason. However, certain table features in CSS3 have been reintroduced for specific types of formatting. So, although tables still are not general formatting tools, they have key functions for displaying data sets and for CSS3 general formatting.

This chapter explores the new CSS3 properties that you can use for accomplishing general formatting layouts, but the chapter's main focus is on tabular data display. *Tabular data* is nothing more than data laid out in a table for ease of reading and not primary layout structures.

CSS3 TABLE PROPERTIES FOR HTML5

In a classic statement of double messages, the World Wide Web Consortium (W3C), the official body that sets the standards for HTML5, states emphatically, "Tables must not be used as layout aids." Then in a note following that admonition, the same document states, "There are a variety of alternatives to using HTML tables for layout, primarily using CSS positioning and the CSS table model."

What this means is that, in general, table elements should not be used for layouts other than tabular data. However, if you need tables in layouts, use CSS3 table properties.

The reason for this admonition is that when CSS became available, all layout was to be done with CSS. In order not to dissuade designers and developers from using the CSS3 table properties (only), W3C added the note that it was okay to use CSS3 table properties and attributes in layout. So, if you're familiar with all the old warnings about not using table elements in layout, rest assured that CSS3 table properties are fine for design — up to a point.

In order to see what this CSS3 feature can do for a design, the first step is to look at the CSS3 `display` property value of `table` and `table-cell`. The display property can be envisioned as a layout statement. The values within the display map out how the display is to be arranged. One of the easiest ways to make a display is to use the table and table-cell values. It might be helpful to think of the table property as a big container and the table-cells as the individual cells in the container. As far as more sophisticated designs are concerned, table-cells are pretty close to a table as a design tool and all the associated problems inherent in it. So, use it for simple applications where you just need a few columns to achieve a simple task.

The CSS3 format for setting up displays uses predefined classes, a user class, or an ID. The display property is assigned a simple table or table-cell as a value. The following is an example (within a style definition):

```
.story {
    display: table;
}
.col1 {
    display: table-cell;
    width: 250px;
    padding-right: 20px;
    color:#cc0000;
}
```

The `story` class simply defines the display property as a table. The col1 class, which you can place inside the table, is displayed as a table-cell, and it's helpful to think of it as such. The following code (`DisplayTable.html` in this chapter's folder at www.wiley.com/go/smashinghtml5) shows how to set up a design that can be used to display text and graphics in two columns.

```
<!DOCTYPE HTML>
<html>
<head>
```

```
<style type="text/css">
body {
    font-family:Verdana, Geneva, sans-serif;
    font-size:12px;
}
h1 {
    font-family:"Arial Black", Gadget, sans-serif;
    width:520px;
    text-align:center;
    color:#005500;
}
.story {
    display: table;
}
.col1 {
    display: table-cell;
    width: 250px;
    padding-right: 20px;
    color:#cc0000;
}
.col2 {
    display: table-cell;
    width: 250px;
    color:blue;
}
</style>
<meta http-equiv="Content-Type" content="text/html; charset=UTF-8">
<title>Table with Display Property</title>
</head>
<body>
<header>
  <h1>2010 World Cup</h1>
  <div class="col1"><img src="cupImages/us.gif"></div>
  <div class="col2"><img src="cupImages/england.gif"></div>
</header>
<br>
<article class="story">
  <section class="col1">During the 2010 FIFA World Cup in South Africa, each country
was represented by one team. The United States was made up of players from all over
the U.S., where soccer has been played by youth teams for the last 40 years.
However, soccer has not caught on with the same enthusiasm in the United States as
it has in the rest of the world—where it is known as "football." Nevertheless, the
U.S. team did well, winning its class in the first round of play.</section>
  <section class="col2"> One of the few nations that has more than a single country
represented in World Cup play is the United Kingdom. In the first round of play,
the United States and England, represented by the St. George flag (rather than the
Union Jack), played to a tie. The tie delighted the Americans and dismayed the
English. Like the U.S., England made it to the second round, and, like the U.S.,
they, too, failed to move on to the next level.</section>
</article>
</body>
</html>
```

The `story` class is a container for ordering different sections that are assigned `col1` or `col2` classes. However, the `col1` and `col2` classes do not have to be placed in a table. Notice that the two graphics — one each in the two different table-cell classes — are defined using `<div>` tags within the `<header>` container. They're then used again inside the `<article>` container that has been assigned a `story` class (table). The two sections have been defined as `col1` and `col2` displays, and although they're not seen in the containers for the two graphics, you can see that different colored text helps to show their separate status. Figure 6-1 shows what you can expect to see in your browser.

Figure 6-1: Using the CSS3 `display` property with table values.

As you can see in Figure 6-1, using table-cells is an easy way to set up multiple columns. When you develop more sophisticated Web sites, you'll want to use more advanced CSS3 display definitions beyond tables and table-cells, but the `table` property in CSS3 is available when you need it.

TABLES AND TABULAR DATA

Keeping in mind that we'll get an electrical shock if we use standard table markups for site design, this next section takes a close look at how to use tables for displaying tabular data.

Tabular data can be anything from a set of numbers to graphics to descriptive text. If you've ever ordered parts for your car (or just about anything else), chances are, the parts are listed in a tabular format. Usually, you'll find a description of the part, the part number, the year model the part is for, the car model, and the price.

The key to understanding tabular data is that it's laid out in rows and columns for displaying information in common categories. Further, the purpose of a table is to clarify information so that the user can find what she needs.

TABLE BASICS

The basic elements of a table are

- The table itself, `<table>`
- The table rows, `<tr>`
- The table cells, `<td>`
- The table headers, `<th>`

Generally, a table caption `<caption>` is used at the top of the table. A clear table generally has clearly marked column and row headings. The cell in the upper-left corner is often left blank so that the first column doesn't label the row heads; however, the standards state that no cell be left empty. So, the corner cell in `BasicTable.html` contains "r/c" to fill the space — for now, at least. The following example shows the basic table elements in a simple table. The row and columns both have headings, and the data cells represent data placed in the labeled rows and columns.

```
<!DOCTYPE HTML>
<html>
<head>
<meta http-equiv="Content-Type" content="text/html; charset=UTF-8">
<title>Basic Table</title>
</head>
<body>
<table>
  <caption>
  Rows and Columns in a Table
  </caption>
  <tr>
    <td>r/c
    <th>Column 1
    <th>Column 2
    <th>Column 3
  <tr>
    <th>Row 1
    <td>data a
    <td>data b
    <td>data c
  <tr>
```

```
    <th>Row 2
    <td>data x
    <td>data y
    <td>data z
</table>
</body>
</html>
```

One of the more interesting aspects of the table tags is that the closing tags are optional. No best practice suggests that closing tags be used or not. Formatting the code so that the rows are clearly delineated is important for making sense out of what you see. By not including the table cell closing tags, the code seems to be a lot clearer and less cluttered, and that's a good thing. So, the closing cell tags are going to be left out unless putting one in will help clarify what's going on in the listing. Figure 6-2 shows what you'll see when you launch the file in a browser.

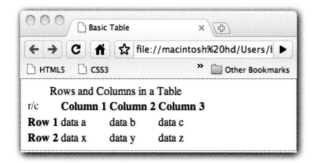

Figure 6-2: A basic table.

Notice that while the `<th>` tags cause the text to be shown in boldface that the table `<caption>` does not. That can be fixed with CSS3, and so can the rest of the table to make it more useful. However, to get started with tables, all you need to understand are the basics.

STYLING A TABLE

You don't use tables for general styling work, but that doesn't mean that you can ignore the style of the table itself. The good news in HTML5 is that borders on tables are not a default state as they had been in previous versions of HTML. In fact, the table border attribute is no longer supported in HTML5. If you want lines around the cells, you have to take that responsibility yourself and add them using CSS3. Borders around cells or anything else must be done judiciously or (in the opinion of many designers) not at all.

ADDING BORDERS WITH CSS3

The renowned information-design thinker Edward Tufte cautions that borders can clutter up the background so much that the data are difficult to read and understand. Although borders clearly separate tabular data, visible borders muddy the waters between the data, making each

data point difficult to easily discern. To see what Tufte means, enter the following script
(BadBorders.html in this chapter's folder at www.wiley.com/go/smashinghtml5)
and look at the page.

```
<!DOCTYPE HTML>
<html>
<head>
<style type="text/css">
table {
     width:400px;
     border-style:groove;
     border-width:thick;
     border-color:#FF5C19;
    color:#C00;
    font-family:Verdana, Geneva, sans-serif;
     font-size:10px;
}
caption {
     font-family:Tahoma, Geneva, sans-serif;
     font-size:24px;
     color:hsl(17, 60%, 40%);
     padding:12px;
}
td, th {
     border-style:solid;
     border-width:thin;
     border-color:#000;
}
</style>
<meta http-equiv="Content-Type" content="text/html; charset=UTF-8">
<title>Borders Are Blinding</title>
</head>
<body>
<table>
  <caption>
  Pet Care
  </caption>
  <tr>
    <td>&#167;
   <th>Cats
    <th>Dogs
    <th>Fish
  <tr>
    <th>Feeding
    <td>Cat food is good
    <td>Doggy treats
    <td>Yucky fish food
  <tr>
    <th>Care
    <td>Scratching post
```

```
        <td>A rubber ball
        <td>Clean tank and air bubbles
  </table>
  </body>
  </html>
```

Figure 6-3 shows the results, but before looking at it, examine the CSS3 code carefully. Also, the value &#167 is a character code for a symbol entered using code instead of the keyboard. All UTF-8 characters can be entered this way. Certain symbols such as the greater-than (>) and less-than (<) characters must be entered using this method; otherwise, the parser reads them as part of a tag. Now, take a look at Figure 6-3 to see the page with the borders.

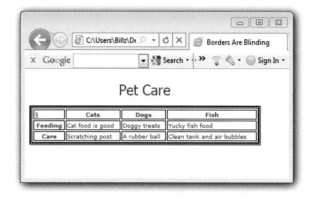

Figure 6-3: Borders can interfere with data clarity.

When trying to read the different data elements, the borders get in the way. To fix that, all you have to do is add padding to the borders and height to the cells. In the style, change the `td` and `th` element definitions to the following:

```
td, th {
     height:50px;
     border-style:solid;
     border-width:thin;
     border-color:#000;
     padding:20px;
}
```

All that you changed is the height of the cell and the space between the border and the text (padding). However, the difference is significant, as you can see in Figure 6-4.

With the added space around the data, the cell value is far clearer. The cells aren't too pretty, but that's easy to take care of — just remove them.

Figure 6-4: Adding space within table cells.

DATA CLARIFICATION WITH BACKGROUND COLORS

Back in the old days, computer printouts were done on paper with alternating background colors to make it easier to separate individual records. (Records and rows are used interchangeably in this context.) As you saw, heavy borders intruding on each data cell detract from clarity. That's why the older computer printouts used different background colors. So, instead of separating records by borders, you need to see how to do so using colors (see ColorRows.html in this chapter's folder at www.wiley.com/go/smashinghtml5).

```
<!DOCTYPE HTML>
<html>
<head>
<style type="text/css">
td {
    width:70px;
}
body {
    font-family:Verdana, Geneva, sans-serif;
    font-size:10px;
}
caption {
    font-family:"Arial Black", Gadget, sans-serif;
    font-size:12px;
    font-weight:500;
    color:#360;
```

```
        background-color:hsla(113, 46%, 91%, 1);
    }
    .money {
        text-align:right;
    }
    table {
        background-color:#FFC;
    }
    .alt1 {
        background-color:hsla(113, 46%, 91%, .8);
    }
    </style>
    <meta http-equiv="Content-Type" content="text/html; charset=UTF-8">
    <title>Color Separation</title>
    </head>
    <body>
    <table>
      <caption>
      Sick Thinking Games, Inc.
      </caption>
      <tr>
        <th>Name
        <th>Acct No.
        <th>Amount
      <tr class="alt1">
        <td>Joe Doaks
        <td>ID065212
        <td class="money">$92.83
      <tr>
        <td>Jane Franco
        <td>ID034986
        <td class="money">$17.78
      <tr class="alt1">
        <td>Fernando Rodriguez
        <td>ID019921
        <td class="money">$221.83
      <tr>
        <td>Benny Jet
        <td>ID073456
        <td class="money">$320.45
    </table>
    </body>
    </html>
```

By default, the `td` element left-justifies text, which is desirable in most cases. However, with floating point numbers (numbers with decimal points), numbers are clearer using right-justification. So, one of the style sheet classes included a `money` class to right-justify financial data.

The entire table is given a light yellow background. However, the background color of the table doesn't affect the materials in the `<caption>` container; so the `caption` element gets a color background compatible with the table's. Further, the table, while relatively small, wants to optimize it for small portable devices, so the text is set to 10px (10px is pretty close to 10-point text). Figure 6-5 shows the results (with a few more records added to fill up the vertical screen) on a mobile device.

Figure 6-5: Alternate row viewing in a table on a mobile device.

By using a color with less than 100 percent opacity (some transparency), the alternating green is slightly mixed with the light yellow background color. The caption background color is the same as the alternating row green, but it has 100 percent opacity (solid) and you can see it has a slightly different tint. The `th` elements inherited the table's background color but serve well as column labels without any other adjustments.

The cell widths are set to a non-relative value (70px) because the width reflects the fact that the table is optimized for mobile viewing. As a result, the names can take up double rows and not detract from either the design or the table's functionality.

COMPLEX TABLES

The term complex implies tables that are difficult to understand. Actually, complex tables are solutions to tricky problems. If you're using tables to organize data coming out of a database, chances are good that you can use a pretty standard table with a measured set of rows and columns all the same size.

When you begin to use a table to display data for just about anything, including data coming from a database, you may encounter situations in which something happens to change the neat set of rows and columns, and you have to make adjustments to fit more into a single row or column than originally planned.

In order to understand complex tables, you need to understand the idea of a cell. A table is nothing more than a collection of cells ordered into rows and columns. The intersection of a column and row is the cell. In HTML5, you create cells using the <td> and <th> tags. Figure 6-2, earlier in this chapter, shows basic cells organized into rows and columns.

USING THE ROWSPAN AND COLSPAN ATTRIBUTES

To change a cell's default characteristic of an intersection between a single row and column, you need to use a td element's attributes, rowspan and/or colspan. Each attribute is assigned a positive integer value that expands a cell to cover multiple rows or columns. Figure 6-6 shows a standard table made up of equal-size cells and a comparative table with expanded rows and columns.

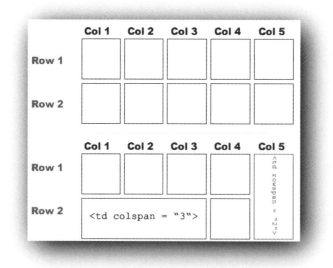

Figure 6-6: A table with equal-size cells and a table with rowspan and colspan.

Figure 6-6 shows that the first cell in Row 2 in the bottom table took up the space of three cells in Row 2 in the top table. In Col 5 of the bottom table, both Row 1 and Row 2 were collapsed into a single cell taking up both rows. Importantly, the top table has ten cells and the bottom table has only seven cells. When you code tables with `rowspan` and `colspan`, you'll use fewer `<td>` tags compared to a table that does not (see `RowColSpan.html` in this chapter's folder at `www.wiley.com/go/smashinghtml5`).

```html
<!DOCTYPE HTML>
<html>
<head>
<style type="text/css">
caption {
    font-family:"Arial Black", Gadget, sans-serif;
    color:#C60;
}
table {
    font-family:Verdana, Geneva, sans-serif;
}
td, tr {
    border-style:solid;
    border-width:thin;
    border-color:#ccc;
  width:120px;
    padding:5px;
}
</style>
<meta http-equiv="Content-Type" content="text/html; charset=UTF-8">
<title>Colspan and Rowspan</title>
</head>
<body>
<table>
  <caption>
  Rowspan and Colspan
  </caption>
  <tr>
    <td rowspan="2">Row A and Row B
    <td>Column 2a
    <td>Column 3a
    <td>Column 4a
  <tr>
    <td>Column 2b
    <td>Column 3b
    <td>Column 4b
  <tr>
    <td>Row C
    <td>Column 2c
    <td colspan="2">Column 3c and Column 4c
</table>
</body>
</html>
```

This example uses a very light gray border so that you can better see the spans — vertically and horizontally. However, you don't need the borders to use spans. In fact, without borders, it can be difficult to distinguish where the spans actually exist, which can be a good thing. Figure 6-7 shows the actual table with the two spans.

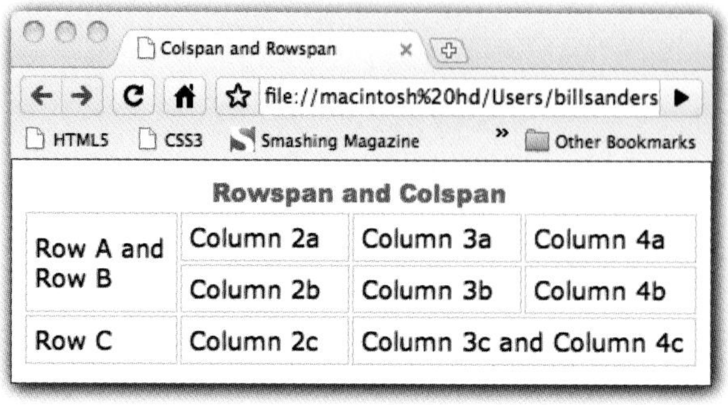

Figure 6-7: Adding vertical and horizontal spans.

You can see that the table in Figure 6-7 has 10 cells where a full 4-by-3 table would have 12. Likewise, in the listing, you can see ten `<td>` tags. Both `colspan` and `rowspan` can be a little tricky, but if you think of them in terms of cell mergers, they're a little easier to understand and work with.

PRACTICAL SPANS IN TABLES

When creating complex tables using `colspan` and `rowspan`, the exercise may seem to be one in futility because a practical application doesn't seem that obvious. Alternatively, you may look to do the whole thing in CSS3 without any use of table elements or attributes. So, the following walks through a simple but typical scenario where spanning cells is a practical solution.

Consider a Web development/design firm that has set up project management using tables as a simple way to keep track of a project's progress. The production team is divided into the following groups, each with a separate record:

- Team coordinator (1)
- Design team (4)
- Rich interactive application (RIA) design (2)
- Front-end development (3)
- Back-end development (2)

The columns for the project include the following:

- Task
- Project
- Team members
- Due date

That should be simple enough to understand and complex enough to be useful. The irony of making this table is in adding the spans where only one item is in the cell. It's almost counter-intuitive because the column for the team members will have several rows within the other cells that have a `rowspan` the size of the team size. The following program (`SpanProject.html` in this chapter's folder at `www.wiley.com/go/smashinghtml5`) illustrates how this is done.

```
<!DOCTYPE HTML>
<html>
<head>
<style type="text/css">
/* F2F0E6,595443,A6A08D,3A3F59,8D91A6 */
caption {
    font-family:"Arial Black", Gadget, sans-serif;
    color:#3A3F59;
}
table {
    font-family:Verdana, Geneva, sans-serif;
    background-color:#F2F0E6;
  padding:5px;
    border-collapse:collapse;
}
td, tr {
    padding-right:8px;
    font-size:11px;
    border-collapse:collapse;
}
.bluish {
    background-color:#8D91A6;
}
.brownish {
    background-color:#A6A08D;
}
</style>
<meta http-equiv="Content-Type" content="text/html; charset=UTF-8">
<title>Project Tracker</title>
</head>
<body>
<table>
  <caption>
  Project Plan
  </caption>
  <tr>
    <th>Task
    <th>Project
    <th>Team
    <th>Due Date
  <tr class="bluish">
    <td>Coordinator
    <td>Cold Fire
```

```
        <td>Emma Peel
        <td>01-21-2012
      <tr class="brownish">
        <td rowspan="4">Design Team
        <td rowspan="4">Cold Fire
        <td>Sancho Panza
        <td rowspan="4">10-01-2011
      <tr class="brownish">
        <td>John Watson
      <tr class="brownish">
        <td>Edward McMahon
      <tr class="brownish">
        <td>Vanna White
      <tr class="bluish">
        <td rowspan="2">Rich Interaction<br>
          Design
        <td rowspan="2">Cold Fire
        <td  rowspan>Garth Algar
        <td rowspan="2">11-12-2011
      <tr class="bluish">
        <td> John McIntyre
      <tr class="brownish">
        <td rowspan="3">Front End<br>
          Development
        <td rowspan="3">Cold Fire
        <td>Barney Rubble
        <td rowspan="3">12-15-2011
      <tr class="brownish">
        <td>Ethel Mertz
      <tr class="brownish">
        <td>Paul Schaffer
      <tr class="bluish">
        <td rowspan="2">Back End<br>
          Development
        <td rowspan="2">Cold Fire
        <td  rowspan>Louise Sawyer
        <td rowspan="2">01-15-2012
      <tr class="bluish">
        <td>Andy Richer
  </table>
  </body>
  </html>
```

Basically, the <td> tags that include a rowspan attribute are those that have to be large enough to match the number of team members that will be in the same row. Figure 6-8 shows how the page appears in a browser.

The most important thing to remember about tables is that they should be used judiciously. They aren't general design tools, but you can use CSS3 to design the look of tabular data set in table elements. So think, "Tabular data, tables; non-tabular content, CSS3 only."

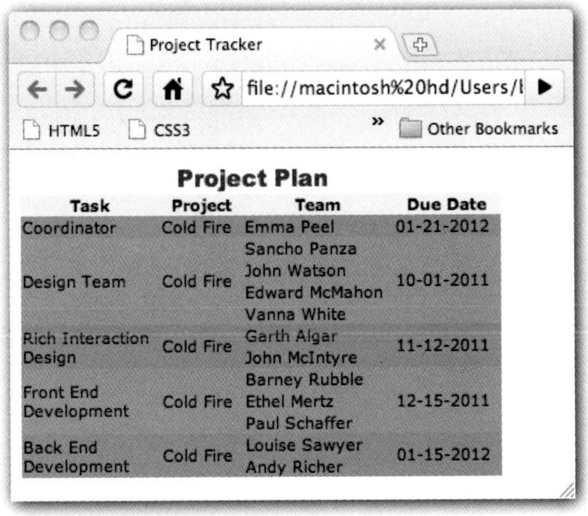

Figure 6-8: Multiple and differential rowspans.

TAKE THE WHEEL

Figure 6-9 shows the end result of the challenge table. It has headers at the top and bottom, and the background colors for the rows are at 20 percent and 40 percent opacity. See if you can replicate it with HTML5 and CSS3.

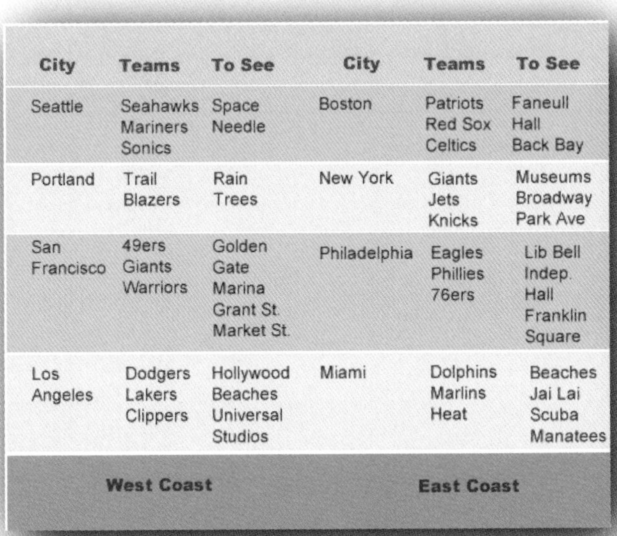

Figure 6-9: Challenge table.

Feel free to change the regions, cities, teams, and comments — especially if you're a New York Yankees fan. You can substitute cities from all over the world and include hockey, rugby, soccer (football), cricket, and women's teams. Just get the table to look like the one in Figure 6-9.

7 ALL ABOUT LINKS

THE MAJOR CAPABILITY of Web pages besides displaying text, graphics, and media is loading other pages. Using Web pages, people — including designers and developers — tend to think of *going somewhere* or *getting something*. We even think of helping users with site maps and navigation tools that imply that they're on some kind of trip. The navigational issues are important and are discussed in Chapter 8.

However, this chapter looks at how links load other Web pages, as well as how they're used to access alternate style sheets. Included in this examination are the different attributes that are related to loading pages, the details of accessing a page, and CSS3 properties used to both style links and to launch interactive features in those properties.

THE LINK ELEMENT AND ITS KEY ATTRIBUTES

The major link element is the a element. So, most of this chapter will focus on the `<a>` tag. However, before doing that, the `<link>` tag is important to consider. It, too, loads pages, and while the files loaded using the link element cannot be seen, they're an important kind of data-loading feature that needs to be understood for optimum use.

The attributes used with both `<a>` and `<link>` tags share attribute characteristics with all HTML5 elements, so they can be treated just like an attribute for `<h1>`, `<body>`, or any other HTML5 tag. However, the attributes used with link elements tend to focus on loading files (`.html`, `.css`, and `.js`) rather than on appearance.

The link element itself is part of the metadata content and is found within the head container at the top of a Web page. In Chapter 3, you saw how to use link to load external CSS files. In the first section, I show you how to set up your Web page to load mutually independent style sheets.

ALTERNATE STYLE SHEETS

In an attempt to make Web pages as accessible to as many users as possible, the new HTML5 browsers have pop-up menus that allow you to select from more than one style sheet. Using the `<link>` tag with the rel attribute set to `alternate stylesheet`, you can include as many style sheets as you want, and the user can select which she likes best. Here's the general format:

```
<link rel="stylesheet" type="text/css" href="default.css" title="default">
<link rel="alternate stylesheet" type="text/css" href="other.css" title="alternate">
```

The ref value `alternate stylesheet` is an entity that is different from the `alternate` value that I cover in the next section. You can load as many style sheets as you want; however, the user can only change to an alternate style sheet — not to a regular style sheet.

To see how the alternate style sheets work, this next example begins with two different external style sheets saved in files named `warm.css` and `cool.css`. Then, the Web page code creates the code that loads the warm style sheet as the default, and users may choose to switch between the two styles.

Warm Color Theme

```
@charset "UTF-8";
/* CSS Document */

body {
    /*FFE0A3,7F7D78,FFFAF0,7F7052,CCC8C0 */
    font-family:Verdana, Geneva, sans-serif;
    font-size:11;
    background-color:#FFFAF0;
    color:#7F7052;
}
```

```css
h1 {
    font-family:"Arial Black", Gadget, sans-serif;
    color:#7F7D78;
    text-align:center;
}
h2 {
    font-family:"Lucida Sans Unicode", "Lucida Grande", sans-serif;
    background-color:#CCC8C0;
    color:#FFE0A3;
}
```

Cool Color Theme

```css
@charset "UTF-8";
/* CSS Document */

body {
    /*056CF2,0F88F2,52B5F2,85D3F2,F2F2F2 */
    font-family:Verdana, Geneva, sans-serif;
    font-size:11;
    background-color:#F2F2F2;
    color:#056CF2;
}
h1 {
    font-family:"Arial Black", Gadget, sans-serif;
    color:#52B5F2;
    text-align:center;
}
h2 {
    font-family:"Lucida Sans Unicode", "Lucida Grande", sans-serif;
    background-color:#85D3F2;
    color:#0F88F2;
}
```

The warm and cool color schemes use identical CSS3 code, save for the color values. In that way when we compare them, everything except the color palette will be the same. The following Web page (`AlternateStylesheets.html` in this chapter's folder at www. wiley.com/go/smashinghtml5) uses both CSS external files with one being the default (`stylesheet`) and the other the alternate (`alternate stylesheet`):

```html
<!DOCTYPE HTML>
<html>
<head>
<link rel="stylesheet" type="text/css" href="warm.css" title="Warm View (Default)">
<link rel="alternate stylesheet" type="text/css" href="cool.css" title="Cool scene">
<meta http-equiv="Content-Type" content="text/html; charset=UTF-8">
<title>Alternative External Style Sheets</title>
</head>
<body>
```

```
<h1>Warm and Cool</h1>
<h2> Switch between Warm and Cool </h2>
To switch, select View > Page Style [or Style] from your browser menu and choose the
  one you want. Use either the Opera or Firefox browser to start, and then test the
  other HTML5 browsers.
</body>
</html>
```

The rest of the usage is up to the browser. In testing the different HTML5 browsers, at the time of testing only the Opera and Firefox browsers actually had menu items for selecting different style sheets. If you plan to use alternate style sheets with a general set of browsers, be sure to test them with this program first. Figure 7-1 shows the default setting in the Opera browser with the style sheet selection open.

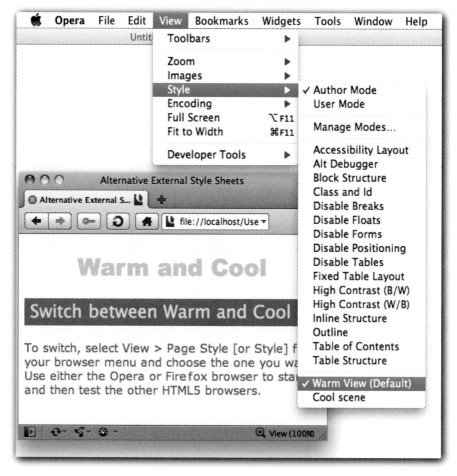

Figure 7-1: Displaying the warm style on the Opera browser.

As you can see in Figure 7-1, the Opera browser path View > Style menu shows the title of the default CSS3 style — Warm View (Default). If users want to switch to the alternate style sheet, they simply select the Cool scene. Figure 7-2 shows the Firefox browser selecting the alternate style sheet.

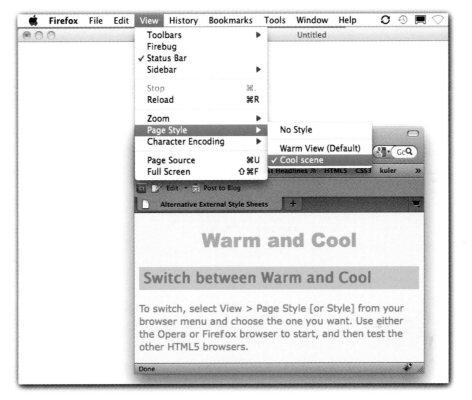

Figure 7-2: Switching style sheets in Firefox.

In Firefox, the menu to select style sheets is slightly different, but like the Opera browser, it provides users with the opportunity to change styles dynamically if they want.

LINK ICONS

Next to using the `rel` attribute for assigning style sheets, the most used value is for setting up a small icon to represent the page. Graphic icons can be assigned to the `rel` attribute using the following format:

```
<link rel="icon" href="graphic.png" sizes="32x32"/>
```

In earlier versions of HTML, the relation value was `shortcut icon` but just `icon` works as well.

In setting up the following example (`LinkIcon.html` in this chapter's folder at www. wiley.com/go/smashinghtml5), several <meta> tags are used as well. They contain information about the page used by search engines, and although they're always helpful, they aren't required for setting up the link relation to an icon.

```
<!DOCTYPE HTML>
<html>
<head>
<meta name="application-name" content="HTML5, CSS3"/>
<meta name="description" content="HTML5 Linking icon"/>
<meta name="application-url" content="LinkIcon.html"/>
<link rel="icon" href="LinkAnchor.png" sizes="32x32"/>
<meta http-equiv="Content-Type" content="text/html; charset=UTF-8">
<title>Page Icon</title>
</head>
<body>
Link icon
</body>
</html>
```

In testing the icons with four different browsers (Safari, Chrome, Opera, Firefox), the icons only showed up on the Opera and Firefox browsers. Internet Explorer (IE) was not tested because at the time of this writing, Microsoft was still developing IE9. Also, none of the mobile browsers displayed the page icon. Figure 7-3 shows where the icons (a small green anchor) appear on the Opera and Firefox browsers.

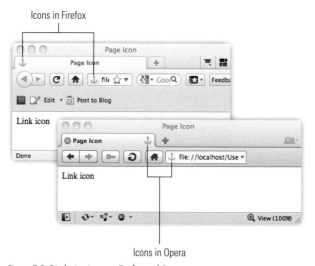

Figure 7-3: Displaying icons on Firefox and Opera.

In creating an icon, I used a .png file set to the default 32 x 32 pixels. You can use different sizes, but the limits are not clear; however, they are set to where the height and width are the same.

PREFETCHING

A new HTML5 value for the `rel` attribute in the `link` element is `prefetch`. Suppose you have a page that is a little "hefty" — it's got some big content like large graphics, video, or audio. Before users go to the page, wouldn't it be nice to preload the page (graphics and all) so that when they click on the link, everything is ready for them? That's what prefetching is. While the browser is idle, prefetching gives it something to do. For example, the following uses prefetch to load a video:

```
<link rel="prefetch" href="Test.mov">
```

So when the user goes to the page with the video, it has already started loading — or it may be completely loaded and ready to go. Here are some other examples:

```
<link rel="prefetch" href="monkeys.html">
<link rel="prefetch" href="monsterTrucksFull.png">
<link rel="prefetch" href="http://www.sandlight.com">
<link rel="prefetch alternate stylesheet" ="http://wherever.org/fall.css"> href
<link rel="prefetch" href="sumVa.mp4" title="Summer vacation">
```

Before you start planning to use the `prefetch` value with every page that links to a "heavy" page, remember that its value is dependent on whether users are likely to go to that page. For example, suppose you're creating a Web site for a big department store, and users select from several different graphic displays of products. If the Web page prefetches all the graphics in the selection matrix, it's going to add a heavy load to the user's computer. So, instead of getting a crisp response, loading the selected page could be sluggish because it has all the other graphics in memory that have been prefetched.

One way to optimize prefetch is to organize your pages so that links to a heavy page have a path that limits pre-loading. Pages that include media that require a good deal of load time should have a path to them that has only a few choices with heavy loads.

OTHER LINK ATTRIBUTES

Other than the `rel` attribute, the other `link` attributes include:

- `href`: Points to external style sheets and icons.
- `media`: Specifies the kind of media for the `link` — screen, PDF, print; if no value is assigned to media, the default is "all."
- `hreflang`: Provides the language of a resource and is purely advisory.
- `type`: Identifies the type of file content, such as "text/css" — the MIME types.
- `sizes`: Specifies the dimensions of an icon, such as 32x32, 48x48, and other sizes used for graphic figures used as icons.
- `title`: Has a real value when using alternative style sheets, but otherwise it's advisory.

As you've seen in the examples using the `rel` attribute, these other attributes are often used in conjunction with `rel`.

133

PAGE LINKS

The a element in HTML5, as well as in previous versions of HTML, is one of the key elements in the language. Its primary use is to serve as a means to load a page using the href attribute. Without the href attribute, the <a> tag can serve as a placeholder, but for all intents and purposes, the a element is really a combination of the element and the attribute. That's why we tend to think in terms of a href or an <a href> tag rather than just the a element by itself. This section examines the nuances of the a element with the focus on the href attribute, but the first topic is using the rel attribute with the a element.

MORE OF THE REL ATTRIBUTE

The rel attribute is related to more than just the link element, and while most of the rel values assigned to link also apply to the a and area elements, only a subset is examined here. The full list of applicable values for the rel attribute in the a element include the following:

- alternate
- archives
- author
- bookmark
- external
- first
- help
- index
- last
- license
- next
- nofollow
- noreferrer
- prev
- search
- sidebar
- tag
- up

Of these, several are for organizing navigation, and these will be discussed more in Chapter 8. For example, index, first, last, prev, and next (among others) all refer to navigation order. I'm introducing them here so that when navigation in a larger context is discussed in Chapter 8, you'll be familiar with the concepts. Other values assigned to the rel attribute in the a element context have more to do with identifying certain characteristics, such as the link's author or a help link, and I discuss them first.

Author relations

Sometimes, a Web page includes the page's author, and you may want to contact her. To help identify the relation, an `author` value can be assigned to the link. A common link for such situations is the `mailto:` keyword used in an `href` assignment. For example, the following listing (`AuthorLink.html` in this chapter's folder at `www.wiley.com/go/smashing html5`) uses the `author` value along with the `mailto:` link.

```
<!DOCTYPE HTML>
<html>
<head>
<style type="text/css">
/* FFF8E3,CCCC9F,33332D,9FB4CC,DB4105  */
body {
     font-family:Verdana, Geneva, sans-serif;
     font-size:11px;
     background-color:#CCCC9F;
     color:#33332D;
}
h1 {
     background-color:#33332D;
     color:#9FB4CC;
     font-family:"Arial Black", Gadget, sans-serif;
     text-align:center;
}
h2 {
     background-color:#DB4105;
     color:#FFF8E3;
}
a {
     text-decoration:none;
     font-size:9px;
     color:#DB4105;
}
</style>
<meta http-equiv="Content-Type" content="text/html; charset=UTF-8">
<title>Author</title>
</head>
<body>
<header>
  <h1>All about HTML5</h1>
</header>
<article>
  <header>
    <h2>  Herein lies the Wisdom of the Ages </h2>
  </header>
  <section> Whoaaa!&#8213;<em>Wisdom of the Ages?</em>&#8213;That's a lot of respon-
  sibility! Why not&#8213;<em>The best I can do since 2010?</em>
    <p> Who wrote this thing anyway?</p>
    <h3>He did!&#8595;</h3>
```

```
      <footer>
        <nav><a href="mailto:bill@billzplace.net" rel=author>Bill Sanders</a></nav>
      </footer>
    </section>
  </article>
</body>
</html>
```

In creating the author e-mail link, the a element is styled to get rid of the underline — the default style for links — and replaces it with a small but noticeable color. To some extent, the entire page draws focus to the link, as you can see in Figure 7-4.

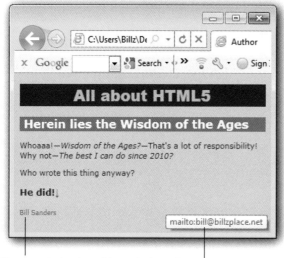

When cursor is placed over link to author's e-mail...

... a message appears in the lower-right corner.

Figure 7-4: Using the author e-mail link.

The cite element can be confused with the author value assigned to the rel attribute in an a element. First, cite is an independent element, and second, it italicizes the content in a cite container. For example, the following snippet shows how both keywords are used in the same paragraph:

```
<p>Most of the quotes can be found in the works of <a href="http://www.willieS.com"
  rel="author">William Shakespeare</a>, especially the famous reference book,
  <cite>Camford's Complete Works of the Bard</cite>.</p>
```

The text in that code generates:

> Most of the quotes can be found in the works of William Shakespeare, especially the famous reference book, Camford's Complete Works of the Bard.

As you can see when you place that code in a Web page, the `author` value is advisory and the `cite` element changes the appearance of the text. In some respects, both are advisory in that each calls attention to the content — one in the code, and the other in the screen display.

Hierarchical and sequential link types

You can organize your links using both hierarchical and sequential link types. The hierarchical `rel` values include `index` and `up`. The `up` value refers to a level up in the hierarchy, and `index` refers to the very top. For example, the following code references a directory that is the top of the hierarchy, three levels up from the calling page.

```
<a href="/" rel="index up up up">Home</a>
```

The clearest path in the example is made by referencing both the `index` and the number of `up` levels.

The sequential link types include `first`, `last`, `next`, and `prev` with each keyword relative to a page within a sequence. For example, the following code goes to the next page relative to a page in the sequence:

```
<a href="page4.html" rel="next">Page 4</a>
```

The implementation of these link types is different for different browsers, and they're better used with the `link` element to map out a site's organization relative to a given page than to direct a page using the `a` element.

PAGE ANCHORS AND IDS

In addition to linking directly to a page, you can link to a specific location on a page. One way to link directly to a location on a page is to assign an anchor to a tag on the page using the `name` attribute. For example, the following code will jump to the position on the current page where the "developer" name is found:

```
<a href="#developer">Developers</a>
```

To set up the target using an anchor, just assign a tag the name of the anchor like the following:

```
<div name="developer">
```

In testing the anchor technique on HTML5 browsers, it failed to work on several. The HTML5 browsers seemed to have adopted using CSS3 to create IDs and use them exclusively. The following example (`AnchorID.html` in this chapter's folder at www.wiley.com/go/smashinghtml5) shows how to use IDs as anchors:

```
<!DOCTYPE HTML>
<html>
<style type="text/css">
/*D4CBA0,BD4A14,804130,4F3C33,6D7F59*/
```

```
body {
    font-family:Verdana, Geneva, sans-serif;
    background-color:#D4CBA0;
    color:#804130;
}
h1 {
    font-family:"Arial Black", Gadget, sans-serif;
    color:#4F3C33;
    background-color:#BD4A14;
    text-align:center;
}
h2 {
    color:#6D7F59;
}
h3 {
    margin-left:15px;
    color:#4F3C33;
}
a {
    font-family:"Trebuchet MS", Arial, Helvetica, sans-serif;
    font-size:11px;
    color:#BD4A14;
    text-decoration:none;
}
nav {
    text-align:center;
}
#fsquirell { };
#cats { };
#dogs { };
</style>
<head>
<meta http-equiv="Content-Type" content="text/html; charset=UTF-8">
<title>Anchors</title>
</head>
<body>
<article>
<header>
  <nav><a href="#fsquirrel">Flying Squirrels</a>  | <a href="#cats">Cats</
  a>  | <a href="#dogs">Dogs</a></nav>
  <h1>Caring for Pets</h1>
  Just in case you're not interested in Flying Squirrels, you can select the "Cat"
  or "Dog" anchors and go right to your topic of interest. </header>
<section ID="fsquirrel">
  <header>
    <h2>Care and Handling of Flying Squirrels</h2>
  </header>
  <h3>Hangars</h3>
  <h3>Runways</h3>
```

138

```
    <h3>Flight Training</h3>
    <h3>Airline Food</h3>
    <h3>Baggage (these squirrels have lots of it...)</h3>
</section>
<section ID="cats">
  <header>
    <h2>Care and Handling of Cats</h2>
  </header>
  <h3>Kitty Basket</h3>
  <h3>Scratching Post</h3>
  <h3>Litter Box</h3>
  <h3>Cat Food</h3>
  <h3>Toy Mouse and Catnip</h3>
</section>
<section ID="dogs">
  <header>
    <h2>Care and Handling of Dogs</h2>
  </header>
  <h3>Dog House</h3>
  <h3>Walks</h3>
  <h3>House Breaking</h3>
  <h3>Dog Food</h3>
  <h3>Chew Toys and Balls</h3>
</section>
<footer>
  <nav><a href="#fsquirrel">Flying Squirrels</a>  | <a href="#cats">Cats</
  a>  | <a href="#dogs">Dogs</a></nav>
</footer>
</body>
</html>
```

When using CSS3 IDs for anchors on mobile devices, you'll find that your design is not quite as constrained for the small screen sizes. As you can see in Figure 7-5, anchors make it easy to navigate a page on a mobile device.

In Figure 7-5, the screen on the left is the initial page on an Opera Mini browser. When the Dogs link is tapped (or clicked on a non-mobile device), the page jumps down to the dog information. Notice that the menu is both at the top and bottom of the page. Generally speaking, if your page is long enough to require IDs for moving around the page, you should have a top and bottom menu. If the page is very long, you can give the nav element an ID and then have each section link to the menu.

If you want to set up a link directly to an ID or anchor, you simply add #name to the URL. For example, if somewhere else on your site (or even another site), you want a direct link to the material about cats. You'd simply create the following link:

```
<a href="http://my.domain.com/AnchorsID.html#cats">
```

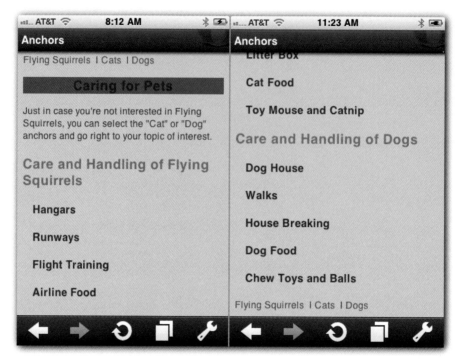

Figure 7-5: Using IDs for anchors.

From within the same directory, you would write:

```
<a href="AnchorsID.html#cats">
```

In Chapter 8, you'll see how to use IDs and anchors in planning a navigation design strategy.

TARGETS

Up to this point, all the links have been ones that replace the calling page with a new page to be loaded in your browser window. However, you can use the `target` attribute with the `<a>` tag to assign different ways for a page to appear — known as the browsing context. You may select from the following browsing contexts using `target`:

- `_self` replaces the current page; default if no context is assigned.
- `_blank` opens the new page in a new browser window — a new browsing context.
- `_parent` opens the new page in the "parent" document of the current page. The parent document is typically the browser windows that caused the current page to open.
- `_top` opens the new page in the full body of the current browser window.

These browsing contexts are assigned as shown in the following snippet:

```
<a href="somePage.html" target="_blank">
```

The underscore in naming all the browsing contexts is required. So, something like target ="blank" would not work — it has to be target="_blank".

In older versions of HTML, the `frame` and `frameset` elements were widely used and both could be named as `target` values. Likewise, the _parent and _top browsing contexts would be used to open a page in a different frame. In HTML5, the major use of the `target` attribute is to select the _blank browsing context over `_self` (default).

New browsing contexts in computer browsers

When you use the `target` attribute in the a element to create a _blank browsing context in your computer, the current page remains on the screen and the requested page appears in a new browser window or tab. The following program (`Link2Target.html` in this chapter's folder at `www.wiley.com/go/smashinghtml5`) is a simple illustration of how this works.

```html
<!DOCTYPE HTML>
<html>
<head>
<style type="text/css">
h1 {
    font-family:"Arial Black", Gadget, sans-serif;
    color:#060;
}
a {
    color:#900;
}
h3 {
    font-family:Verdana, Geneva, sans-serif;
}
</style>
<meta http-equiv="Content-Type" content="text/html; charset=UTF-8">
<title>Open New Page</title>
</head>
<body>
<header>
  <h1>Original Page</h1>
</header>
<nav>
  <h3><a href="http://www.w3.org" target="_blank">World Wide Web</a></h3>
</nav>
</body>
</html>
```

Figure 7-6 shows your screen when you test the program on your computer and click the link.

Depending on your browser's setting, your new page may appear in a new tab instead of a separate window. You can drag the tab to create a separate window so that both pages can be viewed simultaneously.

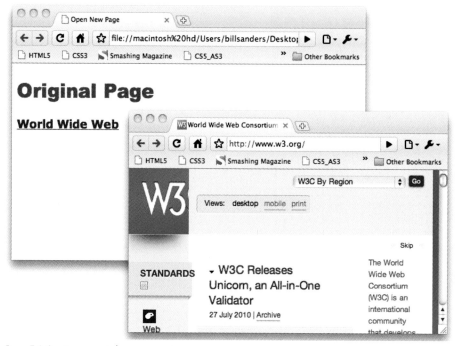

Figure 7-6: Opening a new window on a computer screen.

New browsing contexts in mobile browsers

When a Web page uses a `_blank` browser context in a mobile device, you do not have the ability to see multiple pages in a single viewing window. Instead, the calling page is treated as a previous page (Opera Mini) that can be accessed by pressing a back arrow or some other method. The Safari browser for the iPhone has a pages icon in the lower-right corner that shows the number of currently loaded pages. When the user taps the pages icon, up to eight pages can be viewed in a window where the user can slide them to view them sequentially. Figure 7-7 shows the pages context in a Safari browser on an iPhone.

If the page is opened using a `_blank` browsing context in the mobile Safari browser, it does not have a back link as in the Opera Mini browser; however, it's opened in a new browser window alongside the calling page.

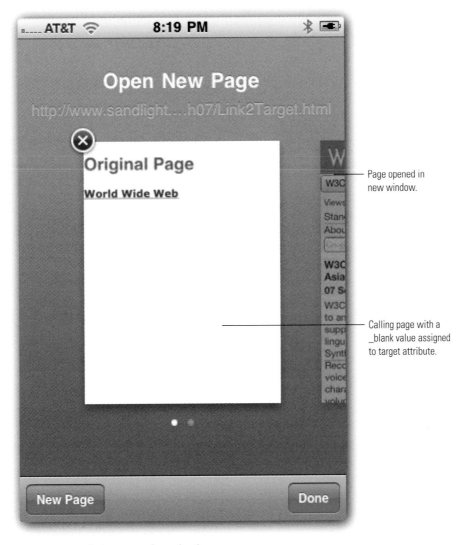

Page opened in new window.

Calling page with a _blank value assigned to target attribute.

Figure 7-7: Viewing multiple pages in Safari on the iPhone.

USING IFRAMES

The `iframe` element declares an inline frame. Using inline frames, you can load other Web pages or other media within a single Web page. The element represents what is called a nested browsing context. The "Targets" section in this chapter discusses different browsing contexts in terms of different windows and tabs. A *nested browsing context* occurs when one page is nested inside another page. Essentially, an `<iframe>` tag places one Web page inside another.

You may wonder why you would want one Web page inside another one. Why not just open a new window or tab? One reason is to allow users to get an idea of what may be in the pages and then link to whichever the user finds most interesting, relevant, or appropriate.

Other uses of iframes include placing thumbnail images on a page, and then allowing the user to select different thumbnails to bring up the full-size image. This allows you to build a single Web page where the user can view several different images by selecting image links that bring up the image in the same page — all without having to use JavaScript or Ajax.

NESTING WEB PAGES

The HTML5 `iframe` element has several attributes; some of which are new to HTML5. However, to get started, all you need to know is the basic tag and how it's implemented. The following is the bare bones `<iframe>` tag with a Web page embedded:

```
<iframe src="http://www.w3.org"></iframe>
```

That tag simply places the source Web page in the upper-left corner of the calling page. To better see the options and control over the iframe, the following program (`iframeWeb.html` in this chapter's folder at www.wiley.com/go/smashinghtml5) embeds two different Web pages inside itself and add several attributes that you can see.

```
<!DOCTYPE HTML>
<html>
<head>
<style type="text/css">
/*657BA6,F2EDA2,F2EFBD,F2DCC2,D99379*/
body {
    background-color:#F2EDA2;
}
h1 {
    font-family:Verdana, Geneva, sans-serif;
    color:#657BA6;
}
</style>
<meta http-equiv="Content-Type" content="text/html; charset=UTF-8">
<title>Iframe Web</title>
</head>
<body>
<!DOCTYPE HTML>
<html>
<body>
<article>
  <header>
    <h1>Before iframes</h1>
  </header>
  <section>
    <iframe name="info" width="480", height="320" sandbox="allow-same-origin"
  seamless src="http://www.smashingmagazine.com"></iframe>
```

```
    <iframe name="info2" width="480", height="320" sandbox seamless src="http://www.
  w3.org"></iframe>
   </section>
   <footer>
     <h1>After iframes</h1>
   </footer>
 </article>
 </body>
 </html>


 </body>
 </html>
```

In the two <iframe> tags, you can see several attributes, some of which you've seen in other elements. The iframe element itself has seven attributes plus HTML5 global attributes. The element attributes are

- src
- srcdoc
- name
- sandbox
- seamless
- width
- height

Of these seven, srcdoc, sandbox, and seamless are new. At the time of this writing the srcdoc has not been implemented in any of the tested browsers, but when it is, it navigates to a text/HTML file with information specific for the iframe. The sandbox attribute, available in the Google Chrome browser, is used for restricting the types of content and functionality that can be provided in an iframe, for security reasons. The seamless attribute has not been implemented either, but when it is, all links will be opened in the parent browsing context instead of the nested browsing context — inside the iframe. Older browsers and HTML5 browsers that have not yet implemented them ignore all these new iframe attributes. Therefore, you can add the attributes to <iframe> tags to set up good habits so that when they're available, they can help add security to your Web pages. Figure 7-8 shows how the embedded pages appear on a computer screen.

The h1 headings before and after the embedded pages show that the embedded pages are not subject to the CSS3 style of the parent page. Also, you can see that each page is inside another page — before and after the insertion of the two other Web pages.

If you look at the code, you'll see that their dimensions (320 x 480) suggest the viewing resolution for a mobile device. However, when tested on a mobile device, the iframe opened up to display the entire embedded pages. No scroll bars appear in the mobile browsers, so the only alternative to show the entire contents of the embedded pages is to allow them to be thumb-scrolled horizontally and vertically within the iframe. Initially, this may seem to be a deal breaker for iframes in mobile devices; however, in Chapter 8, you'll see how iframes can be used as single-page Web sites optimized for mobile browsers.

Figure 7-8: Embedding Web pages inside a Web page.

TAKE THE WHEEL

Setting up a Web site of your own can be a lot of fun, and one of the tasks is to get all the links working in concert. In the next chapter, you'll learn about navigation strategies, but for now you need some practice in getting a set of links and icons ready. Here's your challenge:

1. Create three Web pages. Include several sections with headings and subheadings so that each will go beyond a vertical screen viewing area. (In other words, the viewer would have to scroll down in order to see the bottom sections.)

2. On each of the Web pages, set up a link to an icon (see "Link icons" in this chapter). It's up to you whether you want each page to have a page icon (all different) or a site icon (all the same).

3. Create two different CSS3 style sheets (external) and provide alternate styles and access to them on all the pages (see "Alternate style sheets" in this chapter).

4. Create a third style sheet that has nothing but IDs that will be used as anchors. Place an ID in each section of your pages.

5. Finally, create links on each of the three pages that will link to the other two pages and all the IDs on each page.

Make this exercise fun for yourself. You can create pages to do anything you want. There's no reason to be serious (unless you have a client in mind!). So, don't worry about the content, but make it exactly what you'd like.

8

NAVIGATION STRATEGIES

GETTING AROUND A Web site is generally known as *navigation,* and HTML5 recognizes that fact by introducing a `<nav>` tag. With simple sites, navigation is simple. However, bad or inadequate navigation can invade virtually any Web site. By the same token, good navigation can make even the most complex site easy for the user to find what he wants.

Because this book focuses on HTML5, this chapter shows how to set up different navigation systems using specific HTML5 elements. However, before starting on the more specific tags that are to be used, you need to understand some general Web navigation concepts.

WEB NAVIGATION CONCEPTS

When thinking about navigation, Web designers consider

- **Interface design:** Jennifer Tidwell best describes interface design for the Web in her book *Designing Interfaces*. Many of the processes and patterns that Tidwell discusses are covered in this chapter as well, but with nowhere near the depth and scope as Tidwell does, so if you want more information on this subject, be sure to check out her book.
- **Information design:** In a far broader topic, information design, Edward Tufte has shown how different kinds of information can be presented so that it's best understood. Of special interest to Web navigation design is the notion that information is the interface. In other words, navigation is information arranged so that users can find what they want.

Neither Tidwell's nor Tufte's concepts can be summarized in a tidy definition. The idea of interaction is one of responding to another action, such as two people having a discussion. That's social interaction and it's something we do all the time — including interaction mediated by the computer, such as text chats. The same concept applies to treating a Web page as a stand-in for another person. The user does something, and the Web page responds from a finite set of choices created by the designer. The better the job that the designer does, the more natural it feels to the user. Trying to create an environment of comfortable interaction is the goal of good interaction design.

DESIGNER NAVIGATION AND USER NAVIGATION

Navigation design contains an almost limitless number of possibilities, and you want to set up your navigation so that users easily can get around. The first thing to ask yourself is, "Who is the typical user?" Then, say to yourself, "It ain't me, babe." If you remember the title to that old Bob Dylan song, you'll be on the right track. Jennifer Tidwell points out that a maxim in interface design is, "Know thy users, for they are not you!" Two corollaries can be added to that maxim:

- The better the designer, the more likely the interface will be bad.
- Excellent developers almost always make bad interfaces.

So, if you aspire to be either a great designer or a developer, you're likely to make a bad interface unless you pay attention. Here's why: Great designers focus on how the page looks, not on the users' ability to navigate a site. Designers want to display their creativity, and that's a good thing. However, when that creativity is such that users can't navigate from one page to another, there's a problem.

One of the worst user interfaces ever devised was on New York's Museum of Modern Art (MoMA) site. The navigation was based around a stack of cubes with no labels. Users were supposed to place their mouse over each cube and a label would appear with the name of the linked item. In order for the MoMA site to work, some fancy coding was required under the hood. The code would warm the cockles of any developer's heart, but it led to a disaster because, like the designer, the developer was thinking about what a talented coder he was and not about the user experience. Getting the link name to pop up when the mouse moves over it takes some coding talent that the designer did not posses. So, if you want to make a really terrible navigation system combine the best designer and the best developer!

Can you be a good designer and/or developer and still create good interfaces? Sure, but you have to think about it. You must take the view of your typical user into consideration. Who are your users? Are they children or adults? Is your audience men, women, or both? What age group? What is the user's style? Are they businesspeople? If so, what kind of business and where are they in the organization? Are they managers or are they the people who do the actual work? Find out who your users are. (You already know who you are.)

If you're a designer and you're making a Web site for other Web designers, do you want to show them what a good designer you are or how they can become better designers? Likewise, if you're a developer and you're making a site for other developers, you definitely want to show them code that will allow them to do some seriously sick programming. Developers want to see some code. However, designers do not want to see code — they're more interested in design tools and techniques, not code. (Of course designers, love CSS3 code!) Work what your user base wants into your navigation plan.

The very best way to find out if your interface is good is to test it with typical users. If you're making an educational site for third-graders, you want third-graders to test it. Likewise, if you're selling haute couture to wealthy women, you don't want teenage girls to test your navigation. It may take a little extra time, but you'll have a far better site if you test your site with the type of audience who will use it.

Knowing your users does not mean that you have to have dowdy design or use low-end technology in your site. What it means is that you need to get to know your users and find out what they think your site will do for them. You're not going to change your users. Make your site for them, not for you. If the site is not for your users, they won't return.

GLOBAL NAVIGATION

Global navigation in Web pages refers to broad navigation categories that can be placed on every page in a Web site. Global navigation helps users keep track of where they are in a site, so no matter where they go, they'll see a familiar road map.

In mapping out a trip from Santa Barbara, California, to Ocean City, New Jersey, you'll find major interstate highways. The links go from I-210 > I-15 > I-40 > I-44 > I-70 and finally to I-76. These might be considered the global elements in the 3,000-mile trip from coast to coast. However, between the major interstate highways, you'll find smaller connector roads such as CA-134E that connects US-101 with I-210.

Similarly in global navigation, you must consider navigation between the major links. For example, suppose you have a big site with the global navigation broken down into three categories:

- Animal
- Vegetable
- Mineral

That's certainly global and links would fit nicely on every page like the following:

Animal | Vegetable | Mineral

However, within each of those general categories, you're going to need something more specific. For example, suppose a user wants to find a breed of dog — a Greater Swiss Mountain Dog. The following path would be a possible one depending on the designer:

Animal
    Mammal
        Dog
            Breeds
                Greater Swiss Mountain Dog

Each submenu will have lots of choices, so let's consider what elements are available in HTML5 to handle these navigation paths from global navigation.

Using lists in global navigation

One way to approach global navigation is to use lists. For example, consider the following script (ListNavigation.html in this chapter's folder at www.wiley.com/go/ smashinghtml5) that uses global navigation and local navigation.

```
<!DOCTYPE HTML>
<html>
<head>
<style type="text/css">
/* 3C514C,98AB98,D3DFD3,A6A47D,8C1616 */
body {
    color:#3C514C;
    background-color:#D3DFD3;
    font-family:Verdana, Geneva, sans-serif;
```

```
        }
        h3 {
            color:#8C1616;
            background-color:#A6A47D
        }
        a {
            color:#8C1616;
            font-size:11px;
        }
        </style>
        <meta http-equiv="Content-Type" content="text/html; charset=UTF-8">
        <title>Global Navigation</title>
        </head>
        <body>
        <nav> <a href="#">Animal</a> | <a href="#">Vegetable</a> | <a href="#">Mineral</a> |
          <ul>
            <h3> Animals</h3>
            <li><a href="#">Mammals</a></li>
            <li><a href="#">Fish</a></li>
            <li><a href="#">Birds</a></li>
            <ul>
              <h3> Mammals</h3>
              <li><a href="#">Dogs</a></li>
              <li><a href="#">Cats</a></li>
              <li><a href="#">Other</a></li>
              <ul>
                <h3> Dogs</h3>
                <li><a href="#">Golden Retriever</a></li>
                <li><a href="#">Red Setter</a></li>
                <li><a href="#">German Shepherd</a></li>
                <li><a href="#">Greater Swiss Mountain Dog</a></li>
              </ul>
            </ul>
          </ul>
        </nav>
        </body>
        </html>
```

Just from looking at the code, you may suspect that this kind of navigation system will quickly overwhelm the page. Figure 8-1 shows what appears even though the possible choices have been drastically cut.

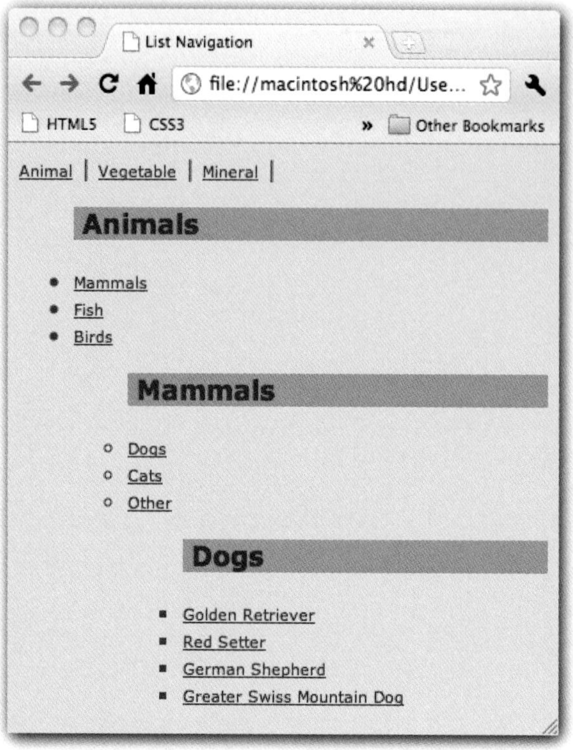

Figure 8-1: List navigation.

With a large enough screen and abbreviated choices such as those used in the example, it may be possible to have a navigation system using the `<ul>` tags. However, with the list system of navigation on mobile devices, the best advice is, "Don't even think about it!" Figure 8-2 shows how the navigation takes up the entire window in a mobile device.

Clearly, as you can see in Figure 8-2, some other system of navigation is required so that the topic can be viewed. The navigation system takes up the entire page. In fact, it looks more like a site map, which I discuss later in this chapter, but it can't be used in global navigation.

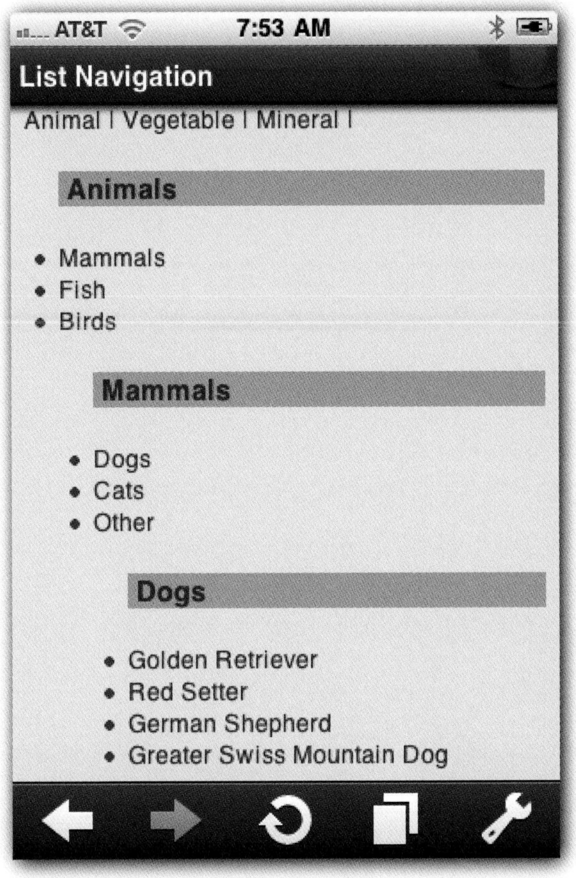

Figure 8-2: List navigation crowds the display area on a mobile device.

Drop-down menus and global navigation

An alternative approach to global navigation using text links is to use elements that can provide more information in a smaller place. One such element is the <select> tag. The select element displays the first item in a list of options that can be seen only when the user clicks on the select window that appears. The format is made up of a <select> tag along with an <option> tag nested within the select container. Each option container contains an object that is visible when the drop-down menu opens. The following snippet shows the basic format:

```
<select id="animals" name="global1">
    <option value="horses">Horses</option>
    <option value="dogs">Dogs</option>
    ...
</select>
```

This can be a handy way to place all of a site's links into a small area for use as a global menu. You can nest as many <option> tags inside the <select> container as you want. In order to see how this can be set up as a global navigation system, the following HTML5 script (SelectNav.html in this chapter's folder at www.wiley.com/go/smashinghtml5) illustrates a simple example.

```
<!DOCTYPE HTML>
<html>
<head>
<meta http-equiv="Content-Type" content="text/html; charset=UTF-8">
<title>Drop-Down Menu</title>
</head>
<nav>
  <label for="animals">Animals </label>
  <select id="animals" name="global1">
    <option value="horses">Horses</option>
    <option value="dogs">Dogs</option>
    <option value="cats">Cats</option>
    <option value="rabbits">Rabbits</option>
    <option value="raccons">Raccoons</option>
  </select>
  <label for="vegetables">Vegetables </label>
  <select id="vegetables" name="global2">
    <option value="carrots">Carrots</option>
    <option value="squash">Squash</option>
    <option value="peas">Peas</option>
    <option value="rice">Rice</option>
    <option value="potatoes">Potatoes</option>
  </select>
  <label for="minerals">Minerals </label>
  <select id="minerals" name="global3">
    <option value="tin">Tin</option>
    <option value="gold">Gold</option>
    <option value="copper">Copper</option>
    <option value="iron">Iron</option>
    <option value="mercury">Mercury</option>
  </select>
</nav>
<body>
</body>
</html>
```

With that many HTML5 tags, you might expect a much larger Web page. However, as Figure 8-3 shows, very little space is taken up.

The HTML5 code has no CSS3 to format the text, and as you can see, the default body font is a serif font and the default menu font is sans-serif. When you use CSS3 for styling, work with the <select> tag for style instead of the <option> tag. If you style the option element, you can style the font family with good results, but other styling is unpredictable between different browsers.

Figure 8-3: Displaying menu choices with the `<select>` tag.

If the categories appear a bit shallow, you can add greater detail in an outline format using the `<optgroup>` tag. With each tag, a new subgroup is added. You can nest them in several levels if you wish. The following listing (`Optgroup.html` in this chapter's folder at www. wiley.com/go/smashinghtml5) shows how the `optgroup` element is used in conjunction with the `<select>` and `<option>` tags.

```
<!DOCTYPE HTML>
<html>
<head>
<style type="text/css">
select {
        background-color:#F2EFBD;
        color:#657BA6;
        font-family: Verdana, Geneva, sans-serif;
}
</style>
<meta http-equiv="Content-Type" content="text/html; charset=UTF-8">
<title>Stratified Drop-Down Menu</title>
</head>
<nav>
  <label for="animals">Animals</label>
  <select id="animals" name="global1">
  <optgroup label="Dogs">
    <option value="hounds">Hounds</option>
    <option value="work">Work</option>
    <option value="terrier">Terriers</option>
    </optgroup>
  <optgroup label="Horses">
    <option value="race">Race</option>
    <option value="work">Work</option>
    <option value="show">Show</option>
    </optgroup>
    <optgroup label="Rabbits">
    <option value="pets">Pets</option>
```

155

```
            <option value="pests">Pests</option>
            <option value="easter">Easter</option>
          </optgroup>
       </select>
    </nav>
    <body>
    </body>
    </html>
```

For some reason, different browsers have different displays of the category headings generated by the `optgroup` element. Figure 8-4 shows how the same menu looks on different browsers.

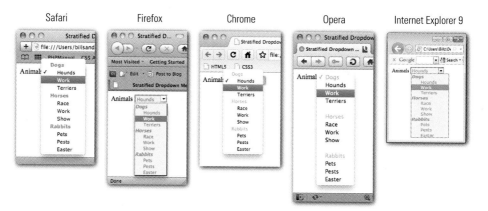

Figure 8-4: Using the `<optgroup>` tag.

Of the four browsers tested, Firefox stands out as unique. The `optgroup` headings are italicized and the color combinations are preserved when the menu opens. The other browsers display the correct color scheme only when the menu is closed. (Will this give designers another challenge? Yes!)

USING JAVASCRIPT TO CALL A LINKED PAGE

Any global navigation system needs a way to call different Web pages and the drop-down menus need a way to call a selected item. Up to this point, the `<a>` tag has done a good job of taking care of links, but you probably noticed the drop-down menus have no links. The `<select>` tag needs to work with the `form` element (which is covered in detail in Chapter 14) and a JavaScript function. (Chapter 12 has more details on getting started with and using JavaScript.) On the HTML5 side, the following snippet shows the essentials:

```
<form name="menuNow">
    <label for="animals">Animals</label>
    <select id="animals" name="global1" onChange="optionMenu()">
      <option value="animals/horses.html">Horses</option>
      <option value="animals/dogs.html">Dogs</option>
```

The names of the `form` and `select` elements are important because JavaScript uses the names as a path to the selected `option`. (If you're familiar with arrays, the options are all treated as array elements.)

The JavaScript is placed in a separate file because if you're going to be using it with a global navigation system, you don't want to have to rewrite it with every page. The following JavaScript should be saved in a text file named `globMenu.js`.

```
function optionMenu()
    {
            var choice = document.menuNow.global1.selectedIndex;
            var urlNow = document.menuNow.global1.options[choice].value;
            window.location.href = urlNow;
    }
```

What that reflects is the HTML5 Document Object Model (DOM). The `document` is the Web page, `menuNow` is the name of the `form` element, `global1` is the name of the `select` element, and `selectedIndex` is the selected option. Because the `selectedIndex` is a number between 0 and the number of options in the `<select>` tag container, it can be used to choose the array element (option), which is selected. Whatever value is stored in the option is passed to the variable named `urlNow`. For example, the following line has a relative URL of `animals/dogs.html`:

```
<option value="animals/dogs.html">Dogs</option>
```

The final line in the JavaScript, `window.location.href = urlNow`, has the same function as the following HTML5 line:

```
<a href="animals/dogs.html">
```

In this context, a different JavaScript function would have to be written for each `<select>` tag because the function uses a specific reference to that tag (`global1`). More sophisticated JavaScript could be developed to use variables for the different element names, but the function employed here is relatively short and easier to implement.

To test this out yourself, create simple Web pages with the following names:

- `horses.html`
- `dogs.html`
- `cats.html`
- `rabbits.html`
- `raccoons.html`

The Web pages can just have names on them — nothing fancy. Then, in the same directory, enter the following HTML5 code (`SelectNavJS.html` in this chapter's folder at www. wiley.com/go/smashinghtml5).

```
<!DOCTYPE HTML>
<html>
<head>
<script type="text/javascript" src="globMenu.js" />
<meta http-equiv="Content-Type" content="text/html; charset=UTF-8">
<title>Drop-Down Menu</title>
</head>
<body>
<article>
  <header>
    <nav>
      <form name="menuNow">
        <label for="animals">Animals</label>
        <select id="animals" name="global1" onChange="optionMenu()">
          <option value="animals/horses.html">Horses</option>
          <option value="animals/dogs.html">Dogs</option>
          <option value="animals/cats.html">Cats</option>
          <option value="animals/rabbits.html">Rabbits</option>
          <option value="animals/raccoons.html">Raccoons</option>
        </select>
        <label for="vegetables">Vegetables</label>
        <select id="vegetables" name="global2">
          <option value="carrots">Carrots</option>
          <option value="squash">Squash</option>
          <option value="peas">Peas</option>
          <option value="rice">Rice</option>
          <option value="potatoes">Potatoes</option>
        </select>
        <label for="minerals">Minerals</label>
        <select id="minerals" name="global3">
          <option value="tin">Tin</option>
          <option value="gold">Gold</option>
          <option value="copper">Copper</option>
          <option value="iron">Iron</option>
          <option value="mercury">Mercury</option>
        </select>
      </form>
    </nav>
  </header>
</article>
</body>
</html>
```

Test the page using with Google Chrome or Opera — at the time of this writing, those were the only two browsers that had implemented this aspect of HTML5.

For the time being, you won't be doing anything with the second two drop-down menus, but at the end of the chapter you'll be given an opportunity to complete them with a few additions to the JavaScript file.

CREATING CONSISTENCY

One of the most important features of a good navigation system is consistency. The user has to be able to know where to find the navigation system no matter where she is in the site. If one page has the navigation at the top and the next page does not, in the same site, users may not know where they are relative to where they started or where they're going. One of the most misquoted pieces of wisdom about consistency can be found in Ralph Waldo Emerson's essay, "Self-Reliance." By quoting only a part of Emerson's thought, many people are misled to believe that consistency is wicked. That famous misquote is ". . . consistency is the hobgoblin of little minds. . . ." What Emerson fully wrote is, "A foolish consistency is the hobgoblin of little minds, adored by little statesmen and philosophers and divines. With consistency a great soul has simply nothing to do." The reason that the quote is important is that Emerson never said that consistency is a bad thing. Foolish consistency is the problem — not consistency. When it comes to navigation consistency is essential, and by all means avoid foolish consistency. In other words, don't put a bad navigation system together and then repeat it because it's consistent. As far as a great soul having nothing to do, that may be a good thing. With consistency, you don't have to reinvent the navigation system with every new page. A great soul would have different consistencies for different audiences and types of sites; but within the site, the consistency is constant.

In her work on grouping elements, Jennifer Tidwell talks about using color-coded sections to assist users in keeping track of where they are. Using colors, you can add clarity to global navigation. The three global categories that have been selected for navigation — animal, vegetable, and mineral — can be a good example of multiple-consistency (each menu is consistent with the other menus). For the animal category, you might use brown tones; for the vegetable category, green tones; and for the mineral category, nickel tones. Figure 8-5 shows an example where the global navigation is in place and the different pages have a color scheme that differentiates them from one another and at the same time places each in the appropriate grouping.

Figure 8-5: Global navigation and color grouping.

In Figure 8-5 note that the global navigation incorporates the color palette of the respective categories. It would be foolish consistency to insist that the color schemes be the same. However, the global navigation is consistent and each page is consistent with the other pages in the same category.

VERTICAL AND HORIZONTAL NAVIGATION

Besides using the horizontal plane along the top and bottom of a page for navigation, inter-face designers often reserve part of the side of a Web page for navigation. Figure 8-6 shows the general design for this approach.

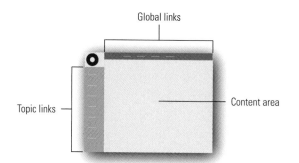

Figure 8-6: Vertical and horizontal navigation.

When using horizontal and vertical link planes, the user can see all the global links and the links for the current topic simultaneously. More of the viewing area is taken up by the navigation system, but with the larger monitors becoming standard on computers, this isn't that much of a problem. With electronic tablets like the iPad that have smaller screens, it cuts into the usable viewing area, but not a great deal. However, on mobile phones, especially when viewed vertically, the content space is severely reduced.

To create an area for a vertical link area with HTML5, you just need to set up a two-column page below the area generally reserved for the logo and global navigation bar.

APPLYING CSS3 PSEUDO-CLASSES

When dealing with more complex navigation systems, you may want to consider CSS3 pseudo-classes. These are class definitions added to an element. For navigation, the following four pseudo-classes are important because they're associated with the <a> tag:

- `link`
- `visited`
- `hover`
- `active`

Each has the same formatting as other elements, but they're declared with the element name separated by a colon. For example, the following code snippet shows how the `hover` pseudo-class is styled:

```
a:hover
{
     color:#A69055;
}
```

When that code is added to a style sheet, whenever the mouse hovers over the link (<a> tag), it will change the color to the `hover` definition. Of course the colors defined for the <a> tag have to be different from the `hover`, but you can add subtle or blatant signals to the user that the text is a link. Likewise, you can change other features using the pseudo-classes. The following examples will give you an idea:

```
<!DOCTYPE HTML>
<html>
<head>
<style type="text/css">
a {
     font-family:Verdana, Geneva, sans-serif;
     font-size:11px;
}
a:link {
     color:#cc0000;
     text-decoration:none;
}
a:hover {
     font-size:14px;
}
a:visited {
     color:#00cc00;
     text-decoration:none;
}
a:active {
     background-color:#ffff00;
}
</style>
<meta http-equiv="Content-Type" content="text/html; charset=UTF-8">
<title>Pseudo Classes in Links</title>
</head>
<body>
<a href="#">Click here</a>
</body>
</html>
```

When using pseudo-classes for navigation, you want to keep the user in mind. Adding strange effects with pseudo-classes can be fun, but you need to ask whether the effects will assist or confuse users. If you can add an effect that users associate with making choices, then that effect is likely to be helpful. For example, making the font larger when the mouse is over it was an idea taken from the Macintosh dock where icons enlarge when the mouse passes over them. However, you might want to ask whether turning the link another color and changing the text decoration is a good idea for a visited class. Does it really help the user? Also, try it on different browsers and see if the results are consistent. Remember that just because you can change a link's appearance doesn't mean you have to.

UNDERSTANDING THE HTML5 MECHANICS OF VERTICAL NAVIGATION

The most important part of creating a vertical section to use for navigation in your site is sectioning a portion of the page where you can place the links. This example uses the `<aside>` tag to set off the vertical navigation. However, because it's navigation, the `<nav>` tag is used as well so that any JavaScript references to the Document Object Model (DOM) can recognize the section as one used for navigation. The following listing (VertHor.html in this chapter's folder at www.wiley.com/go/smashinghtml5) shows how.

```
<!DOCTYPE HTML>
<html>
<head>
<style type="text/css">
/*141919,2D2B21,A69055,C9B086,FFB88C --Japanese Art*/
body {
        font-family:"Trebuchet MS", Arial, Helvetica, sans-serif;
        color:#2D2B21;
        background-color:#C9B086;
        font-size:12px;
}
.content {
        display:table-cell;
        width:600px;
        padding:15px;
}
aside {
        display:table-cell;
        width:100px;
        background-color:#FFB88C;
        padding-right:5px;
}
h1 {
        font-family:Papyrus;
        color:#2D2B21;
        text-align:center;
}
h2 {
        color:#A69055;
}
a {
        font-family:Verdana, Geneva, sans-serif;
        font-size:10px;
        text-decoration:none;
```

```
        color:#141919;
    }
a:hover {
        color:#A69055;
    }
.centerNav {
        text-align:center;
    }
.indentNav {
        margin-left:15px;
    }
</style>
<meta http-equiv="Content-Type" content="text/html; charset=UTF-8">
<title>Web Services Galore</title>
</head>

<body>
<img src="designLogo.png" width="64" height="66" align="left">
<nav class="centerNav"> <a href="#">Graphic Design</a> |  <a
  href="#">Development</a> |  <a href="#">Interface Design</a> | 
  <a href="#">Site Architecture</a></nav>
<header>
  <h1> Honorable Web Services</h1>
</header>
<aside>
  <nav class="indentNav"> <a  href="#">Overview</a><br>
    <br>
    <a href="#">Navigation</a><br>
    <br>
    <a href="#">RSS Subscription</a><br>
    <br>
    <a href="#">Iframes</a><br>
    <br>
    <a href="#">CSS3 Navigation Styles</a><br>
    <br>
    <a href="#">Audience Identification</a><br>
    <br>
    <a href="#">Focus Group Testing</a><br>
    <br>
    <a href="#">Adding Mobile Options</a><br>
    <br>
  </nav>
</aside>
<section class="content">
  <header>
    <h2>Interface Design</h2>
  </header>
  Honorable Web Services has full interface design services. You may choose from the
  following list, selecting just the services you want.
  <ul>
    <li>Simple text link interfaces</li>
```

```
        <li>Drop-down menus </li>
        <li>Button links</li>
        <li>Datalist links</li>
        <li>Iframe navigation</li>
        <li>Navigation styling</li>
    </ul>
    Select one of the links on the left to see more information. Also be sure to check
    out our services in graphic design, development, and architecture in the menu along
    the top of the page.</section>
</body>
</html>
```

When you run this program, you can see that although it provides a wide variety of user choices, it's clear. The global navigation along the top provides all the main choices. Then on each page within a global collection, users are able to select choices specific to the selected topic. Figure 8-7 shows what you can expect to see when you test the program in an HTML5 browser on a computer screen.

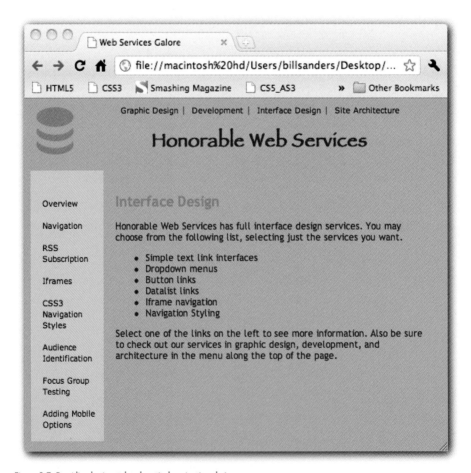

Figure 8-7: Providing horizontal and vertical navigation choices.

When you look at the same page on a mobile device, the space taken up on the left where the vertical menu has been placed pushes the content downward. Users have to scroll more. Also notice that the horizontal menu along the top is pushed in so that it now takes up two roles. Figure 8-8 shows the results on a mobile browser.

For mobile devices, two-tier horizontal navigation bars — that do not push content below the viewing area — may better serve you. As you can see in comparing Figures 8-7 and 8-8, the horizontal navigation bar breaks into two tiers in the mobile device without taking up much room. However, the vertical navigation bar pushes into the content area and forces more content (including the navigation bar itself) below the viewing area.

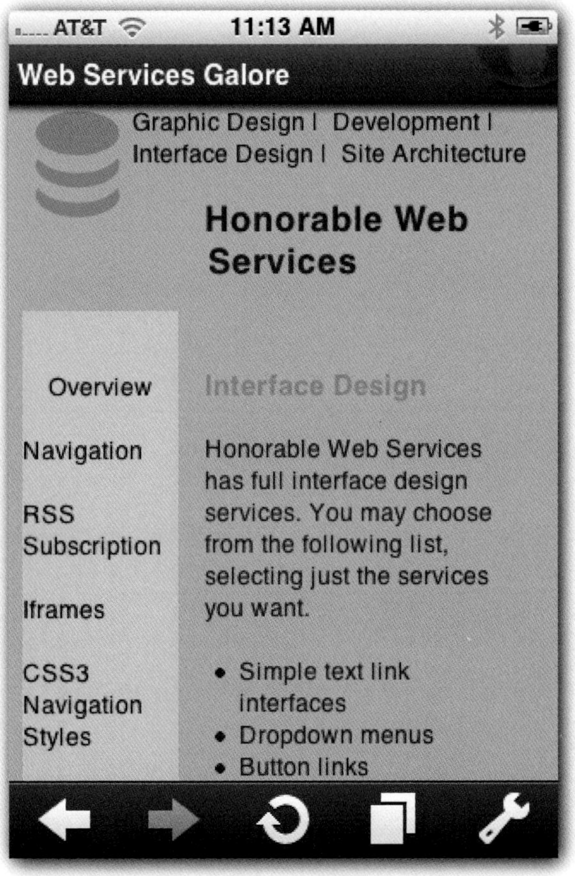

Figure 8-8: Vertical and horizontal menus on a mobile device.

USING GRAPHIC ICONS IN NAVIGATION

In addition to using text to link to other pages, you also can use graphic files — JPEG, PNG, or GIF. Using graphic images for linking can help users quickly find what they're looking for. For example, a right or left arrow quickly can be identified as linking to the next or last page.

Such images transcend language differences and help a wider audience base. Likewise, younger children are more likely to understand certain symbols than they are certain words.

The format for using images for identifying links is the same as it is for text. However, instead of placing text in an <a> container, you use an image reference. The following code snippet shows the basic format:

```
<a href="page2.html"><img src="arrowRight.jpg"></a>
```

Users see an arrow icon and click it instead of a text message. Often, designers will use both text and an image to send users to another page, as shown in the next snippet:

```
<a href="page2.html"><img src="arrowRight.jpg">Next Page</a>
```

Also, some designers create icons with text embedded in the symbol, as shown in Figure 8-9.

Figure 8-9: Link image with text.

One advantage designers find in using graphic text is that they can use any font they want without fear that the user won't have that particular font in his system. It also helps to keep users from getting lost because graphic symbols with text are easy for the user to spot and understand.

SINGLE-PAGE WEB SITES WITH IFRAMES

Think of a Web site as a loading zone. Whenever, you click a link, you load another page — graphics and all. Sometimes, all you want to do is load just one thing. That saves the user from having to wait for all the other stuff to load or reload. If you know a bit of JavaScript and Ajax, you can do that, but what about with just HTML5? The answer is yes!

This section examines how to link to graphics and change the graphic in an iframe. When creating applications designed specifically for mobile devices, you want to use as little bandwidth as possible. By changing just one thing on a Web page, the mobile device just has to load or reload a single item, so the response time is less.

LINKING TO A GRAPHIC

Generally, when we think of adding graphics to a page, we think of the <img> tag. After all, that tag is what we use to place graphics on a Web page. However, you also can use the <a href> tag to load a graphic. Instead of assigning a Web page path to the href assignment, assign a graphic. For example, the following line of code loads a blank page with a graphic:

```
<a href="myGraphic.jpg">My Graphic</a>
```

When users click on the link text, the current page disappears, and the graphic appears in the upper-left corner of a new page.

Placing a graphic in an `iframe` element works just like placing a Web page in an iframe (see Chapter 7). The link is to the target within the iframe and instead another Web page. That means that the current Web page stays in place, and the graphic opens in the iframe.

The following script uses graphic icons for the navigation. However, instead of navigating to another page, the navigation places a different graphic in the main viewing area — an iframe. By making miniature versions of the graphic to be displayed (called thumbnails), users see their selection first in the navigation design. That is, the thumbnails guide users to the full-size view.

MAKING AND USING THUMBNAIL ICONS

To prepare for the application, first create full-size versions and thumbnails of all the graphics. The full-size graphics and the thumbnails should all be the same size. In the following example, the full-size graphics are set to 250 x 312 pixels, and the thumbnails are set to 63 x 79 pixels. Thumbnails need to be small enough to serve as navigation buttons but large enough for users to get an idea of what the larger graphics will look like. Notice that the iframe dimensions are the same as the full-size graphics. Once the graphics are prepared, they're placed in separate directories for the thumbnails and full-size graphics. (The names, thumbs and portraits are used in the following example [`IFrameNavigation.html` in this chapter's folder at `www.wiley.com/go/smashinghtml5`].)

```
<!DOCTYPE HTML>
<html>
<head>
<style type="text/css">
/*F2CF8D,401E01,F2AA6B,8C3503,F28D52*/
body {
    font-family:Verdana, Geneva, sans-serif;
    background-color:#F2CF8D;
    color:#401E01;
    font-size:11px;
}
h1 {
    font-family:"Harrington", Arial, sans-serif;
    font-size:36px;
    color:#8C3503;
    margin-left:10px;
}
h4 {
    font-family:"Arial Black", Gadget, sans-serif;
    color:#8C3503;
    margin-left:86px;
}
aside {
```

```
        margin-left:10px;
    }
    h5 {
        margin-right:40px;
    }
    </style>
    <meta http-equiv="Content-Type" content="text/html; charset=UTF-8">
    <title>Iframe Navigation</title>
    </head>
    <body>
    <!DOCTYPE HTML>
    <html>
    <body>
    <article>
      <header>
        <h1>Portrait Studio</h1>
      </header>
      <aside>
        <iframe name="fullSize" width="250", height="312" seamless src="portraits/man.
    jpg"></iframe>
      </aside>
      <section>
        <nav> <a href="portraits/man.jpg" target="fullSize"><img src="thumbs/thumbMan.
    jpg"></a> <a href="portraits/woman.png" target="fullSize"><img src="thumbs/thumb-
    Woman.png"></a> <a href="portraits/boy.jpg" target="fullSize"><img src="thumbs/
    thumbBoy.jpg"></a> <a href="portraits/girl.png" target="fullSize"><img src="thumbs/
    thumbGirl.png"></a>
          <h4>Select portrait</h4>
        </nav>
      </section>
      <section>
        <h5> All of the creations are by a little-known artist, <b>Mo Digli Anni</b>,
    from Spunky Puddle, Ohio. By clicking on the thumbnail buttons, you can send the
    image to the larger viewing window. </h5>
      </section>
    </article>
    </body>
    </html>
```

When you test the example, you'll see the man's portrait and then the four thumbnails of the man, woman, boy, and girl beneath the image inside the iframe. Figure 8-10 shows the page on a computer monitor screen.

As you can see in Figure 8-10, users are instructed to click on the thumbnail buttons to view the different "portraits." The interface is fairly intuitive and users know what to expect when they click on one of the graphic buttons. The best part is that only the graphic for the selected portrait is loaded into the iframe instead of loading a new page with all the graphic buttons and other page materials.

Figure 8-10: Images used for navigation.

USING IFRAMES ON MOBILE DEVICES

In testing the application on a mobile device, the results depended on the HTML5 mobile browser in use. Figure 8-11 shows the Opera Mini browser on the left; as you can see, the text beneath the images is formatted to be readable. However, at the time of testing, the Opera Mini seemed to reload the entire page as each button was selected.

The image on the right in Figure 8-11 is from the Safari mobile browser. The text at the bottom didn't follow the CSS3 formatting and ran off to the right side of the screen. However, the images in the `iframe` worked perfectly, and as each thumbnail button was clicked, the full-size image loaded without reloading the entire page.

169

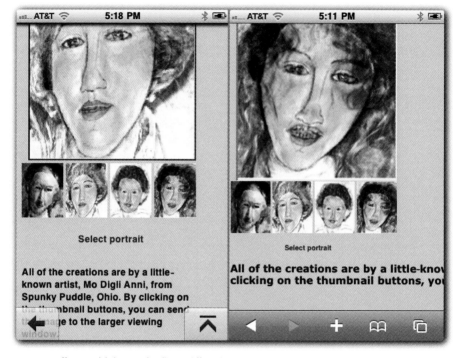

Figure 8-11: Different mobile browsers handle text differently.

Several different kinds of businesses and social networking sites use similar applications. For example, professional photographers use thumbnails of their photographs that users click to view the full-size images. Likewise, social networking sites can use similar pages to display and load pictures of each users' friends without having to leave the page.

Because mobile devices have such small display areas, using iframes in navigation designs is quite helpful. Trying to click small text links can be difficult, but as you can see in both mobile browsers in Figure 8-11, the graphic buttons are easy to see and tap for loading the full-size image or other materials into the iframe space.

TAKE THE WHEEL

This chapter has two different challenges:

- **JavaScript challenge:** The first challenge is to complete the JavaScript linkage in the section "Using JavaScript to Call a Linked Page." The HTML5 page named Select NavJS.html has three different <select> tags — one each for animals, vegetables, and minerals. Only the animal <select> tag contains a JavaScript event function. By adding two more functions to the JavaScript file (globMenu.js) that are similar to the first function but with a different name, you should be able to create functions for the <select> tags for the vegetable and mineral menus. (It's basically a matter of copying and pasting the original function and pasting it twice and then just changing the function name.) Then, just add the OnChange attribute to the two other <select> tags. The second two <select> tags have names of global2 and global3 that you can add to the JavaScript functions — notice where global1 is located in the original JavaScript. (Don't worry if you can't do this exercise! Without knowing JavaScript, it can be tricky.)

- **Iframe challenge:** You can put as many iframe elements in a page as you want. Suppose you want to compare different sets of objects — cars, clothes, or mobile devices. For example, let's say that you were building a site to compare different models of Fords and Toyotas. The Fords appear in the left iframe and the Toyotas in the right. Below each iframe, are links that bring up different types of cars — economy, sedans, hybrid, vans, trucks, and SUVs. Each brand of automobile has links beneath it so that you can bring up comparable ones — such as two hybrids. See if you can create such a site — using content of your choice. (By the way, Edward Tufte, the information design authority, strongly urges comparative information to be presented so that users can view it in the same eyespan — what you can see in a single view.)

Both of these challenges use the materials in this chapter, and they can be applied to many different applications.

MEDIA IN HTML5

9 IMAGES

ONE OF THE most exciting features of HTML5 is the ability to use Scalable Vector Graphics (.svg) files. Artists who use programs like Adobe Illustrator that create vector graphics can save their files as .svg files and put them right into their Web pages. Because .svg files contain vector graphics, images can be made larger or smaller without losing their resolution as bitmapped graphics do. However, you still can use your favorite bitmapped graphics in .jpg, .gif, or .png format for static display.

This chapter seeks to clarify using graphics on the Web in terms of the main types of images that are

likely to be used, how to place them where you want on your Web page, and how to optimize them for Web use. Much of this chapter, out of necessity, must use graphic applications that you may not have. These applications include Adobe Illustrator, Adobe Photoshop, and Adobe Fireworks. However, you can substitute other applications you may own, such as Microsoft Paint or Corel Draw. Finally, for drawn graphics and photographs, you're going to have to rely on your own skills, both in terms of artistic abilities and ability to use graphic drawing programs. (In a pinch, you can download public-domain image files from the Web in the file type you need.)

THE BASICS OF HTML5 IMAGE FILES

A fundamental truth about graphic files on the Web is that they have weight. Weight, in the context of an HTML5 page, refers to file size measured in terms of the number of pixels stored in an image. Generally speaking, larger and higher-quality images have more pixels. The consequence of size for the Web is that heavier graphics take longer to move over the Internet and load into an HTML page. If you've ever stared at a Web page waiting for a big graphic to load, you know that it can be frustrating and cause your mouse button finger to start twitching, wanting to hit the Back button on the browser.

By understanding something about the different file types and how to optimize their size, you can better adjust the files and get the most out of images on your page — both in terms of how they look and how long they take to load.

FORMATS AND PIXELS MATTER

What matters most on a screen is how an image looks. The appearance of an image depends to a great extent on the monitor's resolution. The higher the resolution of a monitor or mobile device's display, the better the image is going to look. At the same time, a graphic with more information is going to look better than a graphic with less information. That also means that a graphic that takes up more screen space is going to require more information than a smaller image and take longer to load.

To better see what needs to be understood to create good-looking graphics that don't take up much bandwidth and load quickly requires a closer look at the different types of Web graphic formats. The next four subsections provide a brief overview of each format.

Scalable Vector Graphics (SVG)

Vector graphics are drawings created using mathematical formulas that specify points and then draw lines between the points. Bitmapped graphics place color "bits" at different points. For example, if you draw a straight line in vector graphics, the computer takes Point A and Point B and draws a line between them. The same line drawn with bitmapped graphics specifies all the points to place bits to make up the line. (That explanation oversimplifies the process but provides a rough idea of the difference between vector and bitmapped graphics.)

Because vector graphics use formulas, when a graphic is changed, it doesn't become pixilated as bitmapped graphics do. Imagine a line 100 pixels long that you want to change to 400 pixels long. With vector graphics, all that has to be changed is the distance between two points. With bitmapped graphics, you have to add an additional 300 pixels. If you try to change a bitmapped graphic line in a Web page by changing its width from 100 pixels long to 400 pixels long, it stretches out the original 100 pixels to cover a width of 400 pixels, and that's why it looks pixilated.

Another important new feature of SVG graphics is the ability to change different aspects of the image dynamically. Using JavaScript, you can take an .svg file displayed on a Web page and dynamically change it — not by switching figures but by actually changing a parameter.

Fortunately, some recently provided tools help create separate regions to be changed and generate the code needed to make the changes (see the section, "Application for Dynamic SVG files from Adobe Illustrator CS5 files" later in this chapter.)

Graphic Information Format (GIF)

The good thing about GIF files is that they can produce some of the smallest files and they support background transparency. In large part, that's because they can handle only 256 colors and obtain transparency by turning off one of the colors. The set of colors known as "Web safe" are based on the fact that GIF files can handle only 256 colors. This format is extremely limiting for designers who want a larger color palette, and the format is not recommended for digital photographs other than black-and-white ones with limited gray tones.

One format for GIF files is an animated one. If an animated GIF is loaded, it begins playing — sequentially flipping through the images — displaying animated actions. Because the animated GIF is contained in a single file, it can be loaded directly into an HTML5 page using the `<img>` tag. Typical animated GIF files are relatively short. Otherwise, the pack of files within the animated GIF file is too large for quick loading.

Besides the limited number of colors available for GIF creations, CompuServe and Unisys held a copyright on the format and set up a licensing requirement. Rather than worry about getting sued, most developers simply opted for other graphic formats.

Joint Photographic Experts Group (JPEG)

Most digital photographs on the Web use the JPEG format. Likewise, any more complex graphics with several colors and shades prefer JPEG for preserving the look intended by the photographer or artist. As a result, most of the images on Web sites that display services or products are in the JPEG format. JPEG files tend to be larger than GIFs, but with the increased bandwidth on the Internet, the size is not as problematic as it once was.

The JPEG format doesn't support transparency like GIF files, and it doesn't have an animated format. Further, JPEG files use what is called lossy compression, which can reduce the image fidelity. Compared to lossless compression that supports an exact replication of the original data, lossy compression is considered more of an approximation of the original data that makes up the image.

The standard JPEG format is open source and requires no licensing permission. Interestingly, some patented features for JPEG can require licensing, but these features have not been included in most JPEG files so developers and designers can use JPEG format freely.

Portable Network Graphics (PNG)

In part, the PNG format was developed as an alternative to the patent license requirements in the GIF format. However, the development was also motivated by the desire to have more than 256 colors and a lossless display. The PNG format also supports transparency and an alpha channel.

At one time, not all browsers supported the PNG format and some developers didn't use it, despite its many advantages. However those days are long gone, and any browser that supports HTML5 will support PNG. As a result, any HTML5 developer or designer can use PNG files without fear of the browser not being able to load them.

PRESERVING LAYERS IN WEB GRAPHICS

One of the big advantages of PNG files is that they preserve layers. Designers who use tools like Adobe Illustrator, Adobe Fireworks, and Adobe Photoshop organize their graphics in layers. A simple application of a layer is labeling a photograph. For example, suppose you have a photograph that you label and save as a JPEG file, as shown in Figure 9-1.

Figure 9-1: A JPEG image with embedded label.

After you finish the graphic and save it as a JPEG file, you realize that it's mislabeled. It's a morning glory, not a daisy. Because the file is saved in JPG format, the layer with the Daisy label is not preserved. When you edit the file, you'll find that the label is fused with the rest of the graphic.

With a PNG file, not only are the layers preserved, but if you use a transparent background, it picks up the background of your Web page, and the transparency is preserved. Figure 9-2 shows that the simple swapping of layers fixes the label problem and provides a transparent background.

With multilayered graphics, preserving the final Web image in PNG format will save editing time. In this particular example, in a JPEG file, erasing the wrong label and replacing it with the correct one in a space below the main image is not too difficult. However, with more complex graphics that include several layers, rather than having to redo the entire graphic, designers can just edit the layer.

Figure 9-2: PNG file with preserved layer and transparent background (shown in a graphic editor).

The only unfortunate problem in preserving layers in a PNG file is that it increases the size of the file. The JPEG file is only 33 kilobytes (KB) and the PNG is 225 KB. However, in the next section, you'll see how to reduce the size of a file so that you may be able to maintain layers and still have a file that loads quickly.

WORKING WITH GRAPHIC FILE SIZES

Given the different kinds of Web graphic files that can be loaded, the temptation is to use the type that has the smallest file size. Indeed, in some cases, that is the way to go. However, when your site needs the highest quality, the trick is to see how to get the highest quality with the lowest bandwidth use — the format with the smallest settings. Unless you're using SVG format, remember the key Web bitmapped graphic dictum:

Do not ever change a bitmapped graphic's dimensions with HTML5 attributes within an element.

You can change a graphic's dimensions all you want with a graphics application like Adobe Photoshop or Microsoft Paint. But when you change the size of a bitmapped graphic using HTML5 attributes like width and height, your results, especially when you attempt to enlarge an object, tend to either pixilate or crush the object. Figure 9-3 shows three GIF images, and you can see that the enlarged graphic has jaggy edges and the pixels are beginning to appear as little boxes.

Figure 9-3: An enlarged GIF using HTML5 attributes.

The middle figure is the original one with original dimensions. Had a graphic tool been used to enlarge the image, it would appear un-aliased (without jagged edges). You can see the same thing happen with digital photographs, as shown in Figure 9-4.

The original image is on the far left. The enlarged image shows jagged edges and the image is beginning to blur. The image on the far right is so small, it's difficult to see much detail and determine the extent to which it appears crushed (pixels pushed together to distort). Use the following program (ImageDistortion.html in this chapter's folder at www.wiley.com/go/smashinghtml5) to test some of your own graphics.

```
<!DOCTYPE HTML>
<html>
<head>
<meta http-equiv="Content-Type" content="text/html; charset=UTF-8">
<title>Web graphic distortion</title>
</head>
<body>
<!-- Original -->
<img src="photo.jpg" width="100" height="127">
<!-- Enlarged 400% -->
<img src="photo.jpg" width="400" height="508">
<!-- Reduced 50% -->
<img src="photo.jpg" width="50" height="63.5">
</body>
</html>
```

Figure 9-4: Enlarged JPG digital photo using HTML5 attributes to enlarge and shrink.

To find the width and height of a graphic, use the mouse pointer to select the image file and then

■ In Windows, right-click it and select Properties → Details and read the Width and Height values. You can find the dimensions of a graphic file by moving the mouse over the file.

In Mac OS X, Ctrl+click the image file and select Get Info. In the More Info section view the Dimensions showing Width x Height.

Most Web tools, such as Dreamweaver, provide code hinting at the image dimensions. Likewise, virtually all graphic-editing programs show the image's dimensions when the file is loaded.

181

USING GRAPHIC APPLICATIONS TO MODIFY IMAGE FILE SIZE

When discussing an image's size, two different meanings are used:

The size of the file in terms of its dimensions

The number of bytes it takes up

Usually, in this discussion the context should make it clear which sense of size is being used, but for the most part, the term size refers to the number of bytes in a file, and dimensions refers to the size of the image on the screen.

Adobe Photoshop is a commonly used application for making adjustments to graphic size and quality. Further, Photoshop provides visual information that designers and developers can use to decide how much byte reduction the graphic can take before its appearance suffers. Figures 9-5 and 9-9 show this process. (Figures 9-6 through 9-8 show information about the files and how they appear on a Web page.)

Figure 9-5: Image and size information display in four-way view.

Changing JPEG file sizes

Beginning with a very large TIFF file that must be converted to either a PNG, JPEG, or GIF file, the file-editing process begins with three levels of quality — maximum, medium, and low. Figure 9-5 shows the original TIFF file and three JPEG renderings.

The original TIFF image in the top-left corner is over a half a megabyte, and it needs to be slimmed down significantly and converted into a format that HTML5 browsers can read. The top-right figure in JPEG format is set to the maximum quality — 100. On the bottom row, the bottom-left figure is low quality set to 2, and the bottom-right figure is considered medium quality, set at 60. The smallest Web file is only 8.6K and the largest is 127.1K. A quick glance shows very little difference with this particular image.

To get a more definitive idea, the two extremes of Web quality settings are saved to disk. Then (on a Macintosh) each is viewed for the size settings as shown in Figure 9-6.

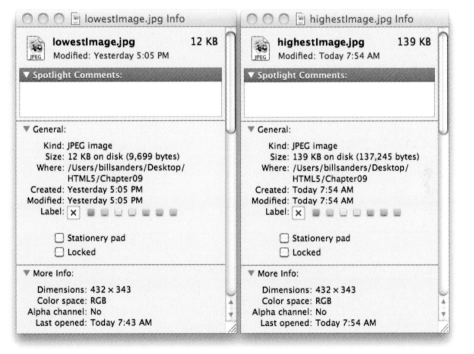

Figure 9-6: Checking image file properties.

In looking at Figure 9-6, you can see that both have identical dimensions (432 x 343), but one has 12 KB of information and the other has 139 KB. The reason for beginning adjustments by comparing the best and the worst quality as implied in the file size is that visual differences are more apparent. Perception studies have found that examining minute differences tends to gloss over those differences, whereas extreme differences are clear, so when you begin making adjustments, it's better to start with the big differences. Figure 9-7 shows the two files on a Web page.

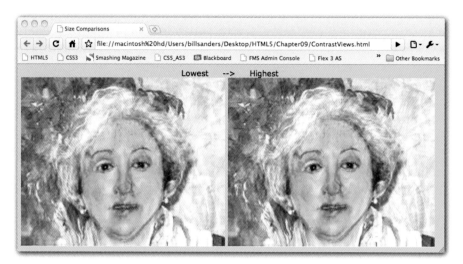

Figure 9-7: High-quality and low-quality JPEG files on a Web page.

As you can see, the lowest-quality image (left) and highest-quality image (right) are very similar. In the context of other materials on a Web page, some quality differences may appear. However, images that have the characteristics of those two shown in Figure 9-7 don't suffer much in appearance on the Web when file size is reduced.

A bigger difference with JPEG files sizes can be seen with digital photos. In Figure 9-8, the photo on the left is the lowest quality (8K) and the one on the right (115K) is the highest, with corresponding file sizes.

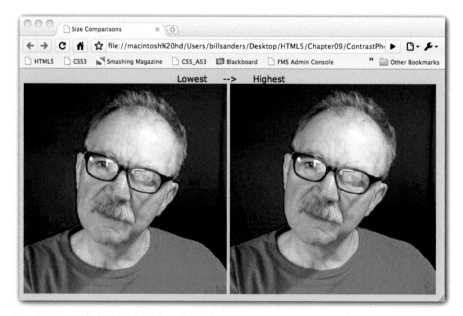

Figure 9-8: Low- and high-quality digital photos in JPEG format.

The differences between the two photos with the different settings is minimal, but the difference in the kilobytes is quite large — 8K versus 115K. On a video monitor, the image in Figure 9-8 on the left has poorer definition around the edges, but if the primary audience has very low bandwidth available, cutting down the size of JPEG files won't significantly cut down on the quality of the image.

The image in Figure 9-8 was photographed with a Webcam, and digital photographs taken with higher-quality cameras show far more detail that may be lost with the loss of information taken out when a file size is reduced. However, very high-quality digital photos have to be reduced significantly in size to be practical for the Web.

Good lighting saves bandwidth

Regardless of the kind of camera you're using, a well-lighted image is going to look better than a poorly lighted one. Everything we see (and your camera sees) is the reflection of light off objects. If you pay just a little attention to the lighting of your subject, your digital images will look better.

You don't need a lighting studio to take good photographs, but by adding light correctly, your digital photo is going to look better, and you'll be able to remove more information from the file and still have it look good enough to put on the Web. Here are some tips:

Use diffused light. If you take a picture on a cloudy day, the pictures generally turn out better. That's because the clouds diffuse the light. (If you've ever seen those photos where the unfortunate subjects have to line up and squint into the sun, they not only look squinty, the photos are overexposed.) For indoors, aim a light at white paper and let it bounce the light onto the subject. A crumpled up piece of aluminum foil flattened out does a good job of diffusing light.

Use natural light where possible. If you're taking indoor photos, open the curtains and blinds and let in the natural light.

Changing PNG and GIF file sizes

Turning now to changing file sizes with PNG and GIF files, the differences tend to be more significant with the reduction of file size and the accompanying information that is removed. Take a look at Figure 9-9, and you can immediately see that the different settings have different quality levels.

In Figure 9-9, the top two images are GIF files and the bottom two are PNG. When GIF files are reduced, they lose colors. The top-left image has only 32 colors and the one on the right has 256 (which isn't a whole lot either). In comparing the sizes of the two GIF files, the one on the top-left is only half the one on the right. Compare that with the different quality levels using JPEG files in Figure 9-5.

The two PNG files are labeled PNG-24 (left) and PNG-8 (right). The PNG-8 format has only 128 colors, while PNG-24 can handle millions of colors. The 8 and 24 refer to 8-bit and 24-bit color processing. In a nutshell, PNG-24 is of a higher quality.

Figure 9-9: Changing PNG and GIF file sizes.

Changing SVG file sizes

Unlike the bitmapped graphics, changing SVG graphic sizes is simple and doesn't hurt the look of the image. The following Web page code shows a 500 x 400 `.svg` file displayed in different sizes determined by the width and height attributes: The following script (`SVG.html` in this chapter's folder at `www.wiley.com/go/smashinghtml5`) uses a single `.svg` file to display many different sizes without distortion.

```
<!DOCTYPE HTML>
<html>
<head>
<meta http-equiv="Content-Type" content="text/html; charset=UTF-8">
<title>SVG Test</title>
</head>
```

```
<body style="background-color:#BAD9CB" >
<!-- Safari, Chrome and Opera -->
<img src="logo500x400.svg" width=100 height=80>
<img src="logo500x400.svg" width=200 height=160>
<img src="logo500x400.svg" width=300 height=240><br>
<img src="logo500x400.svg" width=500 height=400>

<!-- Firefox and Opera
<object width=100 height=80 type="image/svg+xml" data="logo500x400.svg"></object>
<object width=200 height=160 type="image/svg+xml" data="logo500x400.svg"></object>
<object width=300 height=240 type="image/svg+xml" data="logo500x400.svg"></
  object><br>
<object width=500 height=400 type="image/svg+xml" data="logo500x400.svg"></object>
-->
</body>
</html>
```

At the time of this writing, Firefox did not use the <img> tag with .svg files but required the <object> tag instead. The Opera browser worked with both formats. Figure 9-10 shows the results. As you can see, the logo in Figure 9-10 looks the same no matter what size it's displayed in.

Figure 9-10: An SVG image changed by changing attributes with no distortion.

Grayscale on Internet Explorer

One interesting note in working through file sizes is the use of a special CSS property recognized only by Internet Explorer. Some designers use grayscale settings to reduce the size of their graphics or for the effect of grayscale. If you want an interesting option using Microsoft Internet Explorer, you can write a little CSS code to convert color files to grayscale. Use the following snippet in a style definition:

```
<style type="text/css">
img {
     filter:gray;
}
</style>
```

Figure 9-11 shows a color figure (Figure 9-8) that is turned into a grayscale using CSS only.

Figure 9-11: Using Internet Explorer CSS grayscale filter.

Using this technique is a quick way to see how the figure looks in a grayscale before rendering it in a grayscale mode. If you're updating a site, and you want to view the images on the page in grayscale, you can add the CSS and test it on Internet Explorer first. If you want to keep the file size down and the quality up, a JPEG image in grayscale instead of color will cut the file size in half.

PLACING IMAGES AND CREATING FLEXIBLE WEB PAGES

The <img> tag is the primary one used to call up graphics, and although CSS3 is the primary tool for getting things to go where you want on a Web page, you can use certain <img> attributes to help out. This section examines options you have for placing text where you want it to go on your Web page and how to use certain key attributes with the <img> tag.

IMAGE PLACEMENT WITH THE ALIGN ATTRIBUTE

To start looking at placement, consider the align attribute of the <img> tag. The one advantage is that there is no easier way to quickly position the image relative to the text. The following script (ImagePlacement.html in this chapter's folder at www.wiley.com/go/smashinghtml5) illustrates this.

```
<!DOCTYPE HTML>
<html>
<head>
<style type="text/css">
/*048ABF,049DBF,F2F2F2,595959,0D0D0D*/
body {
    background-color:#F2F2F2;
    color:#0D0D0D;
    font-family:Verdana, Geneva, sans-serif;
}
h1 {
    font-family:"Trebuchet MS", Arial, Helvetica, sans-serif;
    color:#595959;
    background-color:#049DBF;
    text-align:center;
}
h2 {
    color:#048ABF;
}
</style>
<meta http-equiv="Content-Type" content="text/html; charset=UTF-8">
<title>Simple Placement</title>
</head>
<body>
<article>
  <header>
    <h1>Web Developer's Gym</h1>
  </header>
  <section>
    <header>
      <h2>Developer's Workout</h2>
    </header>
    <figure> <img src="webDeveloper.gif" width="250" height="263" align="left"
  align="workout"> </figure>
```

```
        You know you've been thinking about it. Isn't it about time you started working
    on your &lt;alt&gt; and tags? Build up your elements and attributes in HTML5 at the
    Web Developer's Gym. Once you get going, you can add a little &lt;canvas&gt; tag
    work and get into some serious CSS3. The gym is open 24/7 for your convenience—and
    you can access it anywhere worldwide! All your friends have joined, and just look
    at them—they're even adding video to their Web pages! You can do it, too! Don't let
    another day go by with you wishing that you could be a Web developer. Start today!
        </section>
    </article>
    </body>
    </html>
```

The right and left placement of the image is simple. All that's required is the assignment of
`"left"` and `"right"` values to the `align` attribute. Figure 9-12 shows the placement of the
image in both the left and right positions.

Figure 9-12: Image placement with the align attribute.

In Figure 9-12, the page on the right looks okay, but the page on the left jams the text right up
against the image. Also, the page is wholly dependent on the user's page settings and size. In
other words, using the `align` attribute for placing images can make your page look awful.
Figure 9-13 shows two other views of the same page that transform its look.

In Figure 9-13, the figure on the left shows the text scattered all over the page, while the figure
on the right, a mobile device, shows the image just fine, but the text is just one word wide,
snaking along the side of the picture. The rest is below the view area.

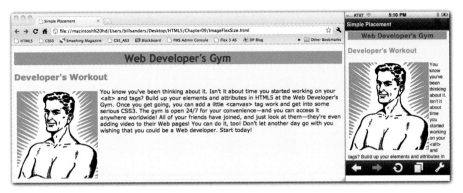

Figure 9-13: Different views of a page.

FLEXIBLE IMAGE SIZE WITH A LITTLE JAVASCRIPT

In Chapter 12, you'll understand this information better, but I need JavaScript in this section to show how your pages can be more flexible by having different-size images. JavaScript has a little property called `navigator.appVersion`. When that property is placed into a script, you can find out information about the hardware being used to load the Web page. If you find out that the page is being loaded into a mobile device, instead of loading the full-size image into the Web page, it loads the smaller one.

To make this work, take the same GIF file used for the original Web page created in the previous section, and make a second one about one-third the size of the original. Create a folder, and name it `flexImages`, and place both the large and small GIF files. Name the large file, `WebDeveloper.gif` and the smaller one `lilWebDeveloper.gif`, and place them both in the `flexImages` folder. Then enter the following program (`ImageFlex Size.html` in this chapter's folder at `www.wiley.com/go/smashinghtml5`) and save it in the same directory as the `flexImages` folder.

```html
<!DOCTYPE HTML>
<html>
<head>
<script type="text/javascript">
var envir=navigator.appVersion;
envir=envir.substring(5,11);
var imageNow=new Image();
var showNow;
function showImage()
{
    if(envir=="iPhone" || envir=="(iPhon")
    {
        showNow="flexImages/lilWebDeveloper.gif";
    }
    else
    {
        showNow="flexImages/WebDeveloper.gif";
    }
```

```
        imageNow.src=showNow;
        document.pix.src=imageNow.src;
}
</script>
<style type="text/css">
/*048ABF,049DBF,F2F2F2,595959,0D0D0D*/
body {
        background-color:#F2F2F2;
        color:#0D0D0D;
        font-family:Verdana, Geneva, sans-serif;
}
h1 {
        font-family:"Trebuchet MS", Arial, Helvetica, sans-serif;
        color:#595959;
        background-color:#049DBF;
        text-align:center;
}
h2 {
        color:#048ABF;
}
img {
        padding:5px;
}
</style>
<meta http-equiv="Content-Type" content="text/html; charset=UTF-8">
<title>Flexible Image Size</title>
</head>
<body onload="showImage()">
<article>
  <header>
    <h1>Web Developer's Gym</h1>
  </header>
  <section>
    <header>
      <h2>Developer's Workout</h2>
    </header>
    <figure> <img src="flexImages/WebDeveloper.gif" name="pix" align="left"> </
  figure>
    You know you've been thinking about it. Isn't it about time you started working
  on your &lt;alt&gt; and tags? Build up your elements and attributes in HTML5 at the
  Web Developer's Gym. Once you get going, you can add a little &lt;canvas&gt; tag
  work and get into some serious CSS3. The gym is open 24/7 for your convenience—and
  you can access it anywhere worldwide! All your friends have joined, and just look
  at them—they're even adding video to their Web pages! You can do it, too! Don't let
  another day go by with you wishing that you could be a Web developer. Start today!
  </section>
</article>
</body>
</html>
```

First, try out the program on your computer. You should see exactly what you saw when you originally tested it (refer to Figure 9-12). Now, try it out in a mobile browser. Instead of a large image pushing all the text to one side, you see a smaller image surrounded by text, just like the one on your computer. That's because the Web page was able to use the JavaScript to determine whether the page was loaded by an iPhone or some other platform or device.

Place the Web page file and both of the images in their folder into the same directory on a server. When you test it, it looks like it was made for the iPhone, but it was really made for the iPhone or any other device. Using this and other JavaScript code, you can do a lot more with HTML5 than you can with just HTML5 by itself.

Figure 9-14: Displaying a small graphic for a mobile device.

The JavaScript used in the example is as minimalist as possible. However, the logic of it can be outlined as follows:

Place the contents of `navigator.appVersion` into a variable named `envir` (short for environment).

Because `navigator.appVersion` generates a long description, get only the part of the results that either shows iPhone or not.

Create a new image object named `imageNow`.

Initialize a variable named `showNow` (that you'll use in the function).

Create a function that asks, "Is this an iPhone environment or not?" If it is an iPhone environment, then use the small graphic; otherwise, use the big graphic. (In an Opera Mini quirk, JavaScript returns `" (iPhon"` as the first six characters of `navigator.appVersion`; so, the code has to query whether it found `" (iPhon"` or `"iPhone"` — this goes to show just how accommodating JavaScript can be.)

Of course, there are a lot more types of mobile devices available, and you'd have to change the JavaScript code to add more to the list of mobile devices besides iPhone, but the logic is the same — just a bit more JavaScript.

By the way, if you've never done anything with JavaScript, don't expect to understand the code in the Web page markup. This demonstration just shows what can be done with JavaScript. The future of the Web needs to include many different kinds of Web-browsing platforms, and this little demonstration is just a taste of what you can do. (If you're an experienced JavaScript developer, you can create something a bit more elegant!)

APPLICATION FOR DYNAMIC SVG FILES FROM ADOBE ILLUSTRATOR CS5 FILES

Adobe Illustrator CS5 (AI) has an added feature, Adobe Illustrator CS5 HTML5 Pack, available at `http://labs.adobe.com`. It's designed to allow graphic designers using AI to easily convert their `.ai` files to `.svg` files containing parts that can be dynamically changed using HTML5. To give you an idea how it works, the following example begins with a simple graphic image in AI. It has two layers, and on one of the layers, the designer wants variable color that can be coded in HTML5. The layer to be given a variable feature is selected and viewed in the Appearance panel (as shown in Figure 9-15).

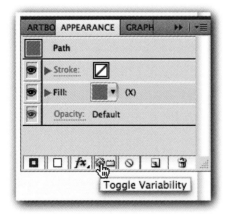

Figure 9-15: Fill is set as a variable in Adobe Illustrator CS5.

The (X) in Figure 9-15 indicates that the Fill is a variable that can be changed with HTML5. In order to access the feature to be changed (the fill color in this case), AI generates code for the SVG file format that can be viewed and/or saved during the conversion from an .ai file to an .svg file. During the conversion process, the designer clicks the Show SVG code button, and finds the layer name of the variable feature. In this example, the specific SVG code was the following:

```
<g id="Button">
     <ellipse fill="param(SVGID_2__FillColor) #A35563" cx="50" cy="50" rx="40"
 ry="40.5"/>
</g>
```

The id with the value Button is from the name of the layer in AI. The param name value is SVGID_2__FillColor, which is automatically generated by AI.

In order to work the SVG information into an HTML5 program, the .svg file must be referenced in an <object> element and the parameter in a <param> tag. The JavaScript file Param.js is also automatically generated by AI and must be loaded in the <head> container in order for Firefox to correctly parse the code. The following code (AI2svg.html in this chapter's folder at www.wiley.com/go/smashinghtml5) works with Firefox, Safari, Chrome and Opera browsers but with some differences in display.

```
<!DOCTYPE HTML>
<html>
<head>
<script src="Param.js"></script>
<meta http-equiv="Content-Type" content="text/html; charset=UTF-8">
<title>AI -> SVG</title>
</head>
<body>
<article>
  <section>
    <figure>
      <object type="image/svg+xml" data="butnBkground.svg">
        <!--No param tags -->
      </object>
    </figure>
    <figure>
      <object type="image/svg+xml" data="butnBkground.svg">
        <param name="SVGID_2__FillColor" value="#cc0000" />
      </object>
    </figure>
  </section>
</article>
</body>
</html>
```

In order to illustrate the sequence of processes, Figure 9-16 shows the original AI file and the results of the output in Opera when the page AI2svg.html loads.

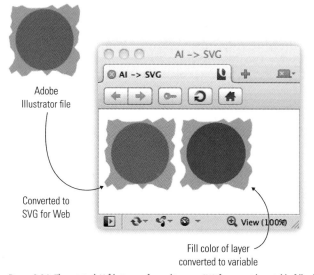

Adobe
Illustrator file

Converted to
SVG for Web

Fill color of layer
converted to variable

Figure 9-16: The original AI file is transformed into an SVG format with variable fill color.

The `Param.js` and `.svg` files must be in the same folder as the HTML5 page, just as external CSS3 and graphic files are expected to be either in the same folder as the HTML5 that calls them or in the path specified by the HTML5 code. The best part, though, is that designers and developers can focus on the HTML5 tags while Adobe Illustrator CS5 takes care of generating the JavaScript and the parameter names. Of course, this means that designers can use vector graphics and have dynamic features in their AI creations.

TAKE THE WHEEL

This first exercise is a Web treasure hunt. You can find a lot of free tools on the Web that can be used to alter the size of a graphic file — both in terms of dimensions and number of bytes in the image. Even if you have a tool like Adobe Photoshop or Microsoft Paint, go find an application on the Web that works on your computer. (You can find several if you want.)

Take an existing graphic file that is not in JPEG, PNG, or GIF format. For example, find a graphic with a `.tif` or `.tiff` extension. (It can be a digital photograph or a drawn graphic — or some combination of both.) Then do the following:

1. **Convert the file to JPEG, PNG, *and* GIF format.**

   Now you have four files — the original and three Web formats.

2. **Make a second copy of all Web graphics, naming the second one so that it indicates it will be low quality.**

   For example, if you have a file named `car.jpg`, copy it and name the second copy `carLow.jpg`.

3. **Using the image application you found on the Web, create the highest- and lowest-quality file for each of the three file types.**

4. **Using HTML5 and CSS3, create a Web page with three rows. On the left side place the highest-quality images, and on the right place the lowest quality.**

5. **Between all the images, place fill text of your choice.**

   This is a good time to look up lorem ipsum on the Web. Figure 9-17 shows the general format.

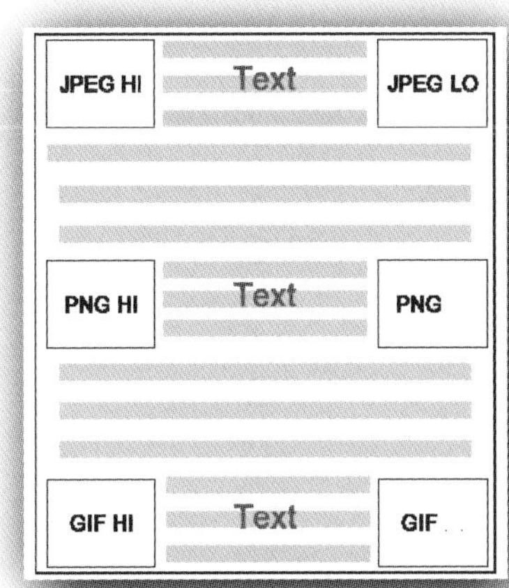

Figure 9-17: Displaying the different types and qualities of graphics in text.

This exercise has two purposes:

   To provide you with an exercise in placing text — work with CSS3 from this chapter and previous chapters. Using the align attribute in the `<img>` tag has serious limitations.

   To drive home the idea that all changes to images must be done using software that changes the characteristics of an image before you put your Web page together.

For those who want to do more with vector graphics, try out the Adobe Illustrator CS5 HTML5 Pack. If you do not have Adobe Illustrator CS5, you can download a 30-day trial free. Try creating variables out of different parts of an AI design using multiple layers with names that become the ID name of the parameter you'll change.

10 SOUND

ADDING SOUND TO Web pages allows developers to create a wide range of Web sites. Sites that play music, provide instruction, or add sound effects certainly widen the range of possibilities of what you can do with HTML5. This chapter examines how to prepare sound for the Web and how you can use sound to help your Web pages make some noise.

You'll learn how to work with the different `<audio>` tag attributes and settings. Also, you'll see how different browsers handle sound and different sound files. As with graphics, specialized programs are available to create audio and edit it. So, after examining the basic HTML5 elements and attributes, this chapter goes on to show you how to create sounds for your Web site.

THE BASICS OF AUDIO IN HTML5

One of the most exciting new tags in the HTML5 collection is `<audio>`. With it you can play audio files using the speakers on your computer or headset on a mobile device. The basic format to select a sound file to play is:

```
<audio src="jazz.mp3"></audio>
```

The `src` attribute works just like it does in an `<img>` tag — it's a reference to the source of the file. However, to get the audio to play, you need to look at the attributes.

AUTOPLAY

The `autoplay` attribute is fairly self-explanatory. As soon as the page loads, the sounds begin to play. Before adding the `autoplay` attribute, you want to be sure that all your users are going to be okay with listening to whatever you're playing. One way to guarantee that users will not return to a page is to have a continuous sound that automatically turns on. That concern aside, the following script (`BasicAudio.html` in this chapter's folder at www. wiley.com/go/smashinghtml5) shows how to create a simple page that begins playing as soon as it's launched:

```
<!DOCTYPE HTML>
<html>
<head>
<meta http-equiv="Content-Type" content="text/html; charset=UTF-8">
<title>Basic Audio</title>
</head>
<body>
Audio is between the lines<br>
-----------------------------------------
<br>
<audio src="jazz.wav" autoplay></audio>
<br>
-----------------------------------------
</body>
</html>
```

You can test that script with any browser except Google Chrome because it's the only one that doesn't recognize sound files in the `.wav` format. Use an `.mp3` or `.ogg` sound file instead for Chrome testing.

CONTROLS

As noted, if your sound (music, sound effects, or even just talking) annoys your users, they're not going to return. So, how do you control sound? The easiest way is to add the `controls` attribute. As with `autoplay`, you don't have to give it a value. Just include it within the `<audio>` tag, and it automatically appears. Try the following program (`Controls.html` in this chapter's folder at www.wiley.com/go/smashinghtml5):

```
<!DOCTYPE HTML>
<html>
<style type="text/css">
/* 694703,A83110,E89F06,F5D895,B3CF83 */
body {
      background-color:#B3CF83;
      font-family:Verdana, Geneva, sans-serif;
      color:#694703;
}
h1 {
      font-family:Braggadocio, "Arial Black";
      color:#A83110;
}
</style>
<head>
<meta http-equiv="Content-Type" content="text/html; charset=UTF-8">
<title>Controls</title>
</head>
<body>
<article>
  <header>
    <h1>Jazz Tonight</h1>
  </header>
  <section>
    <p>Click the triangle to start the show: </p>
    <audio src="mists.ogg" controls></audio>
    <p>The || two pipes symbol stops all of this. </p>
  </section>
</article>
</body>
</html>
```

When you run this program, be sure to use a browser compatible with the audio file. (Use a .wav file if the .ogg file type doesn't work with your browser.) Depending on the kind of browser you use, you'll see different player controls. Figure 10-1 shows how the different browsers look. (The Google Chrome browser is shown with the sound actually playing.)

About the only common feature of the audio control bar is the triangle start button on the far left, and the sound on/off toggle on the far right. The stop/pause button is similar as well, but the graphics of each is unique. (The different control bar images may give designers fits as they try to design a page with audio to be fully compatible with all browsers.)

Providing some kind of control for users is essential. The Chrome browser provides a nice big bar so that the user can clearly see where she is relative to the beginning and end of the audio. For instructional audios, the scrubber bar (the vertical bar you can see in the Chrome browser in Figure 10-1) is important so that the student can drag the scrubber bar to review those portions of a lesson that are difficult to understand.

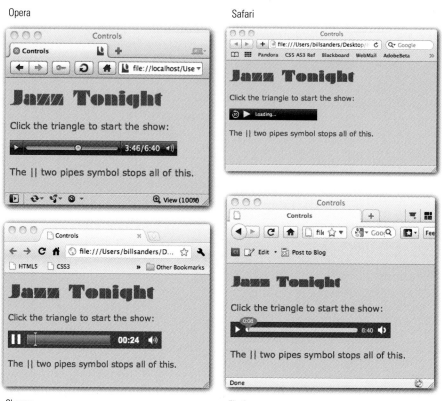

Figure 10-1: Using audio player controls.

PRELOAD

The `preload` attribute of the `<audio>` tag can be an important one because it starts preloading the audio before it's played. In that way, users don't have to sit and twiddle their thumbs while the audio loads after they press play. The simplest format for the `preload` attribute is just like the controls and autoplay — it just needs to be added without a value, as the following shows:

```
<audio src="Shadows.wav" preload controls></audio>
```

When preload is employed, you can use autoplay, but I'm not sure that it makes much sense to do so. Autoplay starts the audio playing as soon as the page loads, while preload is used to load an audio file before the play command is issued by the controller.

You can assign values to the `preload` attribute:

- `none`: Having none as a value may seem strange, but some browsers may be set to automatically preload audio files. However, if the chance of using a particular audio is remote, the developer may decide not to use Internet resources and so assigns the `none` value to the `preload` attribute.

- `metadata`: All audio (and video) files have metadata like duration or some other sound data that the sound author placed in the audio's file. When the chance of using an audio file is low, but (just in case) loading the metadata is reasonable and doesn't take up much in the way of Internet resources.
- `auto`: If the `preload` attribute is present, it automatically preloads the audio file information. The auto assignment simply acts as a reminder that the file is going to preload. (It's the same as not have any value assignment to a `preload` attribute.)

The more varied your audience and the more audio in your Web page, the more you want to provide the `preload` attribute with options.

LOOP

When you want a sound to endlessly repeat itself, you use a loop. The advantage of using a loop is that you can take a relatively short piece of music and have it repeat itself so that it sounds like a full composition. In this way, you can use a minimum amount of Internet resources and have continuous music. The format is like the other attributes that act like Booleans — they're either off or on. The following is an example:

```
<audio src="Shadows.wav" autoplay loop></audio>
```

In that line lies the seeds of its own destruction. For many good reasons, users may want to turn off sound. You can use JavaScript to put together a simple routine that will do that, but it's easier simply to add the `controls` attribute and let the user turn it off. However, some designers, with good reason, would rather not have the audio control anywhere in the design; they believe that some nice music would be an integral part of the design. In that case, start looking up the JavaScript to turn the thing off. No matter how nice a piece of sound is, repeated endlessly it becomes brainwashing, and that's not allowed by the Geneva Convention.

203

BROWSER SUPPORT FOR AUDIO

At the time of this writing, while testing audio formats, I could find no format that all browsers supported. Worse still, no single format is supported by all HTML5 browsers. Table 10.1 shows the breakdown.

Table 10.1   Browsers and Audio Format Support

Browser	MP3	WAV	OGG
Chrome	Yes	No	Yes
Firefox	No	Yes	Yes
Internet Explorer 9*	Yes	No	No*
Opera	No	Yes	No
Safari	Yes	Yes	No

* Microsoft announced that IE9 would be supporting the OGG format, but in the beta version of IE9, it did not.

As you can see, the only audio format that comes close to support by all browsers is .wav. The good news is that .wav files are widely available, and you can find just about any sound you in .wav format. However, if a significant number of your user audience prefers the Google Chrome browser to the others, you're going to need a Plan B.

SAVED BY SOURCE: PLAN B

Usually, if you have to determine which browser is going to work with different resources, you're going to have to break out the JavaScript. Fortunately, HTML5 has an element that can offer up several different audio formats and let the browser select the one that's compatible.

The <source> tag can be placed within the <audio> container with the source and URL of the audio inside the <source> tag. Suppose that you're running a Web site with audio instructional materials — you talk learners through HTML5, for example. Instead of telling everyone that they have to use a certain type of browser, all you need to do is have files for all possible browsers and let the browser pick the one it likes. For example, let's say that you're setting up Lesson #3 on a Web page. The following would provide a selection of files that no browser would pass up:

```
<audio controls>
  <source src="instruction3.ogg">
  <source src="instruction3.mp3">
  <source src="instruction3.wav">
</audio>
```

The chore of making multiple versions of audio files may be annoying, but even if you programmed it in JavaScript, you'd need multiple copies of the media. (In Chapter 9, multiple copies of a graphic file were required for mobile and non-mobile platforms that used JavaScript to sort out whether the page was being viewed on an iPhone or something else.)

TYPE ATTRIBUTE

When setting up several different types of audio sources to be sure that all HTML5-compatible browsers will play it, you can enhance the process by adding the type attribute to the <source> tag. The information in the type attribute tells the browser whether it should even attempt to load the file. For example, the following snippet shows the format:

```
<source src='mists.ogg' type='audio/ogg'>
```

The reason for including a type attribute is to save time. The interpreter in the browser looks at the line and realizes that the type indicates that it can either play it or not. If not, it doesn't even bother trying. For example, suppose you were given a choice of taking two tests — one in HTML5 and the other in quantum physics. Unless you have a background in quantum physics, you're not going to waste your time trying. However, knowing that a test will be in HTML5, you feel like you can give it a shot. It's the same with the type attribute. If it sees the type and determines, "I can't play that," it doesn't try.

If the `type` attribute is not in place the browser will try to load it, and if it fails, it then goes on to the next `<source>` tag and gives it a try.

The following snippet shows all the types:

```
<audio controls>
  <source src="instruction3.ogg" type="audio/ogg">
  <source src="instruction3.mp3" type="audio/mpeg">
  <source src="instruction3.wav" type="audio/wav">
</audio>
```

All values must be valid MIME types. The valid ones follow the `media-type` rule defined in W3C specifications for HTML5. The `type` attribute is optional, but if your site has a lot of traffic, you want to cut out every unnecessary call. The `type` attribute helps you do that. For more help, you need to consider the `codec` parameter in the next section.

SOURCE TYPE CODEC PARAMETER

Generally, if you enter a value for the `type` attribute, all you have to include is the general type. However, when more than a single codec is available, you should add the codecs that the browser can read. Again, specifying the codec is not going to allow the browser to access a certain codec that it would not otherwise be able to do. Rather, it provides a heads-up to the browser so that if it can't read it, the browser doesn't even try. It's like a newspaper vendor asking, "What do you want? We've got papers in English, Spanish, and Mongolian." If you read English and Spanish, you can choose them, but if you know you don't read Mongolian, you don't even try.

Before moving on to a closer look at the codec parameter, be sure to understand what a codec is. The word codec is a combination of the terms compression and decompression. So, when I speak of a codec, I'm talking about how a file is encoded (usually shrunk) and decoded (expanded so it can be played).

The type of codec, even though the file types are the same, can be different. In order to speed up the process of determining whether the file can be read, adding the codec parameter filters out those codec types that the browser can't read. For example, the following are all `.ogg` files with different codecs:

```
<source src="songFest.ogg" type="audio/ogg; codecs=vorbis">
<source src=" songFest.spx" type="audio/ogg; codecs=speex">
<source src="audio.oga" type="audio/ogg; codecs=flac">
```

So remember, codecs and file types are horses of different colors. If your Web pages can use full codec information on a file, you may as well use it. Otherwise, some browsers may attempt to launch the sound only to find that the codec is incompatible.

Some types of audio files are more likely than others to have a wide range of codecs. The following snippet shows typical codecs for all the HTML5 sound files that can be read by HTML5 browsers:

```
<audio controls>
  <source src="sound.ogg" type="audio/ogg; codecs=vorbis">
  <source src="jazz.mp3" type="audio/mpeg; codecs=mp3">
  <source src="Shadows.wav" type="audio/wav; codecs=wav">
</audio>
```

The above snippet does not show all possible codecs of all audio types. However, it represents the typical kinds of codes used in Internet audio.

CREATING AUDIO FILES

Both Windows 7 and Macintosh OS X include programs that you can use to create your own audio files. They come loaded on your computer, and unless you removed them, you should be all set to get started making sound recordings.

Earlier versions of Windows also have a Sound Recorder application, but it looks different from the one used in the example. Also, the Sound Recorder that is part of Windows XP saves files to .wav format, so they're all ready for a Web page. However, the newer version of Sound Recorder that ships with Windows 7 only saves files in .wma format and must be converted to a file type recognized by HTML5 browsers.

WINDOWS 7 SOUND RECORDER

The first thing you want to do when you make a recording is to set up some kind of microphone for the recording. Most computers that run Windows 7 have built-in microphones, and you can use those. Otherwise, you'll need to plug in the microphone you plan to use and make sure it's properly configured. Usually, your computer can find the audio drivers you need, but some microphones come with software drivers that you need to install. Directions for such installations will come with the microphone.

To select a microphone, use the following path: Control Panel > Hardware and Sound > Manage Audio Devices. When the Sound window opens, select the Recording tab. You'll see the selections shown in Figure 10-2.

Your recording selections may be different, but in general you'll either have a line-in or a built-in microphone. When you make a selection, click OK, and you're now ready to open the Sound Recorder application.

From the Start menu, select All Programs > Accessories > Sound Recorder. (If you're running Windows XP, choose All Programs > Accessories > Entertainment > Sound Recorder.) Figure 10-3 shows what the Sound Recorder looks like when it's ready to record (top) and while it's recording (bottom).

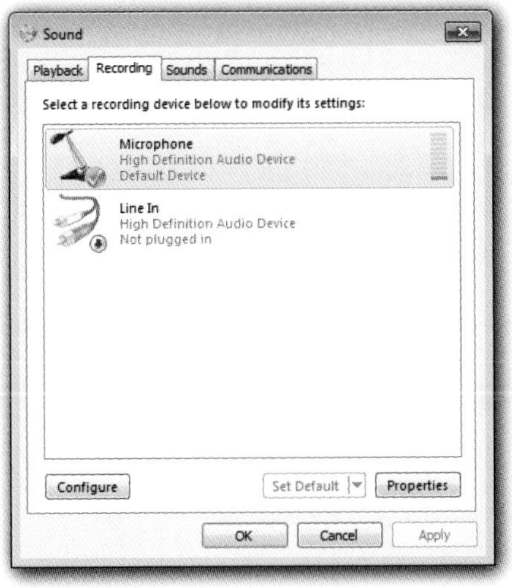

Figure 10-2: Windows 7 recording selections.

Figure 10-3: The Sound Recorder application in Windows 7.

Once you're ready to start recording, click on the red circle, and begin talking. As you talk, you'll see a green bar appear next to the timer in the middle of the recorder bar. If that bar is not moving as you talk, that means your microphone is not working correctly. Otherwise, you'll see the green sound bar bounce in and out as you speak. When you're finished, click on the Stop Recording button — a blue square. (In Sound Recorder in Windows XP, the Stop Recording button is a black rectangle right next to the red circle that starts the recording.)

When you click the Stop Recording button, a new Save As window opens and you can select the directory where you want to save your audio recording. As noted, in Windows 7, the only option is in .wma format (Windows Media Audio). If you're using the Windows XP version, select Save or Save As to open a dialog box to use to choose the directory, filename, and format — which is .wav (but not .wma!).

If you're using the older version of Sound Recorder, you're all set with a .wav file that you can play using the HTML5 <audio> tag. Otherwise, you'll have to convert the .wma file to an acceptable format for HTML5 browsers.

MACINTOSH OS X SOUND STUDIO

Macs come bundled with a program called Sound Studio. Macs also have built-in microphones as well, or you can use an external microphone if you have the correct drivers installed. You can select an external microphone (including ones built into any attached cameras) either from System Preferences > Sound > Input or from Sound Studio. While you're choosing the Input device, any noise will appear in an Input level graphic, so be sure to speak while making the settings so that you can get an idea of the sound level.

To open Sound Studio, select Go > Applications > Sound Studio (folder) > Sound Studio.app from the Finder. When Sound Studio opens, you'll see a timeline and an Input Levels window, as shown in Figure 10-4.

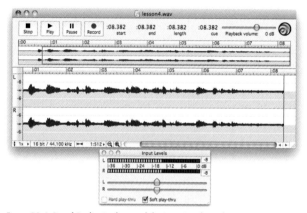

Figure 10-4: Sound Studio timelines and the Input Levels window.

Converting files

If you'll be using audio for general audiences, you're going to need either

 ◆ A sound editor that saves audio files as `.wav` files and either `.mp3` or `.ogg`.

 ◆ A conversion program. A simple search on the Web will reveal several. For example, if you're using the Windows 7 Sound Recorder, you'll need a program to convert from `.wma` format to `.mp3`, `.wav`, or `.ogg`. Generally, the process is quite simple for either Mac or Windows platforms.

A variety of conversion products are available, but several for Windows 7 can be found at `http://software-download.name/audio-converter-windows-7/`. On the Mac, I tested Switch Sound File Converter (`http://download.cnet.com/Switch-Audio-Converter/3000-2140_4-10703967.html`) and found it to be easy to use; it converted typical Mac sound file types (like `.aiff` files) to sound files recognized by the HTML5 browsers. Do a Web search and you'll find far more converters for both Windows and Macs.

To make a recording, click the red Record button. If you want to pause to gather your thoughts, click the Pause button. Once you're finished, click the Stop button and select File from the menu bar. If you choose Save or Save As, you can save the file for HTML5 browsers in `.wav` format. However, if you select Export with QuickTime, the file will be in `.mp3` audio format. So, using Sound Studio on the Mac, you can generate two of the three HTML5 formats available to store your audio recordings.

SOUND EFFECTS: FX ON YOUR DESKTOP

The range of sound effects available on the Web either free or for a price should get you started on just about any sound effect you could want. The best place to start is at FlashKit (`www.flashkit.com/soundfx`). Even though the site is dedicated to Flash, it has over 7,000 (and growing) free, public-domain sound effects from which to choose. What's more, you can download them in either `.wav` or `.mp3` format, so they're already set to be used in an HTML5 Web page. If you search the Web, you can find virtually any sound effect you want.

If you want to record your own sound effects, you can use simple household noises and the sound recording applications on your computer. For example, a dog barking, an airplane flying overhead, or just about any other sound you can hear, you can record. (Be careful with copyrighted music, though!)

TRANSITION SOUNDS

A subtle yet effective interactive sound can be used to add an audio component to page transitions. In a tactile world of buttons, switches and doorknobs, our actions often evoke sounds. You can make your Web links do the same thing. Use the following steps to create a simple transition:

1. **Navigate to** `www.flashkit.com/soundfx`.
2. **Select Sound FX from the home page menu.**
3. **Select Interfaces > Clicks from the Interfaces Categories.**
4. **Select a click sound that you like.**
   If you'd rather, choose a Zoop, Zang or Zing — just be sure it's short in duration.
5. **Download both** `.wav` **and** `.mp3` **versions.**
6. **Rename one file** `click.wav` **and the other** `click.mp3`.
7. **Place the** .mp3 **and** `.wav` **files in a folder.**
   Now, in the same folder where you placed the sound files, place the following two pages (`TransitionSound.html` and `SoundOpen.html` in this chapter's folder at `www.wiley.com/go/smashinghtml5`).

209

Start Page with No Sound

```
<!DOCTYPE HTML>
<html>
<head>
<style type="text/css">
a {
     font-family:Verdana, Geneva, sans-serif;
     color:#cc0000;
     font-size:24px;
     text-decoration:none;
}
</style>
<meta http-equiv="Content-Type" content="text/html; charset=UTF-8">
<title>Transition Sound</title>
</head>
<body>
<a href="SoundOpen.html">Click to Next Page</a>
</body>
</html>
```

Play Sound When Opened

```
<!DOCTYPE HTML>
<html>
<head>
<style type="text/css">
body {
     font-family:Verdana, Geneva, sans-serif;
     color:#cc0000;
     font-size:24px;
}
</style>
<meta http-equiv="Content-Type" content="text/html; charset=UTF-8">
<title>Sound on Open</title>
</head>
<body>
<audio autoplay>
  <source src="click.wav" >
  <source src="click.mp3" >
</audio>
This page clicks.
</body>
</html>
```

Save both HTML5 pages in the same folder along with the two sound files. Test the HTML5 pages with several browsers. When you click the link, it opens a Web page and an <audio> tag with the autoplay attribute should play the click sound right after the page loads. If you have a site where the links go back and forth, the sound plays almost simultaneously with the click action so that it sound as though clicking the link made the sound. Of course, that's the idea. Otherwise, if the page takes even a little while to load, the click sounds when the page comes up — sort of like clicking itself into place.

At the time of this writing, the Opera and Firefox browsers on the Macintosh did not work when the `type` attribute was added to the `<source>` tag, but with Safari and Chrome it did. However, when the `type` attribute was omitted, the Web pages worked fine with all the Macintosh HTML5 browsers. In testing on Windows 7, the latest versions of Firefox and Safari did not generate sound, but both Opera and Chrome did with the same files. (This is why Web developers age quickly.) However, HTML5 is still young, and many of the features of HTML5 are still in development. So, by the time you're reading this, these differences may have been resolved.

INTEGRATING SOUND EFFECTS INTO A WEB PAGE

One feature of sound effects that can make them difficult to work with if you're not using the `controls` attribute is getting them to fire when you want. With plain HTML5, about the only way to fire off a sound is to place a page into an `iframe` and play the audio automatically. With JavaScript, far more elegant and sophisticated solutions are available, but functionally, using `iframe` works.

The following four HTML5 pages are made up of one page that loads three other pages into an `iframe`. As each page loads, it plays a sound effect: a dog bark, a scream, and an explosion. The user sees the `iframe` turn the color of the speaker button that was clicked and hears the sound effect, and no JavaScript was used at all. Figure 10-5 shows what the users see when she clicks on the green speaker icon.

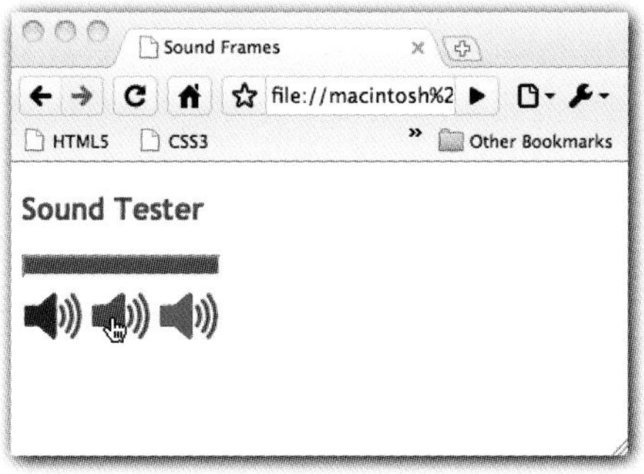

211

Figure 10-5: Triggering sounds using links to an **iframe**.

You'll need to download (or create) three sounds, each in both `.wav` and `.mp3` formats. Use short sound effects and when each of the icon buttons is clicked, the sound plays by the page loading in the `iframe`. The page being loaded has nothing but the sound, and for this demonstration, it has a background color matching the speaker icon color. Place all the pages and the six sound files in the same folder. (The following files are in this chapter's folder at www.wiley.com/go/smashinghtml5: SoundFrame.html, sound1.html, sound2. html, sound3.html.)

A Page with iframe Calls Other pages with Sound Effects

```html
<!DOCTYPE HTML>
<html>
<head>
<style type="text/css">
h3 {
    color:#cc0000;
    font-family:"Trebuchet MS", Arial, Helvetica, sans-serif;
}
</style>
<meta http-equiv="Content-Type" content="text/html; charset=UTF-8">
<title>Sound Frames</title>
</head>
<body>
<article>
  <header>
    <h3>Sound Tester</h3>
    <iframe name="ifSound" width="125" height="10"></iframe>
  </header>
  <section> <a href="sound1.html" target="ifSound"><img src="Redspeaker.gif"
 width="40" height="40"></a> <a href="sound2.html" target="ifSound"><img
 src="Greenspeaker.gif" width="40" height="40"></a> <a href="sound3.html"
 target="ifSound"><img src="Bluespeaker.gif" width="40" height="40"> </a> </section>
</article>
</body>
</html>
```

A Page with a Barking Dog and a Red Background

```html
<!DOCTYPE HTML>
<html>
<head>
<style type="text/css">
body {
    background-color:#cc0000;
}
</style>
<meta http-equiv="Content-Type" content="text/html; charset=UTF-8">
<title>Sound 1: Red</title>
</head>
<body>
<audio autoplay>
  <source src="dog.wav" >
  <source src="dog.mp3" >
</audio>
</body>
</html>
```

A Page with a Scream and a Green Background

```
<!DOCTYPE HTML>
<html>
<head>
<style type="text/css">
body {
    background-color:#060;
}
</style>
<meta http-equiv="Content-Type" content="text/html; charset=UTF-8">
<title>Sound 2: Green</title>
</head>
<body>
<audio autoplay>
  <source src="scream.wav" >
  <source src="scream.mp3" >
</audio>
</body>
</html>
```

A Page with an Explosion and a Blue Background

```
<!DOCTYPE HTML>
<html>
<head>
<style type="text/css">
body {
    background-color:#0000cc;
}
</style>
<meta http-equiv="Content-Type" content="text/html; charset=UTF-8">
<title>Sound 3: Blue</title>
</head>
<body>
<audio autoplay>
  <source src="boom.wav" >
  <source src="boom.mp3" >
</audio>
</body>
</html>
```

You can have a lot of fun testing different sounds. Be sure to test it on different HTML5 browsers. Also, try to make your own sound effects — you can recruit your dog, cat, and parrot (who was once owned by a sailor).

TAKE THE WHEEL

This challenge is to make a talking comic book. Think of a simple story that can be told in four panels. Each panel will have a drawing (or digital photo) but no text. As the user clicks each panel, an audio recording "says" what text would say in a typical comic. You'll have to use an `iframe` to trigger each of the four audio recordings, and each of the comic panels will really be a button to link to the page with the panel's audio. You can use clip art for the panels if you want, and you can enhance the story with sound effects to accompany the audio.

214

11

VIDEO

ONE OF THE most important features added to HTML5 is video. If you've used YouTube, you're aware of the power of video on the Web. Likewise, Adobe Flash users have embedded video in their programs for years. So, video on the Web isn't exactly new. However, the new features of HTML5 make it possible to access video directly from an HTML5 Web page, and that's something that HTML has never been able to do in previous builds without a link to a Flash `.swf` file or some other binary file that streams video independent of the tags placed in an HTML file.

An important caveat to add here is that the video that is displayed by your Web page is not true *streaming video;* instead, it's a type of progressive download. As the video is downloaded from the Web server, it's displayed by the Web page, so it can be slow. In fact, most videos created by Flash hobbyists are very likely to be this kind of video. Streaming video, at this point, requires a streaming video server like Adobe Flash Media Server. However, you can expect to see developments in true streaming as HTML5 video becomes more popular.

If you've read Chapter 10, you'll find many of the video tags familiar. This chapter looks at many of the same tags, like `<source>`, but with an eye to loading and playing video.

MAKING AN HTML5 PAGE WITH VIDEO

To get started with video, you need a video file. You can create one on your computer, or you can download one from the Web. So the question is: What kind of video file? The Tower of Babel made more sense than all the video codecs do, so this section begins with the most ubiquitous of all current video formats, H.264. As a video format, H.264 is usually referred as MPEG-4 or its file extension, .mp4. This video format gained popularity as the first high-definition video format for the Web. Most people first saw it playing on the Web as a Flash .f4v file, and the results were much better than previous Web video.

The key tag used in video is, to no one's amazement, <video>. Just as with an image or audio, the first attribute that you need is a source, and the src attribute is used to identify the source. So, creating Web pages with video is quite simple. The following listing (SimpleVideo.html in this chapter's folder at www.wiley.com/go/smashinghtml5) displays video basics in an HTML5 Web page.

```
<!DOCTYPE HTML>
<html>
<head>
<meta http-equiv="Content-Type" content="text/html; charset=UTF-8">
<title>Simple Video</title>
</head>
<body>
<video src="mbAux1small.mp4" controls preload="auto"></video>
</body>
</html>
```

In order to test and run this file, you need a Safari browser because, at the time of this writing, that's the only browser that it works with. (The browser is free, so go ahead and try it.)

When you run the program, you'll see your video play on the Safari browser. The way the controls are set up, you'll have to wait until you see an image, which means the video is ready. Click the start arrow on the controller and you should see your video play. Figure 11-1 shows what you can expect to see if you play and pause the video.

Obviously, you're going to want your video to play on more than one browser. If your video can be viewed using only a single browser, you're going to miss a lot of users. Fortunately, HTML5 has a simple way of solving the problem. Within a <video> container, you can add as many <source> tags as you want. The source attribute (src) is moved to the <source> tag. If you place several <source> tags in the <video> container, the browser will look at the video files and select the one it knows how to play and automatically play it. If it can play more than a single type of video format, it starts playing the first one it recognizes and ignores all the rest. All this can be done using HTML5 without having to break out JavaScript. The following snippet shows the basic format of accessing video files in this manner:

```
<video>
  <source src="someVid.3gp">
```

```
  <source src="someVid.mp4">
  <source src="someVid.ogv">
  <source src="someVid.webm">
</video>
```

Figure 11-1: Viewing a simple video on the Safari browser.

Although many different formats are around for digital video, the ones that will be used for illustration and discussed in this chapter are the following:

- **H.264:** `.mp4` and `.mov`
- **OGG:** `.ogv`
- **WebM:** `.webm`
- **3GP:** `.3gp`

At the time of this writing (and quite possibly for the future) different formats are going to run on different browsers. However, using the `<source>` tag, you can easily reference several different browsers. For example, the following code (`SimpleVideoSource.html` in this chapter's folder at `www.wiley.com/go/smashinghtml5`) plays the same video on any of the browsers tested, including two mobile browsers.

```
<!DOCTYPE HTML>
<html>
<head>
<meta http-equiv="Content-Type" content="text/html; charset=UTF-8">
<title>Selective Video</title>
</head>
<body>
<video controls preload="auto">
  <source src="multiformats/mbAux1.3gp">
  <source src="multiformats/mbAux1small.mp4">
```

217

```
    <source src="multiformats/mbAux1small.ogv">
    <source src="multiformats/mbAux1small.webm">
</video>
</body>
</html>
```

When I tested the program with different browsers and platforms, all of them were able to find the file format they preferred and play both the video and sound. Figure 11-2 shows the video playing in a Safari mobile browser on an iPhone.

Figure 11-2: Video playing on an iPhone.

The quality of the play was fairly consistent on all browsers. On both the Safari mobile browser and Perfect Browser for the iPhone, other than the screen size, the video quality was quite good. Most important, it loaded quickly.

VIDEO AND BROWSER COMPATIBILITY

Two very different issues must be addressed when discussing HTML5 Web video and compatibility. One is simply which browsers work with which video formats. I'll be using the term video format to refer to a combination of video containers (wrappers in which actual videos are enclosed) and codecs (code-decode technology) — primarily by referring to the extension associated with the files. Technically, there's a lot more about video files than I have room to discuss here, but to get rolling with video, you need to recognize different files by their video extensions and what browsers they'll play on.

Letting the pundits do their job

Technology pundits seem to dwell on the complex and interesting issues surrounding why different companies have chosen particular formats. Apple, Microsoft, Google, Opera, Adobe, and Mozilla selected the file formats they did for reasons that have to do with patents, use rights, licenses, and financial considerations, as well as integrating the technology into other plans they may have. All you need to be concerned with is what works for your Web sites — wondering why one technology is preferred over another by the browser providers is best left to the pundits. You just need to know what will work and how to implement it.

At this point in time, going beyond what can be tested and proven is a bit risky. However, I think that we can look at four different kinds of file containers and codecs and use the four listed at the beginning of the chapter. The 3GP container format is related to MPEG-4, but it's actually an H.263 format, and its primary adoption has been for mobile devices like the iPhone. Table 11.1 shows the compatibility matrix of the major browsers on which video tests have been made or decisions have been made.

Table 11.1   Browsers and Video Format Support

Browser	H.264	OGG	WebM	3GP
Chrome	No	Yes	Yes	No
Firefox	No	Yes	Unknown	No
Internet Explorer 9	*No	No	No	Yes
Opera	No	Yes	Yes	No
Safari	Yes	No	No	Yes
Safari Mobile	No	No	No	Yes

* Microsoft announced that it would support H.264, but IE9 was unable to play MP4 format at the time of testing the beta version of the browser.

Given the array of compatibility between browsers and file formats, you need to know how to convert between the different formats. This next section examines how to do that. The conversion needs to happen first between the file type used by the recording instrument (a camera or screen-sharing application) or video-editing software. The second type of conversion is between the video fully prepared for the Web and the possible types of files required for HTML5 pages. Once all the types of files needed are ready, all you have to do is place them in `<source>` tags within a `<video>` container.

MAKE MINE WEBM: THE MIRO VIDEO CONVERTER

Of all the file formats tested, only Opera worked with the WebM format. However, several other companies who make browsers are also involved in the WebM project, and so in the future, it may prove to be a more important format than it currently is. More information about WebM can be found at the WebM Project site at www.webmproject.org.

One conversion program that was tested and for WebM was the Miro Video Converter. It's simple to use and provides many conversion options — not just to and from WebM. Figure 11-3 shows the Miro Video Converter converting an MP4 into a WebM file.

Figure 11-3: Converting files using Miro Video Converter.

The Miro Video Converter is available free of charge at www.mirovideoconverter.com. The conversion process involves dragging or loading the file to be converted to a central window and then clicking a Convert button. It's very simple and adaptive.

For .ogv files, select Theora from the menu and then click the Convert button. The resulting file has the extension .theora.ogv, but by removing the .theora, you can run it fine with just the .ogv extension. In converting from an .mp4 file to the .ogv file, the file size was reduced from 54MB to 11MB — a fivefold reduction.

CONVERTING TO 3GP: ADOBE MEDIA ENCODER CS5

In converting to 3GP format for displaying on mobile devices, Adobe Media Encoder CS5 (AME) was found to provide many advantages. The encoder ships with several different Adobe products, and for this book I tested it with Adobe Premier while editing MP4 files generated by a high-definition (HD) video camera.

Besides having the ability to convert files into 3GP format, AME was able to do some basic editing itself. The most important function was to reduce the dimensions of the video and, therefore, the file size and the amount of time it took to stream the video over the Internet. This is especially crucial for mobile devices.

Figure 11-4 shows a file that natively was saved in a 720 x 480 format. Then it was reduced to 320 x 212. Typically, videos are formatted in a 4:3 ratio. However, HD format of the video camera used is 16:9, so the dimensions are wider than what you could expect in a video created using a built-in webcam on your computer. When preparing video for the Web, that can be a major consideration. Likewise, when setting the `width` and `height` attributes in a `<video>` tag, don't forget the changed dimensions.

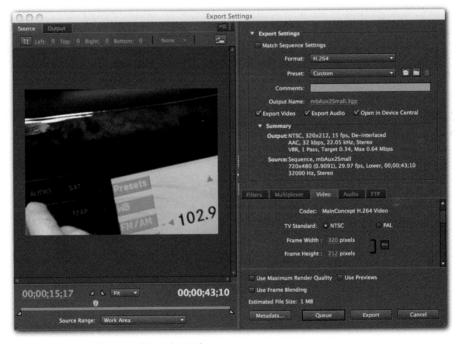

Figure 11-4: Converting files using Adobe Media Encoder.

As you can see in Figure 11-4, AME provides a good deal of file information. In the left panel, it visually displays the file you're currently working with.

When the conversion is complete, AME provides a number of different generic display formats. For example, Figure 11-5 shows what you can expect to see in a mobile device with a horizontal display.

Figure 11-5: Displaying video in Adobe Device Central.

In looking at Figure 11-5, you have an excellent idea of what your video is going to look like in the target device. Adobe Device Central provides several different views so that you can optimize the video prior to placing it on the Web.

MAKING VIDEOS FOR THE WEB

Before turning to the many attributes of the video element, this section considers the whole issue of creating videos and saving them on your computer. The range of types of video available for showing on the Web is wide, and making and storing them is equally varied. Here only four are considered:

- Webcams
- Small camcorders
- Standard camcorders
- Screen video capture

The focus is on getting the materials from the camera into a file format that can be used immediately or converted for use with HTML5.

WEBCAMS

At the time of this writing, most laptop computers come bundled with built-in webcams. Likewise, many desktops do as well. For computers that do not come with built-in webcams, several are available that can be connected to the USB port.

For Windows 7 users, the best software for making videos with the webcam is usually that of the webcam manufacturer. For example, both Logitech and Creative, two companies that manufacture webcams, have excellent software that both records and stores video files that can be converted for Web use. You also can add special effects with the software to your videos.

Also, with Windows 7 and Vista, you can download the newest Microsoft Movie Maker software free from: `http://explore.live.com/windows-live-movie-maker`. Unlike Windows XP, which comes packaged with Windows Live Movie Maker, you have to download the movie-making software from Microsoft if you have the Windows 7 or Vista versions of the OS.

Apple Macintosh computers generally come with built-in iSight webcams. Both iMacs and MacBook laptops have webcams embedded in the top-center of the monitors. The models that don't come with webcams have iSight webcams available that plug into the USB or the Firewire ports.

For creating videos, the Photo Booth application that comes with Mac software can be used to create videos. All files taken with Photo Booth are saved as QuickTime files with the `.mov` extension. These are in MP4 format, and if you change the extension from `.mov` to `.mp4`, they're recognized as the same file.

Webcams are useful for certain kinds of video projects. For making instructional videos for the Web, the instructor can sit in front of the webcam and talk and display materials to the audience. Making Web pages in HTML5 to provide slides supporting the video presentation makes creating an instructional package as simple as making virtually any similar presentation not intended for Web use.

SMALL CAMCORDERS

The primary drawback of webcams for making videos that can be embedded in HTML5 is that they're tied to a computer — either built in or tethered to a USB or IEEE 1394 Firewire port. This makes mobile use of webcams problematic, even for highly portable laptops.

Wireless webcams are available, but they tend to have a limited range and are more expensive. However, several highly portable alternatives are available. The most common are video cameras built into mobile phones. Mobile phones used during the protests following the 2009 Iranian elections provided worldwide exposure of the government retaliation against those who protested election fraud. Because Western journalists were banned from covering the election aftermath, the news coverage was provided by video from mobile phones broadcast on YouTube and announced through Twitter.

A new generation of small HD camcorders have been introduced that are fully portable and save video in a solid state format. For example, the Flip Mino HD with dimensions of 3.94" x 1.97' x 0.63" (H x W x D) is smaller than many mobile phones. Figure 11-6 shows a typical Flip with a company logo embedded in the camera.

Figure 11-6: Small high-definition camcorders are adapted for the Web.

Besides Flip, HD video cameras also are available from Kodak, in the form of the Kodak Pocket Video camcorder. Both the Flip and Kodak camcorders are solid state recorders, so no digital video tapes or removable flash memory cards are required — just as none is required for mobile phones. The small camcorders come packaged with limited video-editing software and save video in H.264 format on both Windows and Macintosh computers.

The quality of the video is as high as much larger and more expensive camcorders, and they're far more portable. They were designed from the ground up for use in creating videos for social-networking sites like Facebook and YouTube; as a result, their native output files are custom-ordered for displaying with HTML5 video elements.

STANDARD CAMCORDERS

The term standard here refers to handheld camcorders with such features as zoom lenses, mini DV tape cassette storage, flash memory cards, and other features that can be placed on larger platforms. The gamut of camcorders has widened to the point where the range is from inexpensive ones used for personal family recordings all the way to those used by independent filmmakers.

Like the (really) small camcorders the standard ones come with USB or IEEE 1394 Firewire connectors. The connectors can them be fed directly into video-editing software like Adobe Premier, Apple Final Cut, or Vegas. The edited video can then be saved to a format that can be used by HTML5 browsers.

SCREEN VIDEO CAPTURE

Screen video capture treats your desktop as a video recording, and a microphone connected to or built into your computer as a video-recording microphone. For example, one of the most established screen-video-capture software packages is Camtasia. It's easy to use and has several features for zooming, panning, and generally simulating a camcorder aimed at your screen. Figure 11-7 shows the basic controls.

Figure 11-7: Screen-video-capture software makes a live recording of your desktop.

Basically, all that Camtasia requires is for the user to select the screen and the microphone and click the Rec button (as shown in Figure 11-7). Available for Windows 7 and Macintosh OS X, it's a widely used software package for trainers and educators who work on a project on the screen so that viewers can follow along.

Another screen video capture application can be found as part of the Apple Quick-Time Player. It automatically saves files in .mov (.mp4) format that are ready to be used with an HTML5 Web site. The recording process is extremely easy, and other than selecting the microphone, it's a one-step start-and-stop recording operation.

VIDEO AND SOURCE ATTRIBUTES

Several different attributes for the `<video>` and `<source>` tags are essential for successful video deployment in HTML5. Once you've created, edited, and converted video for the Web, the next step is to place them in the Web page. This section covers the following `video` element attributes:

- `src`
- `poster`
- `preload`
- `loop`
- `autoplay`
- `controls`
- `width` and `height`

These attributes of the `<video>` tag are discussed in concert with the `<source>` tag because not all browsers read the same file types, so several different sources must be listed. The `<source>` tag allows the browsers to choose which video file is compatible with their own video display functions (as was shown at the beginning of the chapter).

SRC

The `type` attribute is part of the `<source>` tag. As shown at the beginning of the chapter, the `src` attribute is used to select a video file to play. If the browser can't play the assigned file type, it drops down to the next file in the source list. To speed up that process, the `type` attribute lets the browser know what kind of file is waiting to be played and contains a MIME parameter that tells it which codec is in use. This saves the browser from attempting to load the file and failing. Instead, it determines from the type information whether the video file is compatible.

```
<source src="fileName.ext" type="video/type; codecs='c1, c2'">
```

The type assignment can be made with or without the codec. If you don't know the codec, you can leave it blank and rely on the type to let the browser know whether it can play the file. If you know the codec or multiple codecs, you can place more than one codec in the codecs assignment list. Where you're not sure you're better off leaving the codecs assignment blank. The following (`TypeVideoSource.html` in this chapter's folder at www.wiley.com/go/ smashinghtml5) shows the type assignments for the four major types of video files you can use on the Web.

```
<!DOCTYPE HTML>
<html>
<head>
<meta http-equiv="Content-Type" content="text/html; charset=UTF-8">
<title>Selective Video</title>
</head>
<body>
<video controls preload="auto">
  <source src="mbAux1.3gp" type="video/3gpp; codecs='mp4v.20.8'">
  <source src="mbAux1small.mp4" type="video/mp4; codecs='mp4v.20.8'">
  <source src="mbAux1small.ogv" type="video/ogg; codecs='theora, vorbis'" >
  <source src="mbAux1small.webm" type="video/webm; codecs='vorbis,vp8'" >
</video>
</body>
</html>
```

To determine the type and codec of a file, you can find several different programs on the Web. One available at no cost with versions for Windows, Macintosh, and several different Linux operating systems is MediaInfo available at http://mediainfo.sourceforge.net/en.

POSTER

The `poster` attribute is used with large videos and slow Internet connections. It's simple to use, and if you know that it'll take a while for your video to come to the screen and begin playing, the poster gives the user something to look at while waiting. The format is simple as shown in the following snippet:

```
<video poster="message.png">
  <source src="multiformats/mbAux1.mp4" type="video/mp4">
</video>
```

Notice that the `poster` attribute is in the `<video>` tag even though all the file information is in the `<source>` tag. There is no conflict between the video attributes and those in source.

PRELOAD

The `preload` attribute of the `<video>` tag would seem like a natural to include in all Web pages that use video. As soon as the page loads, the video starts loading. That may be important for a page with a single video as the main feature of the page. However, if it's a minor part of the page or if several videos are on a single page, preloading can gobble up resources. So, while useful, the attribute needs to be employed judiciously. It uses the following format:

```
<video preload="auto">
    <source src="mbAux1small.webm" type="video/webm; codecs='vorbis,vp8'" >
</video>
```

The `preload` attribute has several values it can be assigned. They're identical to audio preload values.

- **none:** Having `none` as a value may seem strange, but some browsers may be set to automatically preload video files. However, if the chance of using a particular video is remote, the developer may decide not to use Internet resources and so assigns the `none` value to the `preload` attribute.

- **metadata:** All video files have metadata like duration, width, height, or some other data placed in the source file. When the chance of using a video file is low, loading the metadata is reasonable and doesn't take up much Internet resources.

- **auto:** If the `preload` attribute is present, it automatically preloads the audio file information. The `auto` assignment simply acts as a reminder that the file is going to preload (same as not having any value assignment to a `preload` attribute).

The more varied your audience and the more video in your Web site, the more you want to provide the `preload` attribute with options.

LOOP

A video loop is something that you must plan carefully lest you run off all your viewers. A loop means that the same video is going to start from the beginning again as soon as it ends. The following is an example:

```
<video loop controls>
  <source src="phantom.3gp">
</video>
```

227

Notice that in the above snippet, a `controls` attribute is included. That's so users can stop it if they want. If you set up a loop with autoplay and embed it in your page, you may lose a lot of viewers. If you create a loop advertisement, don't expect people to be attracted to the advertised service or product — they'll notice it, but not in a good way.

There is a certain type of loop, more noted in music than in video, that can be useful. If it's short enough and doesn't have big movements, a loop can take up very few resources and reuse the same video stored in a cache. A demonstration of a process or even an ad that is not annoying can be used in this fashion.

AUTOPLAY

Like the `loop` attribute, the `autoplay` attribute needs to be used with some forethought when employed with video. The `autoplay` is a combination of `preload` and automatically starting the video playing. The format is a Boolean one and setting the autoplay in the `<video>` tag is all it takes to start it.

```
<video poster="wait.jpg" autoplay>
  <source src="phantom.3gp">
</video>
```

In the above snippet, the user has no control to stop the video from playing, but without a `loop` attribute, it will just play once and stop. If the page is meant to be nothing but the video, it's fairly safe to use `autoplay` without a controller. Also, the snippet has a poster to let the view know what's coming, just in case there's a long load. In the context of a Web site when using `autoplay`, be sure to include a link for the next page just in case the user doesn't want to view the video more than once.

CONTROLS

The `controls` attribute generates a graphic control panel beneath the video. It allows the user to perform the following functions:

- Start the video
- Stop the video
- Mute the video
- Control the sound volume
- Time position
- Scrubber control

The controls attribute is a Boolean and is implemented as shown in the following snippet:

```
<video controls>
  <source src="multiformats/mbAux1small.webm">
</video>
```

The implementation of the controller is slightly different on the different browsers (as they are on the audio controller). Figure 11-8 shows the Opera and Chrome browsers displaying the same video.

Figure 11-8: The Opera (left) and Chrome browsers displaying video controller.

The differences in the controls are mostly style, but as you can see in comparing the Opera and Chrome browsers, the Opera browser displays the time in the current video relative to the total time, while the Chrome browser shows only the current time position of the video.

WIDTH AND HEIGHT

Unlike audio, the `width` and `height` attributes in video are very important. The browsers use the `width` and `height` values as hints in rendering the video. The closer the values to the actual size, the better the video looks. The following shows the format:

```
<video width="352" height="288">
  <source src="multiformats/mbAux1small.ogv">
</video>
```

Most videos maintain a 4:3 ratio such as 320 x 240; however, with HD, the ratio is different, and sometimes editing has changed a video's dimensions. You can select a video file and look at its properties, but sometimes you won't be given the dimensions. For example, on a Macintosh OS X, dimension information for `.ogv` and `.webm` files was not provided in a properties query (⌘ + I) The same video in an MPEG4 format, though, showed the dimensions.

TAKE THE WHEEL

This exercise requires a video camera, and it doesn't matter whether it's a webcam or a high-end video camcorder. If you've ever seen a presentation given with Microsoft Power-Point, you know that as a person speaks, the speaker points to different slides with graphics and text. For this exercise, think of something you'd like someone else to understand. Using a combination of images, video and text to create a three-page Web presentation. As users go from one page to another, the video on each page starts automatically, but they have a controller to stop it or make other viewing changes. Include an image to illustrate the topic and text to explain what the presentation is all about. You can sit in front of a webcam to make the video.

IV

DYNAMIC HTML5 TAGS PLUS A LITTLE JAVASCRIPT AND PHP

12 ADDING JUST ENOUGH JAVASCRIPT

JAVASCRIPT IS A Web programming language that you can use with HTML5. It can be used to access certain parts of your Web pages written in HTML5 and do other things that simply cannot be done without JavaScript. This chapter introduces some basic features that are going to be used specifically with HTML5 elements.

JavaScript is considered a scripting language because it's interpreted by the browser at runtime (when you actually open a Web page) rather than compiled and stored on your computer as a binary file. Slightly different versions of JavaScript can creep in with different implementations of the

language on different browsers. Because JavaScript meets an ECMAScript standard (ECMA-262), these differences are slight, and what I'll be discussing in this chapter are only those aspects of JavaScript that you can use with HTML5.

Finally, JavaScript and Java have nothing in common — JavaScript is not based on an interpreted version of Java. They could be named *dogs* and *cats* or *apples* and *oranges* for all they have in common. The name with *java* in it sounded better. So, if you want to look up something on the Web about JavaScript, you won't be helped if you just look for *Java*.

INSERTING JAVASCRIPT INTO HTML5 PAGES

JavaScript programs are placed in the head of a Web page because that part of the Web page loads first, so it's ready when the rest of the page loads. They act very much like CSS3 scripts, and like CSS3 scripts, they can be placed in other places than the page's head. However, for this chapter, I'll keep it simple and all JavaScript will be in the head. For example, try the following program (js1.html in this chapter's folder at www.wiley.com/go/smashinghtml5).

```
<!DOCTYPE HTML>
<html>
    <head>
    <meta http-equiv="Content-Type" content="text/html; charset=UTF-8">
    <script type="text/javascript">
      document.write("A chat with HTML5 is taking place shortly....");
    </script>
    <title>First JavaScript</title>
    </head>
    <body>
</body>
</html>
```

When you test the program, you'll see text on your page and nothing else. The key to understanding the relationship between HTML5 and JavaScript is in the function: document.write(). The document refers to the Web page, and write() is a method that tells the Web page what to do. In this case, write() instructs the program to write the text in quotation marks to the Web page.

JAVASCRIPT IN EXTERNAL FILES

Just like CSS3 files, you can create JavaScript programs in text files and save them externally. The .js extension is used to identify JavaScript files. For example, the following JavaScript program is just one line:

```
document.write("This is from an external file...");
```

Save it as externalJS.js in a text-file format. Next, enter the following HTML5 program and save it in the same folder as the externalJS.js program. The key part of the page is the <script> tag that's used to specify the JavaScript program to use.

```
<!DOCTYPE HTML>
<html>
<head>
<script src="externalJS.js"></script>
<meta http-equiv="Content-Type" content="text/html; charset=UTF-8">
<title>External JavaScript</title>
</head>
<body>
</body>
```

When the Web page opens, you see the contents of the `document.write()` statement. The `write()` method is just a built-in function that expects a line of text to display on the screen. In this case, the text is from an external file; otherwise, it's the same as embedding it in a Web page script.

FUNCTIONS

JavaScript functions are packages of code that are launched when called by the Web page. The advantage of functions is that you can use them to package code and make changes to add new content. The built-in `write()` function only requires that you enter some text for it print to the document (Web page). You don't have to rely on built-in functions but can create your own. For example, the following is an external JavaScript program with a simple function that opens an `alert()` function. (A user function using a built-in function.) Save the following JavaScript program as `nameMe.js`:

```
// JavaScript Document
var name="Little Willie Hacker";
function getName(someName)
{
    alert(someName);
}
getName(name)
```

All functions are followed by parentheses. If required, the developer can put a parameter in the parentheses. In this case, the parameter is called `someName`. When the function is called, the developer places a name, a number, or anything else desired in the space where `someName` is. In this case, a variable labeled name is assigned the value `Little Willie Hacker`. At the bottom of the program, the line, `getName(name)` calls the function, placing the variable into the parameter. The function passes the value of the variable to the `alert()` function within the `getName()` function, so you can expect to see an alert box on the screen when the program launches. The following HTML5 (`JSfunction.html` in this chapter's folder at `www.wiley.com/go/smashinghtml5`) calls the JavaScript that calls the function.

```
<!DOCTYPE HTML>
<html>
<head>
<script src="nameMe.js"></script>
<meta http-equiv="Content-Type" content="text/html; charset=UTF-8">
<title>External Function</title>
</head>
<body>
</body>
</html>
```

That JavaScript program launched as soon as the page loads. A more important use of JavaScript functions lies in its ability to wait for the JavaScript until it needs it. The next section shows how.

EVENT HANDLERS

The real power of JavaScript with HTML5 can be better seen when the program waits until the user does something to launch a script. For example, if the user clicks something, you can launch any JavaScript program you want. You use an HTML5 event handler. The page detects some kind of action (an event) and has a built-in function that recognizes the event.

HTML5 recognizes a lot of events. Some of the events occur automatically — such as when the page loads. Other events occur when users do something with the mouse or keyboard. The elements in Table 12.1 shows a sample of some of the different events handlers.

Table 12.1   A Sample of HTML5 Event Handlers

onchange	onclick	ondbleclick	ondrag	ondragend
ondragenter	ondragleave	ondragover	ondragstart	ondrop
onkeydown	onkeypress	onkeyup	onmousedown	onmousemove
onmouseout	onmouseover	onmouseup	onmousewheel	onpause
onplay	onplaying	onprogress	onloadstart	onload

The general format of all events linked to elements is:

```
<element onEvent = "javascriptFunction()">
```

For example,

```
<body onLoad = "announceSomething()">
```

uses the body element with the onLoad event handler to fire a JavaScript function named announceSomething().

Detecting a variety of events

To see how event handlers work with JavaScript, the following program (ClickDetect. html in this chapter's folder at www.wiley.com/go/smashinghtml5) has three different event handlers and three different JavaScript functions that are launched by the events. The first one sends out an alert when the page loads, the second fires when the top link is clicked, and the third launches an alert when the second link is double-clicked.

```
<!DOCTYPE HTML>
<html>
    <head>
<style type="text/css">
h1, h2 {
    font-family:Tahoma, Geneva, sans-serif;
}
```

```
a {
      text-decoration:none;
      color:#060;
}
</style>

<script type="text/javascript">
function detectLoaded()
{
      alert("Page is loaded.");
}
function detectClick()
{
      alert("You clicked a link.");
}
function detectDoubleClick()
{
      alert("You double-clicked another link.");
}
</script>
<meta http-equiv="Content-Type" content="text/html; charset=UTF-8">
<title>Event Handler</title>
      </head>
      <body onLoad="detectLoaded()">
      <hgroup>
        <h1> <a href="#" onClick="detectClick()">Click This</a></h1>
        <h2> <a href="#" onDblClick="detectDoubleClick()">Double-Click This</a>
        </h2>
      </hgroup>
</body>
</html>
```

The JavaScript functions can be whatever you want them to be, which enables you to interact far more with the users. You can provide instructions, options, cautions, or whatever you want.

Handling with any element

In the "click" area in the previous program, a link tag, <a>, is used to set up the event handler, using the following format:

```
<a href="#" onClick="clickEventHandler()">
```

That kind of code is nothing new to HTML5. It's used here for one simple reason: When the mouse moves over the text within the <a> tag, the cursor changes so that users know that they're over linked text.

However, you can set up an event handler in any element. For example, consider the following Web page (ClickP.html in this chapter's folder at www.wiley.com/go/smashing html5).

```
<!DOCTYPE HTML>
<html>
<head>
<style type="text/css">
p {
      font-family:Verdana, Geneva, sans-serif;
      color:#FF0;
      background-color:#00F;
      font-size:24px;
      text-align:center;
      font-weight:bold;
}
</style>
<script type="text/javascript">
function showArticle()
{
      alert("You just clicked within a <article> container");
}
function showHeader()
{
      alert("You just clicked within a <header> container");
}
function showP()
{
      alert("You just clicked within a <P> container");
}
</script>
<meta http-equiv="Content-Type" content="text/html; charset=UTF-8">
<title>OnClick in any Element</title>
</head>

<body>
<article onClick="showArticle()">
  <header onClick="showHeader()">
  <h1>This is an H1 Element in the Header</h1>
  </header>
  <section>
    <p onClick="showP()">Click This Paragraph</p>
    This is just plain old text in the article container. Click here just to see
  what happens. </section>
</article>
</body>
</html>
```

In looking at the above program, you may have noticed that some events are embedded inside other elements that also have event handlers. For instance, all the elements are inside the `<article>` tag. What will happen when you click on the paragraph that has an event handler? Or the <header>? Are they just going to react to the innermost or outermost event? Look closely at both panels in Figure 12-1.

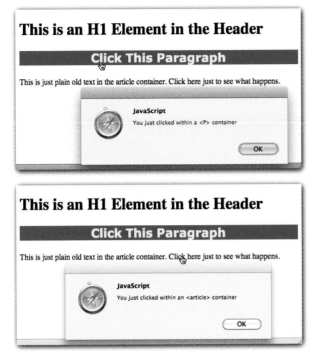

Figure 12-1: Nested event handlers.

In the top panel, as soon as a user clicks the line "Click This Paragraph," the event is reported in the alert box (top panel). Then, when the user clicks the OK button in the JavaScript pop-up, the second alert appears letting him know that he's clicked in the <article> container as well. One way of looking at the events is bubbling up, beginning in the lowest level in the hierarch of elements and then bubbling up to the topmost level.

USING THE DOCUMENT OBJECT MODEL

The Document Object Model (DOM) for HTML5 represents a hierarchy tree. At the base (root) of every Web page or document is the <html> tag, and the rest of the elements in the page are a branch somewhere along the tree. JavaScript uses the DOM for addressing and manipulating a Web page beyond what you can do with HTML5 alone. The entire DOM tree is a representation of the document that resides in your computer's memory.

When any part of the DOM tree is addressed, it does so by referencing an element within the tree, beginning with document. Each element in the tree is addressed in order of the hierarchy beginning with document. The different elements in a Web page are the different properties or methods (built-in functions) of the `document` separated by a dot (.). For example,

```
document.forms.fred;
```

addresses a form named `fred` within a document. The HTML5 markup looks like the following:

```
<form name= "fred">
```

Other times, you'll see a built-in function that does something with the document such as,

```
document.write("This is straight from the Document");
```

which prints text on the screen. Also, the `window` root along with the document has several built-in functions that are useful for manipulating viewing areas of a Web page.

HOW THE DOM WORKS WITH YOUR PAGE AND JAVASCRIPT

To get a better sense of how the DOM works with your page and JavaScript, it helps to see what can be done with a Web page's windows — the viewing part of your Web page. The following (`PageOpener.html` in this chapter's folder at www.wiley.com/go/smashinghtml5) shows how to load a new Window from a current document, leaving the current page in place.

```
<!DOCTYPE HTML>
<html>
<head>
<style type="text/css">
a {
    text-decoration:none;
    color:#cc0000;
    font-size:24px;
}
header {
    text-align:center;
}
</style>
<script type="text/javascript">
function someOtherWindow()
{
    window.open("OtherWindow.html","ow","width=400,height=200");
}
</script>
<meta http-equiv="Content-Type" content="text/html; charset=UTF-8">
<title>Open Other Page</title>
</head>
```

```
<body>
<header> <a href="#" onClick="someOtherWindow()">Click to Open New Window</a> </
  header>
</body>
</html>
```

This page requires a second page to open as a separate window. The following (`OtherWindow.html` in this chapter's folder at `www.wiley.com/go/smashinghtml5`) provides a page to open and, at the same time, the DOM-based script to close the open window.

```
<!DOCTYPE HTML>
<html>
<head>
<style type="text/css">
h1,h4 {
     font-family:Verdana, Geneva, sans-serif;
     color:#930;
}
a {
     text-decoration:none;
     color:#cc0000;
     text-align:center;
}
</style>
<script type="text/javascript">
function shutItDown()
{
     window.close();
}
</script>
<meta http-equiv="Content-Type" content="text/html; charset=UTF-8">
<title>Other Window</title>
</head>
<body>
<h1>This window has an important message. . . .</h1>
<h4>Stand by while I figure out what it is. . . .</h4>
<a href="#" onClick="shutItDown()">Shut the window!</a>
</body>
</html>
```

Figure 12-2 shows what you can expect to see when the Web page opens as second window.

Up to this point in the book, when one page has linked to another page, the current page has disappeared as soon as the user clicks a link. However, with this little JavaScript, you can "talk" directly to the page and tell it you want a new window of a specified size to open while your current window stays open.

Figure 12-2: Opening a second window.

HTML5 ELEMENTS AND THE DOM

In order to give you a better idea of how to work with the DOM in HTML5, certain new elements require DOM references within the tags themselves. One such new element is the <output> tag. At the time of this writing, Opera was the only browser that had fully implemented this new element, so you might want to test it initially with Opera. Before you incorporate it fully with your site, test it with all the other browsers because you may find it very useful as a key HTML5 element.

When you use the <output> tag, you can place the results of a calculation directly on the Web page. You don't have to build a JavaScript function or even a script. However, the materials within an <output> tag must follow the same DOM rules as with JavaScript proper. The output container doesn't require content between the opening and closing tags. However, all the calculations must be within the <output> tag itself.

The output element works in conjunction with the <form> tag that is covered in detail in Chapter 14, but for now the focus is on the DOM structure in the <output> tag's use. The following script (shoppingOutput.html in this chapter's folder at www.wiley.com/go/smashinghtml5) shows how to incorporate the element in a functional HTML5 page.

```
<!DOCTYPE HTML>
<html>
<head>
<style type="text/css">
/*042B45,FFC54F,FFE6BF,E8A5B5,FF0A03*/
body {
    font-family:Verdana, Geneva, sans-serif;
    background-color:#FFE6BF;
    color:#042B45;
}
```

```
input {
    background-color:#FFE6BF;
}
h1 {
    color:#E8A5B5;
    background-color:#042B45;
    text-align:center;
}
h3 {
    color:#FFC54F;
    background-color:#FF0A03;
}
</style>
<meta http-equiv="Content-Type" content="text/html; charset=UTF-8">
<title>Simple Shopping Cart</title>
</head>
<body>
<header>
  <h1>Shopping Calculator</h1>
</header>
<form>
  <input name=cost type=number>
   Cost <br>
  <input name=tax type=number>
   Tax--Enter as decimal percent (e.g., .06) <br>
  <h3>  Total = $
    <output onforminput="value = cost.valueAsNumber * tax.valueAsNumber + cost.
  valueAsNumber"></output>
  </h3>
</form>
</body>
</html>
```

The `<form>` tag has no information beyond the tag itself. For this application, it needs none. Within the `<form>` container, two input forms are named `cost` and `tax`. In the context of the DOM, each is an object with certain properties, one of which is `valueAsNumber`. Whatever number character is in the input form is treated as an actual number instead of a text character. The `valueAsNumber` is a property of the `<input>` tag and not the `number` type that was used in this example. (We could've used a `text` value for the input type and had the same results using the `<output>` tag.) The `number` input form has a "spinner" type of input window, but values in the input window are not automatically converted into numeric data. Figure 12-3 shows the results of the Web page in an Opera browser (the only HTML5 browser that had implemented the `onFormInput` event handler at the time of this writing).

Notice how the `onFormInput` event handler works. As information is entered into the form, the results are calculated and displayed. Initially, the result is NaN (Not a Number) because the tax entry is null, resulting in a non-number result. However, as soon as the tax is entered, the output changes to a number.

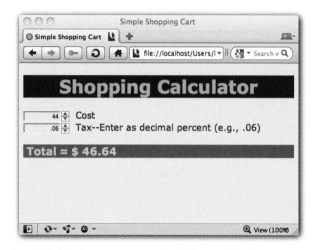

Figure 12-3: Using the `<output>` tag for calculations in Opera browser.

STORING TEMPORARY VALUES

In this brief snapshot of JavaScript, we've looked at a great deal, so if some of it escapes you, don't worry. Most of what you need to know about JavaScript in the context of HTML5 is working with the DOM. In this section, I show you how data are temporarily stored in your computer's memory when looking at a Web page. Users can enter data by clicking a button, a check box, a radio button, or a link, or by using the keyboard. (All of this will be related to what happens with the DOM — trust me.)

In order to use the information that users enter, JavaScript has ways to both store it in memory and make it available later in the session. By examining the different structures in JavaScript, you can get a sense of how this happens.

VARIABLES

A variable is something that changes — it varies. You can think of a variable as a box with a label on it. For example, you might have a box with the label "MobilePhone." In the box, you can place only one thing. You can change what's in the box — what we call the box's value. So, if you have iPhone in your MobilePhone box, you can take it out and put in either a different iPhone (a newer model) or a different phone such as an Android. Now, the box has a different value. The label-value pair (or name-value pair) is the combination of the variable's label and its current value.

You don't have to put in the name of a mobile phone in the MobilePhone box. You can put in anything you want — a tin-can walkie-talkie or a pink elephant. Assign whatever value you want and any type of value, including another variable. If I wanted, I could put in a number — a real number, not just one that identifies something such as a street address. However, a good and practical practice is to use variable names that can be associated with what you expect to

244

put in (or assign to) the variable. For example, if you're making a Web site that expects to be used to enter prices and tax (as was done in the previous section, "HTML5 elements and the DOM"), it makes sense to use meaningful variable names such as "cost" and "tax."

To create a variable, you simply provide a name and assign it a value. For example,

```
billVar="Brought to you by Bill's variable.";
alert(billVar);
```

creates a variable named `billVar`. It then assigns it the value `Brought to you by Bill's variable`. When the variable is placed in the alert function, notice that no quotation marks surround the variable.

Types of data

When you assign values to a JavaScript variable, you can assign any kind you want and then change it to a different type. First, though, you need to have an idea of the different types of data that are available. The following list provides a brief description of each:

- **String:** Treated as text, typically in quotation marks
- **Number:** An actual number (integer or real) that responds to math operations
- **Boolean:** A two-state (true or false, 0 or 1) data type
- **Function:** A set of JavaScript operations contained in a module
- **Object:** An encapsulated collection of properties (variables/arrays) and methods (functions)

You've seen how string variables work. When you put numbers into a string, they're treated as text instead of numbers. For example, the following string treats the "123" exactly like "Elm Street" — as text.

```
funHouse="123 Elm Street";
```

Likewise, if you used the following assignment, you'd still have text and the results would show it:

```
firstNumber="123";
secondNumber="7";
total=firstNumber + secondNumber;
document.write(total);
```

Instead of showing "130" the results show "1237." Next try the following:

```
firstNumber=123;
secondNumber=7;
total=firstNumber + secondNumber;
document.write(total);
```

Now, the results show "130" as expected when you add numbers. Whenever the plus (+) operator is used with text, it's called concatenation and simply strings everything together. If you put any kind of text in a list of numbers to be added, and only one of the numbers is text, all the rest will be treated as text and concatenated.

Different types of variables together

The following program (SimpleVariable.html in this chapter's folder at www.wiley.com/go/smashinghtml5) uses all the different kinds of data. You'll have to look closely at the different data types to determine the expected results. The comments in the code should help you see all the JavaScript data types.

```
<!DOCTYPE HTML>
<html>
<head>
<style type="text/css">
/*BAD9CB,048C3F,7BA651,F2BE5C,F2A950 */
body {
    background-color:#BAD9CB;
    font-family:Verdana, Geneva, sans-serif;
    color:#048C3F;
}
</style>
<script type="text/javascript">
function advertisement()
{
    billVar="Brought to you by Bill's variable.";
    return billVar;
}
//Variable with function
popUpAd=advertisement();
document.write(popUpAd);
//Variable with HTML5 code
cr="<br>";
document.write(cr);
// Variable with string
funHouse=" Elm Street";
// Boolean variable
var fate=true;
// Variable with string
query="Will I find true happiness in HTML5? The answer is: ";
// Variables with numbers
fun=100;
house=23;
// Math with variables
funPlusHouse=fun + house;
// Adding numeric and string variable (concatenation)
showAddress=funPlusHouse + funHouse;
```

```
browser=navigator.platform;
document.write(showAddress);
document.write(cr);
document.write(query);
document.write(fate);
document.write(cr);
document.write(browser);
</script>
<meta http-equiv="Content-Type" content="text/html; charset=UTF-8">
<title>Simple Variable</title>
</head>
<body>
</body>
</html>
```

Depending on the type of computer you use, the browser variable's value will be different. (It certainly varies.) The page was run on both a Windows 7 and Macintosh computer to see how one variable varied. Figure 12-4 shows the different output from the same program.

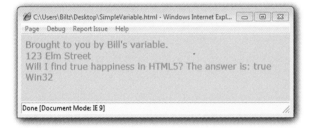

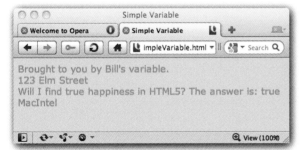

Figure 12-4: Displaying variable computer types on the screen.

The variable value, `navigator.platform` is an object. The `navigator` object has a property, `platform`, that tells what type of computer the browser is running on. In testing the program in Windows 7 (refer to the top panel in Figure 12-4) with a 64-bit operating system, the results show `Win32`. That's because the browsers tested were 32-bit, including an early version of Internet Explorer 9. The `MacIntel` results (refer to the bottom panel in Figure 12-4) were on a Macintosh computer with an Intel processor displayed on an Opera browser.

247

ARRAYS

A variable can have only a single value at one time. The value can be a computed based on a combination of different values, but once it's stored inside a variable, it becomes one. For instance, as shown in the previous section on variables,

```
firstNumber=123;
secondNumber=7;
total=firstNumber + secondNumber;
```

The variable named `total` is the sum of the first two variables. It is a single entity. This would be true were they concatenated as well. So, just remember: Variables can have only one value at a time. Figure 12-5 provides a graphic illustration of the difference between variables and arrays.

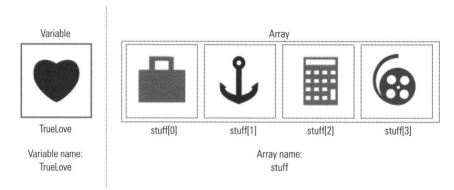

Figure 12-5: Storing data in variables and arrays.

As you can see in Figure 12-5, only a single item is stored in the variable named `TrueLove`, but the array, `stuff`, has lots of, well, stuff. You call each one of the stored datum with the array name with a number in braces. So, `stuff[1]` is an anchor and `stuff[2]` is a calculator.

Some applications require multiple values in a single object, making it easier to recall and store data. Each value in an array is called an element. You reference each by a number, beginning with zero (0) and numbered sequentially (refer to Figure 12-5). Suppose you have an array named `fruit`. You might assign values as shown here:

```
<!DOCTYPE HTML>
<html>
<head>
<script type="text/javascript">
fruit=new Array();
fruit[0]="rasberries";
fruit[1]="peaches";
fruit[2]="apples";
```

```
fruit[3]="plums";
document.write(fruit[1]);
var myFruit=fruit.pop();
document.write("<br>" +myFruit + "<br>");
document.write(fruit.length);
</script>
<meta http-equiv="Content-Type" content="text/html; charset=UTF-8">
<title>Array 1</title>
</head>
</html>
```

The result of the preceding program are the words peaches, plums, and 3 on the screen.
Peaches was pulled out of the array by number reference and placed into a screen output
function. Then using the pop() method, the element on the top of the array was placed into
a variable named myFruit and displayed to the screen. Finally, the pop() method removed
one element from the array and placed it into the myFruit variable, so now the array has a
length of 3 — and that's what's shown on the screen. Each element in an array works just like a
variable. The difference is that it's part of a larger object — the array.

OBJECTS

The final data type used to store values is an object. (Wasn't the Array an object? Yep. You're
already ahead of the game!) All objects are similar to arrays in that they can hold more than a
single value. However, objects have several built-in properties. The properties have either
fixed values (called constants) or values that change depending on the circumstances. Even
the Array object has a built-in property — length. It returns the number of elements in the
array. So, if you add the following two lines to the array program in the previous section,
you'll see how big the array is:

```
. . .
document.write(fruit[1]);
//Add the following two lines
document.write("<br>");
document.write(fruit.length);
```

The value of fruit.length is 4 — it's always one greater than the highest-numbered array
element because the length is the actual number of elements in the array beginning with the
value 1. (It's one-based instead of zero-based.)

Some properties of objects are called methods. A method is a function that does something in
relation to the object. For example, an Array object method is pop(). The pop() method
returns the last element in the array. It's a way that you can assign a variable an object's
method — just as you can assign a variable a function. Let's fix up that program from the last
section again. This time, the variable myFruit is assigned fruit.pop(). That means
whatever is on the top of the array stack is removed. However, if used in a variable assignment, it assigns the removed element to the variable as the following fix-up of the previous
snippet shows:

```
. . .
document.write(fruit[1]);
//Add the following three lines
var myFruit=fruit.pop();
document.write("<br>" + myFruit + "<br>");
document.write(fruit.length);
```

When you test the program from the previous section with the above changes, you'll see that the last added element has a value of plum, and that's what is printed to the screen. However, the length is no longer 4, but now 3. That's because the pop() method removes the element from the array. (By the way, the var in front of the myFruit variable is optional to declare a variable, but it helps to distinguish it from the array elements in this listing.)

Creating your own objects

If you create a few of your own objects, you can get an idea of how objects work in the DOM. Also, to help clarify things, from now on, a reference to an object's properties in general refers to both properties and methods. However, when I get specific in talking about an object's individual parts, the reference will be either to a property (some characteristic of the object) or a method (a function associated with the object).

Making objects is similar to declaring variables and assigning them values. The object itself is sort of a base of operations for doing a lot of different things and having different characteristics. The first step is simply to use a name and the keyword new. For example, the following declares an object named AddingMachine:

```
AddingMachine=new Object();
```

Next, to add a property, you invent a new name for the property and assign it a value. The object name and its property are separated by a dot (.). For example, the following adds a property named firstNumber and assigns it a value of 4:

```
AddingMachine.firstNumber=4;
```

Just like a variable, you can change the firstNumber value to something else.

To add a method (a function) is just as easy. However, instead of using a named function, you use an anonymous one. For example, the following adds the value of two properties for the AddingMachine object and sends them to the screen:

```
AddingMachine.total=function()
{
    document.write(this.firstNumber + this.secondNumber);
}
```

The keyword this is a reference to AddingMachine. It's the same as writing Adding Machine.firstNumber. Notice also that function() has no name — it's anonymous.

Now it's time to put it all together and see what happens (see `UserObject.html` in this chapter's folder at `www.wiley.com/go/smashinghtml5`):

```
<!DOCTYPE HTML>
<html>
<head>
<script type="text/javascript">
AddingMachine=new Object();
//Object properties
AddingMachine.firstNumber=4;
AddingMachine.secondNumber=66;
//Object method
AddingMachine.total=function()
{
     document.write(this.firstNumber + this.secondNumber);
}
//Fire off the method!
AddingMachine.total();
</script>
<meta http-equiv="Content-Type" content="text/html; charset=UTF-8">
<title>Simple Object</title>
</head>
</html>
```

Note that the method `AddingMachine.total()` uses the method `document.write()`. (You can spot methods in JavaScript by looking for the parentheses.) Also, note that to fire off the method, the name of the object and function are listed and off it goes. When you test it, you'll see that the results are the total of the two properties.

Back to the Document Object Model and browser objects

This chapter has covered a lot of territory very quickly. In fact, the last section is the first step in Object-Oriented Programming (OOP). So, if you didn't pick up everything, don't worry. The purpose is to make you more comfortable with the DOM in HTML5. If you understand terms like properties and methods, they won't seem as foreign.

As we get into many of the newer features in HTML5, you'll be better able to navigate through all the terms and understand what's going on. In other words, it'll be easier to learn. That doesn't mean you have to become an OOP programmer to understand this stuff. It just means that a little OOP goes a long way toward helping you understand the DOM and browser objects that come in handy when using elements like `canvas`.

Throughout the book, you've seen objects that belong to the browser. I didn't discuss them as such, but that's what they are. The browser has the following objects that are important to using HTML5. Included are the following:

- `History`
- `Location`

- Navigator
- Screen
- Window

For example, in the "Types of data" section earlier in this chapter, you saw how the `naviga-tor.platform` property was used to find the type of computer in use.

The HTML5 DOM itself has far more objects, and the most used is the `Document` property. The list of objects is the same as the list of elements. So, a list of all the DOM objects is a list of all elements, plus some others that are used in conjunction with the DOM. For example, the following are included in the HTML5 DOM but aren't exactly elements:

- Document
- Event
- Image
- Link
- Meta

Some of these objects we see in tags. For example, the image object is seen in the `<img>` tags. Its properties are similar to the `img` element's attributes. Others, like document are implied in that a Web page is the document. The `event` object is employed in event handling with methods such as `onClick`. The rest are elements, so they should be familiar. But instead of attributes in a tag, expect to find properties with the same names and functions as equivalent attributes.

TAKE THE WHEEL

Data sources are important to understand, and one way to understand them is to practice using different types. The challenge is to do the following:

1. **Select a string — one of your favorite sayings or pieces of information. For example, "All objects are made up of properties and methods."**
2. **Assign the string to a variable and use** `document.write()` **to send it to the screen.**
3. **Break down the string into several separate words and place each word into a different array element and then using the** `array.pop()` **method and** `document.write()` **to display them on the screen in a single message.**
4. **Finally, create an object with a property that is assigned the string that you've selected. Create a method for the property that displays the string to the screen.**

13

THUNDERING YOUR SITE WITH CANVAS

ONE OF THE most important additions to HTML5 is the `<canvas>` tag. With it, you can draw just about anything on an HTML5 page. With just two attributes, `width` and `height`, there's not a lot to remember about attributes. However, the `canvas` element is implemented in what might be called a Document Object Model (DOM) style. Chapter 12 describes the DOM in detail. Essentially, *DOM style* means writing the required JavaScript with references to objects and their methods and properties.

If that kind of talk has you quaking in your flip-flops, relax. Throughout the book, the HTML5 tags (elements) have used attributes, and attributes are just properties of the elements. For the most part, writing JavaScript code is just assigning values to properties, and since you know how to do that from assigning values to attributes — `height="200"`, for instance — there's less that's new about writing this kind of code than you may think.

To help you along, the JavaScript in use employs what you might call "OOP Lite." The DOM represents object oriented programming (OOP) in that all references are to different objects and their properties. By setting up the JavaScript using a similar style — creating objects and then assigning them properties and methods — your code will look a lot like expressions taken from the DOM.

CANVAS BASICS

Because the `canvas` element is a crucial part of HTML5 and works only with HTML5-compatible browsers, the first thing you want to do is to let users know that they need an HTML5 browser. Several methods are available to find out whether canvas works with their browser, but the easiest and most informative (to the user) is to place a message in the `<canvas>` container. Only users without HTML5-compatible browsers see the text in the container. For example, the following line, easily mistaken for the outcry of a drama queen, gets the message across. At the same time it remains invisible to users who have HTML5 browsers:

```
<canvas id="colorScheme" width="600" height="100" >Come on, Jack & Jill! You
  <i>really</i> need to get an HTML5 Compatible browser. You're missing <b>canvas!</
  b></canvas>
```

I dug up an old (really old!) Internet Explorer browser for the Mac. Figure 13-1 shows what appeared when I opened the page with the `<canvas>` tag.

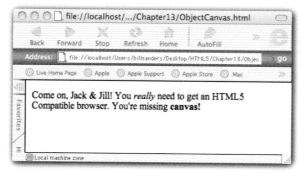

Figure 13-1: Message viewed with a non-HTML5 browser.

Just to be fair, I ran the same program in an early (really early!) version of Internet Explorer 9. As you can see in Figure 13-2, the `canvas` drawing appears, but the message does not.

Figure 13-2: `Canvas` on an HTML5 browser.

We could write something more sophisticated, but the message is the message, so let's leave well enough alone. If you've got an HTML5 browser, everything is Jake. If not, the user finds out why not in a message. (You may want to fine-tune the message for your audience — from Jane Austen to Ivan the Terrible.)

Before we get rolling on creating your own drawings, let's look at one more way that you can keep out of hot water with non-HTML5 users. In addition to adding text, you can add photos or anything else in the `<canvas>` container. For example, the following script (`Canvas-Photo.html` in this chapter's folder at `www.wiley.com/go/smashinghtml5`) provides an alternative to a more sophisticated presentation of a photo image using `canvas`.

```
<!DOCTYPE HTML>
<html>
<head>
<style type="text/css">
body {
    font-family:Verdana, Geneva, sans-serif;
    background-color:#060;
    color:#0FC;
}
img {
    padding-top:10px;
    padding-bottom:10px;
}
</style>
<meta http-equiv="Content-Type" content="text/html; charset=UTF-8">
<title>Fisherkid</title>
</head>
<body>
<body onLoad="CanvasMaster.showCanvas()">
<canvas id="photo" width="300" height="272" >Gentle viewer, if you see this message,
  that means (alas) you don't have an HTML5 browser. (But you can see the photo and
  caption.)<br>
  <figure> <img src="fisherkid.jpg" width="300" height="272" alt="kid fishing"/><br>
    <figcaption>Kid Fishing</figcaption>
  </figure>
</canvas>
</body>
</html>
```

Not only will the non-HTML5 viewer get the message about updating his browser, but he'll get it in the style described in CSS3. He'll also be able to view both the picture and the caption, as shown in Figure 13-3.

If you do use an HTML5 browser, the preceding program presents a big blank green screen with nothing on it. So, be sure that if you're using an alternative for non-HTML5 browsers, you have something actually in `canvas`.

Figure 13-3: Providing alternative materials for non-HTML5 browsers.
© David Sanders

A SIMPLE CANVAS IMPLEMENTATION

When you're working with Adobe Dreamweaver to create an HTML5 page, you can view the page in the Design mode to preview what will show up on the screen. However, with material inside a `<canvas>` container, all you see is the outline. That outline provides an excellent visual picture of how `canvas` allocates a certain part of the page for rendering images even thought it appears as a blank rectangle.

Basically, you're starting off with an empty canvas defined by the `width` and `height` attributes of the `<canvas>` tag. If you think about the first step in creating a canvas on your Web page in terms of stretching a canvas on a frame, it helps you visualize the process.

Understanding the grid

To work successfully with `canvas`, you have to understand the grid and the Cartesian coordinates. Basically, the upper-left corner is the 0,0 position on your page. As you move to the right, the first value increases. If you move 15 pixels to the right, the value becomes 15,0 — this is the x-axis. As you move down, the second value (y-axis) increases. If you moved down 20, the position would be expressed as 15,20. Suppose, that you wanted to use that position as your starting point and create a 100-pixel square. It helps to visualize the position and size relative to the Web page with the grids, but you get a clearer idea of the image you're creating without the grid marks. Using both will help.

Setting up for canvas drawings

Now we're set to fill the blank box. To do so requires JavaScript. The only thing you do with the <canvas> tag is describe the area where you can place your graphics in a rendering context and a reference ID. So, starting small, this first little drawing will begin with the following tag:

```
<canvas id="redHot" width="100" height="100" >
```

This should be pretty familiar. The width and height were simplified to equal 100 pixels, and the new name of the canvas object is redHot. I've already covered the closing </canvas> tag and message in the container. And the rest of the work is all JavaScript programming working with the DOM.

As noted earlier, I'm going to try to simplify things by using a little OOP in the JavaScript to reflect the programming structure of the DOM. So, the first task is to create an object and a method for it.

```
CanvasMaster=new Object();
CanvasMaster.showCanvas=function()...
```

As you saw in Chapter 12, all that does is set up an object and a method for the object — a function that will call the JavaScript operations when we need it.

Next, the program needs a way to access the canvas DOM node. That's the part of the DOM that has canvas and canvas-related methods and properties. The first step is to create an object that holds the DOM node. Instead of thinking of assigning a node to a variable, think of it as creating an instance of an object that has the properties and methods of the canvas object.

```
canvasNow = document.getElementById("redHot");
```

That line creates an object that contains the canvas object named redHot.

Once we have an instance of a canvas object, the program needs a rendering context. About the only context available is one called 2d, suggesting a two-dimensional drawing context. The canvas object (canvasNow) has a method called getContext() to do what it says: get the rendering context.

```
contextNow = canvasNow.getContext('2d');
```

The instance of the rendering context is named `contextNow`. It has the methods and properties of the `2d` rendering context.

Making the drawing

Before going on to the actual drawing, you may be wondering about the `canvasNow` and `contextNow` objects. Aren't those really variables? After all, variables can be assigned objects. Well, that's one way to think about them, but the variables are assigned objects with their own methods and properties. So, aren't they actually instances of objects? When a variable is assigned a real number, it is, for all intents and purposes, a number. You can do math operations just as you can with a literal number. Instead of quibbling about whether the program structures are really variables or objects, just treat them as objects (just as variables with text or numbers can be treated as strings or numbers).

First, assign the drawing a color. You can use any of the techniques available to create a color as described in Chapter 4. This example uses the hexadecimal format:

```
contextNow.fillStyle = '#cc0000';
```

The `fillStyle` property is only for the fill color and not the stroke (outline) of the object.

Next, the fill color needs a shape to fill. To fill a rectangle, use the following:

```
contextNow.fillRect(5,20,100,100);
```

To explain everything in that last piece of code, Figure 13-4 breaks it down.

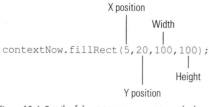

Figure 13-4: Details of the `fillRect()` method.

The first two values place it within the canvas area — not the whole Web page — and the second two values specify the width and height of the rectangle.

The last requirement is actually to carry out filling the rectangle with the specified color. The next line performs that task:

```
contextNow.fill();
```

No matter how many operations are defined, a single `fill()` method takes care of all the fills defined in the larger method.

Now that all the pieces are in place, it needs to be put together in an HTML5 program. The following listing (`SimpleSquare.html` in this chapter's folder at www.wiley.com/go/ smashinghtml5) contains all the script:

```
<!DOCTYPE html>
<html>
<head>
<script language="javascript">
CanvasMaster=new Object();
CanvasMaster.showCanvas=function()
{
    canvasNow  = document.getElementById("redHot");
    contextNow = canvasNow.getContext('2d');

    contextNow.fillStyle = '#cc0000';  // hex value color
    contextNow.fillRect(5,20,100,100); // x, y, width, height

    contextNow.fill();
}
</script>
<style type="text/css">
body {
    font-family:Verdana;
    color:#cc0000;
}
</style>
<title>Red Square</title>
</head>
<body onLoad="CanvasMaster.showCanvas()">
<figure>
  <canvas id="redHot" width="100" height="100" > You're missing the Red Square! Get
  HTML5, comrad! </canvas>
  <figcaption> <br/>
    Red Square </figcaption>
</figure>
</body>
</html>
```

As you can see, the program includes CSS3 and a simple caption along with the appropriate `<figure>` and `<figcaption>` tags surrounding the `<canvas>` tag. The results of this script are shown in Figure 13-5.

Notice that the script also contains a message for non-HTML5 browsers, but because Figure 13-5 shows the `canvas` image, the browser will not display any content in the `<canvas>` container.

259

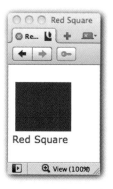

Figure 13-5: Simple canvas drawing
displayed in the Opera browser.

Working with multiple drawings

Now that you see how to create a single drawing, I'll give you a look at creating multiple
drawings. While we're at it, this should also be tested on a mobile device to see how well the
<canvas> tag and JavaScript work in a mobile environment.

The following script (Tortilla.html in this chapter's folder at www.wiley.com/go/
smashinghtml5) is very similar to the script used to create the red square shown in Figure
13-5. However, when drawing multiple objects, their position becomes more important, as the
following script shows:

```html
<!DOCTYPE html>
<html>
<head>
<script language="javascript">
//Color Scheme Values pasted here: 8C6E37,BFA380,593723,736055,261F1E
CanvasMaster=new Object();
CanvasMaster.showCanvas=function()
{
    canvasNow  = document.getElementById("totillaHues")
    contextNow = canvasNow.getContext('2d');

    contextNow.fillStyle = '#8C6E37';    // hex value color
    contextNow.fillRect(5,20,100,100);   // x, y, width, height
                                         // first color

    contextNow.fillStyle = '#BFA380';    // hex value color
    contextNow.fillRect(105,20,100,100); // second color

    contextNow.fillStyle = '#593723';    // hex value color
    contextNow.fillRect(205,20,100,100); // third color

    contextNow.fillStyle = '#736055';    // hex value color
    contextNow.fillRect(305,20,100,100); // fourth color
```

```
        contextNow.fillStyle = '#261F1E ';    // hex value color
        contextNow.fillRect(405,20,100,100); // fifth color

        contextNow.fill();                      // fill all!
        }
</script>
<style type="text/css">
body {
        font-family:Verdana;
        color:#570026;
}
</style>
<title>Feel Like a Tortilla!</title>
</head>
<body onLoad="CanvasMaster.showCanvas()">
<figure>
  <canvas id="totillaHues" width="500" height="120" > No tortillas for you! Get your
  HTML5 browser...pronto! </canvas>
  <figcaption> <br/>
    Tortilla Flat
  </figcaption>
</figure>
</body>
</html>
```

The important parameters in this script are the first two in the `fillRect()` method. They're the x and y positions, and no two squares can be in the same space. The squares are lined up in a horizontal row, so all you need to pay attention to is the x-value because the vertical position is going to be the same.

Once all the `fillStyle()` and `fillRect()` methods are laid out, the drawings require only a single `fill()` method to display them all. Figure 13-6 shows how the figure looks on a mobile Safari browser on an iPhone.

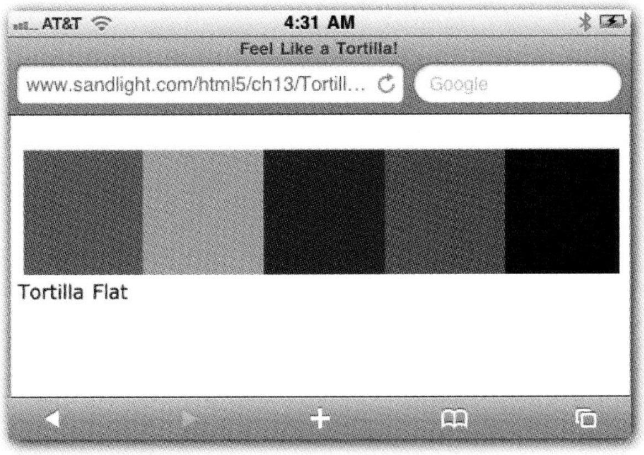

Figure 13-6: Multiple drawings displayed on a mobile browser.

The image in Figure 13-6 may appear vaguely familiar. In Chapter 4, the color scheme program Adobe Kuler had a similar layout, and the colors were developed in Adobe Kuler.

Adding strokes and removing drawings

Two more methods associated with drawing rectangles are `strokeRect()` and `clearRect()`. Both of these methods have parameters similar to the `fillRect()` method — x, y, `width`, `height`. They function the same insofar as specifying which areas to add a stroke or remove a drawing.

The following program (`StrokeAndRemove.html` in this chapter's folder at www.wiley. com/go/smashinghtml5) shows how you can add three methods to the `CanvasMaster` object, which I'll call `addStroke()`, `punchOut()`, and `chomp()`. The first method draws an outline within the canvas area, the second makes a hole in the middle of the rectangle, and the third method removes everything in the defined area.

```
<!DOCTYPE html>
<html>
<head>
<script language="javascript">
//colors: 595241,B8AE9C,FFFFFF,ACCFCC,8A0917
CanvasMaster=new Object();
CanvasMaster.showCanvas=function()
{
    canvasNow  = document.getElementById("strokeAndChomp");
    contextNow = canvasNow.getContext('2d');

    contextNow.fillStyle = '#ACCFCC';
    contextNow.fillRect(5,20,100,100);

    contextNow.fill();
}
CanvasMaster.addStroke=function()
{
    contextNow.strokeStyle='#595241';
    contextNow.strokeRect(7,22,91,76);
}
CanvasMaster.chomp=function()
{
    contextNow.clearRect(5,20,100,100);
}
CanvasMaster.punchOut=function()
{
    contextNow.clearRect(40,45,30,30);
}
</script>
<style type="text/css">
body {
    font-family:Verdana;
```

```
    color:#8A0917;
    background-color:#B8AE9C;
}
a {

    text-decoration:none;
    color:#595241;
    margin-left:16px;
}
</style>
<title>Stroke and Cut</title>
</head>
<body onLoad="CanvasMaster.showCanvas()">
<article>
  <figure>
    <canvas id="strokeAndChomp" width="100" height="100" >You ought to see what
  HTML5 browsers see! Get one now!</canvas>
    <figcaption> <br/>
      Square Work </figcaption>
  </figure>
  <section>
    <p><a href="#" onClick="CanvasMaster.addStroke()">Add Stroke</a></p>
  </section>
  <section>
    <p><a href="#" onClick="CanvasMaster.chomp()">Gobble Up Square</a></p>
  </section>
  <section>
    <p><a href="#" onClick="CanvasMaster.punchOut()">Punch Hole</a></p>
  </section>
  <section>
    <p><a href="#" onClick="CanvasMaster.showCanvas()">Replace Square</a></p>
  </section>
</article>
</body>
</html>
```

This page is formatted for a mobile device. It was tested in Opera Mini on an iPhone, as shown in Figure 13-7.

A blue square appears on the initial load. When you add a stroke line, a frame appears just inside the original image. If you add more strokes, you'll find that the stroke darkens. When you click the Punch Hole selection, a small square appears in the middle of the blue square. The Gobble Up Square selection removes both the image and the stroke. If you click the Add Stroke text after having removed the blue square, you'll see the stroke line only with no blue rectangle.

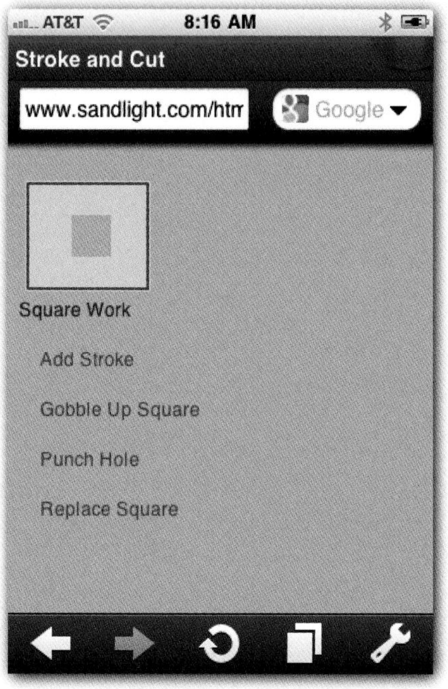

Figure 13-7: Adding a stroke and removing part or all of a rectangle.

IMAGES IN CANVAS AND SHADOWS

One of the fun and simple features of `canvas` is using it with loaded images. Figure 13-3 shows a typical example of what you can load into a Web page using the `<img>` tag. Using the `<img>` tag is okay, but you can make it far more interesting with the `<canvas>` tag.

Loading an image into canvas

To load an image, whether it's a GIF, a PNG, or a JPEG, requires an `Image` object that can be created with JavaScript. Within the method used to create a rendering context, you risk having your user see a blank where the loaded image goes unless you have an event that lets you know that the file has loaded. Fortunately, that's pretty simple to do using the `onLoad` event handler, as the following snippet shows:

```
...
pic = new Image();
pic.onload = function()
{
    contextNow.drawImage(pic,10,10);
}
 pic.src = 'imageName.jpg';
...
```

The rendering context method `drawImage()` expects three parameters:

- **The reference to the file that you're loading:** In this case, the label `pic` is the reference name to the file being used.
- **The *x* and *y* position:** It's a little more involved than using the `<img>` tag, but not much, and this method lets you place the image where you want it within the canvas parameters.
- **The source of the image:** You add the source of the image within the method that creates the rendering context — not unlike the identification using the `img` element.

Adding a drop shadow

Adding a drop shadow to an image gives it a three-dimensional look — it's elevated off the page. The rendering context has four shadow properties:

- `shadowColor="color";`
- `shadowOffsetX=horizontal value;`
- `shadowOffsetY=horizontal value;`
- `shadowBlur=blur value;`

The color can be assigned using any of the methods discussed in Chapter 4. The shadow offsets depend on how big you want your shadow. Experiment with different values, beginning with about 5. In the following example, each is set to 10 to provide enough shadow to make the image rise off the screen but not so much to overwhelm the image. Finally, the blur value can be greater or smaller depending on both the offset values and the amount of blur you want. With greater offset values, you need greater blur values.

To make the shadow have an effect on the image, all shadow properties must be entered before writing the `drawImage()` method. That's all there is to it. The other JavaScript to set up the canvas context rendering is very similar to the drawings in the previous section. The following code (`PhotoShadows.html` in this chapter's folder at `www.wiley.com/go/smashinghtml5`) loads the image and places the drop shadow on it:

```
<!DOCTYPE html>
<html>
<head>
<script language="javascript">
//colors: F4F1BC,736F36,BFB95A
CanvasMaster=new Object();
CanvasMaster.showCanvas=function()
{
    canvasNow  = document.getElementById("picFrame");
    contextNow = canvasNow.getContext('2d');

    pic = new Image();
    pic.onload = function()
```

```
        {
            contextNow.shadowColor ='#BFB95A';
            contextNow.shadowOffsetX=10;
            contextNow.shadowOffsetY=10;
            contextNow.shadowBlur=4;
            contextNow.drawImage(pic,10,10);
        }
    pic.src = 'fisherkid.jpg';
}
</script>
<style type="text/css">
body {
    font-family:Verdana;
    color:#736F36;
    background-color:#F4F1BC;
}
</style>
<title>Frame the Photo</title>
</head>
<body onLoad="CanvasMaster.showCanvas()">
<article>
  <figure>
    <canvas id="picFrame" width="340" height="300" > This is one picture you missed
  because you don't have HTML5. </canvas>
    <figcaption> <br/>
      Photo with Drop Shadow</figcaption>
  </figure>
</article>
</body>
</html>
```

Before putting in your own images, check their size and the size that the `<canvas>` tag has reserved. In this case, there was enough room for both the image (a photograph) and the graphic drop shadow. Figure 13-8 shows the results in a Google Chrome browser.

The color combinations used with the image are important. You'll find that some colors work better than others. The ones used in Figure 13-8 are a monochromatic set based on the colors in the image. As you can see, the shadow nicely lifts the photo off the screen.

Compare the image in Figure 13-3 with the one in Figure 13-8. In Figure 13-3, you see what happens with non-HTML5 browsers; in Figure 13-8, what HTML5 browsers can display. Also, in this latest use of the same digital photo, the non-HTML5 browsers see only the message that they're not seeing the image. If you want, you can add the same image and color scheme without the drop shadow for non-HTML5 browsers.

Figure 13-8: Image and drop shadow with `<canvas>`.
© David Sanders

Working with filters

Before moving on to complex shapes, let's take a look at using filters to add tints to images. The Internet is a huge library of copyright-free photos and drawings; use your favorite search engine to do an image search. (But remember that not every photo you find online is copyright-free — be sure you have permission to use any image you find.) Many of the drawings are in black-and-white and can be a stark contrast to other elements of a page. One way to integrate them is to add a filter, which you can easily do by creating a partially transparent colored shape and place on top of the image. Using `canvas`, this process is quite easy. The key to the process is the following line:

```
context.fillStyle = 'rgba(rn, gn, bn, alpha)';
```

Instead of using a hexadecimal value, it uses RGB with an "alpha" channel — `rgba()` — that controls for transparency. The last parameter is a value between 0 and 1. The higher the value, the more opaque the image will be. By using a value less than 1, you can control the degree of opacity. The rest of the shape matches the dimensions of the image and is positioned in the same space.

To integrate an image with the rest of the page — the plan is to add a color tint using the background color. The following program (`FilterImage.html` in this chapter's folder at www.wiley.com/go/smashinghtml5) adds the image first and then draws the rectangle object on top of it with a transparent fill color.

```
<!DOCTYPE html>
<html>
<head>
<script language="javascript">
//colors: F26A4B,F2D091=rgb(242,208,145)
CanvasMaster=new Object();
CanvasMaster.showCanvas=function()
{
    canvasNow  = document.getElementById("filterFrame");
    contextNow = canvasNow.getContext('2d');

    pic = new Image();
    pic.onload = function()
    {
        contextNow.drawImage(pic,0,0);
        contextNow.fillStyle = 'rgba(242, 208, 145, .6)';
        contextNow.fillRect(0,0,472,306);
        contextNow.fill();
    }
    pic.src = 'dance.gif';
}

</script>
<style type="text/css">
body {
    font-family:Verdana;
    color:#F26A4B;
    background-color:#F2D091;
}
</style>
<title>Filtering Images</title>
</head>
<body onLoad="CanvasMaster.showCanvas()">
<article>
  <figure>
    <canvas id="filterFrame" width="472" height="306" > Not only do you miss the
  filtered image, but you miss the dance! Get an HTML5 browser! </canvas>
    <figcaption> <br/>
      Filtered Image</figcaption>
  </figure>
</article>
</body>
</html>
```

Notice that the sequence first loaded the image and then placed the drawing on top using the following snippet:

```
contextNow.drawImage(pic,0,0);
contextNow.fillStyle = 'rgba(242, 208, 145, .6)';
contextNow.fillRect(0,0,472,306);
contextNow.fill();
```

If the drawing is added first, the image simply sits on top of it as though no filter at all is used. Now, with the added filter, the image better fits in with the page, as Figure 13-9 shows.

Figure 13-9: A filtered image blending in with the background.

Using Adobe Photoshop or some similar image-editing software, you could've added the filter to the image and loaded the filtered image with a standard <img> tag. However, using canvas and HTML5, you can make the changes without any additional software.

CREATING COMPLEX DRAWINGS WITH CANVAS

The simpler shapes are rectangles, and they're terrific for squares and rectangles, but you can only do so much with boxes before you need some lines and curves. This section looks at the following complex drawing elements that are part of canvas. (The context term refers to the name of the rendering context object.)

- `context.beginPath()`
- `context.moveTo(x, y)`
- `context.closePath()`
- `context.lineTo(x, y)`
- `context.quadraticCurveTo(cpx, cpy, x, y)`
- `context.bezierCurveTo(cp1x, cp1y, cp2x, cp2y, x, y)`
- `context.arcTo(x1, y1, x2, y2, radius)`
- `context.arc(x, y, radius, startAngle, endAngle, anticlockwise)`
- `context.rect(x, y, w, h)`
- `context.fill()`
- `context.stroke()`
- `context.clip()`
- `context.isPointInPath(x, y)`

Knowing how to use these methods with a `<canvas>` tag doesn't ensure that they'll look good. The remainder of this chapter examines most of these methods. You should be well on your way to creating many different shapes by the chapter's end.

LINES AND MOVEMENT

The best way to start thinking about using the canvas tools for drawing is to visualize all drawings on a grid, just as you did with rectangles. However, given the relative complexity of freeform drawing, even with straight lines, the beginning point is with images on a grid. Figure 13-10 shows two drawings that can be created with straight lines.

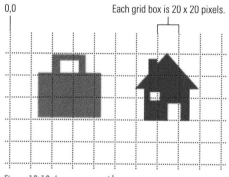

Figure 13-10: Images on a grid.

The grid boxes are 20 pixels wide and 20 pixels high. If you take a pencil and a piece of grid paper (or turn on the grid on a drawing program), you can replicate the images in Figure 13-10. Starting with the left image in Figure 13-10, a typical drawing would consist of the following steps:

1. **Place the pencil at position 40,20 on the grid.**

   To do this with the `canvas` DOM, use `context.beginPath()` and `context.moveTo(40,20)`. This is the starting point.

2. **Draw a line from the starting point to about 72, 20 for the top of the briefcase handle.**

   Use `context.lineTo(72,20)` for the `canvas` equivalent.

3. **Move the pencil down to about 72, 38.**

   Use `context.lineTo(72,38)` for a `canvas` drawing.

4. **Continue in this manner until the outline of the briefcase is complete.**

5. **When you want to draw the inside of the handle, pick up your pencil, move to where you want to start drawing the inside of the handle.**

   With `canvas` you use `context.moveTo(x,y)` to begin in a new position and then use `context.lineTo(x,y)` to finish up. However, you do not have to reuse `context.beginPath()`.

6. **In a pencil and pen drawing, as soon as your drawing is complete, you have the outline of the briefcase. With canvas, you have to include context.stroke() to add the lines.**

When you come to the next-to-last point in your drawing, you can use the `context.closePath()` method to go the point you started, and that is used in the program. The following script (`SimpleLineDrawing.html` in this chapter's folder at `www.wiley.com/go/smashinghtml5`) provides all the steps.

```
<!DOCTYPE html>
<html>
<head>
<script language="javascript">
//colors: 8C6E37,BFA380
CanvasMaster=new Object();
CanvasMaster.showCanvas=function()
{
    canvasNow  = document.getElementById("simpleDraw");
    contextNow = canvasNow.getContext('2d');
    contextNow.beginPath();
    contextNow.moveTo(40,20);
    contextNow.lineTo(72,20);
    contextNow.lineTo(72,38);
    contextNow.lineTo(88,38);
    contextNow.lineTo(88,78);
    contextNow.lineTo(28,78);
    contextNow.lineTo(28,38);
    contextNow.lineTo(40,38);
    contextNow.lineTo(40,20);
    contextNow.closePath();
    contextNow.moveTo(46,26);
    contextNow.lineTo(66,26);
    contextNow.lineTo(66,38);
```

```
            contextNow.lineTo(46,38);
            contextNow.closePath();
            contextNow.stroke();
    }
    </script>
    <style type="text/css">
    body {
            font-family:Verdana;
            color:#000000;
    }
    </style>
    <title>Filtering Images</title>
    </head>
    <body onLoad="CanvasMaster.showCanvas()">
    <article>
      <figure>
        <canvas id="simpleDraw" width="90" height="80" > If you can identify the draw-
      ing, you win a jillion dollars! Oh, I'm sorry . . . looks like you don't have an
      HTML5 browser.</canvas>
        <figcaption> <br/>
          Picasso Was Here</figcaption>
      </figure>
    </article>
    </body>
    </html>
```

Figure 13-11 shows what you can expect to see. (If you worked out the coordinates on your own, yours probably looks better!)

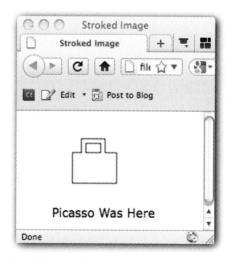

Figure 13-11: Image drawn in canvas.

So far so good, but the original briefcase is brown, so it's going to need some color. The way to color is the same as it is for rectangles: Use `context.fillStyle ="color"`. The complex drawing methods include `context.fill()` to fill in an outline. So, taking out the `context.stroke()`, replacing it with `context.fill()`, and adding a `fillStyle` method should do the trick. Figure 13-12 shows the results.

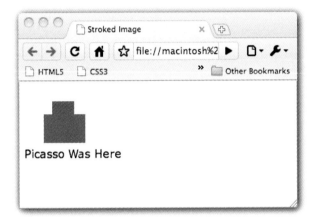

Figure 13-12: The filled image covering the handle.

In looking at Figure 13-12, you can see that the outline and color are correct, but instead of a handle there's a block. Whenever a series of drawing methods are used without beginning a new path, and then when the `context.fill()` method is called, it fills it to the beginning of the path. As a result, everything is filled and not just the parts you want.

To fix this, two `context.fill()` methods are employed. One is at the end of the first outline of the briefcase, and the second is at the end of the outline for the handle. The first is filled with brown, and the second is filled with white. Additionally, a second `context.beginPath()` is added at the beginning of the drawing of the handle. The following program (`SimpleLineDrawingFilled.html` in this chapter's folder at www.wiley.com/go/smashinghtml5) has all the code revised to generate the filled image.

```
<!DOCTYPE html>
<html>
<head>
<script language="javascript">
//colors: 960, fff, 000
CanvasMaster=new Object();
CanvasMaster.showCanvas=function()
{
     canvasNow  = document.getElementById("briefCase");
     contextNow = canvasNow.getContext('2d');
     contextNow.beginPath();
     contextNow.moveTo(40,20);
     contextNow.lineTo(72,20);
     contextNow.lineTo(72,38);
```

273

```
        contextNow.lineTo(88,38);
        contextNow.lineTo(88,78);
        contextNow.lineTo(28,78);
        contextNow.lineTo(28,38);
        contextNow.lineTo(40,38);
        contextNow.lineTo(40,20);
        contextNow.closePath();
        contextNow.fillStyle ="#960";
        contextNow.fill();
        contextNow.beginPath();
        contextNow.moveTo(46,26);
        contextNow.lineTo(66,26);
        contextNow.lineTo(66,38);
        contextNow.lineTo(46,38);
        contextNow.closePath();
        contextNow.fillStyle ="#fff";
        contextNow.fill();
    }
</script>
<style type="text/css">
body {
        font-family:Verdana;
        color:#000;
}
</style>
<title>Filled Line Drawing</title>
</head>
<body onLoad="CanvasMaster.showCanvas()">
<article>
  <figure>
    <canvas id="briefCase" width="90" height="80" > If you can identify the drawing,
  you win a jillion dollars! Oh, I'm sorry . . . looks like you don't have an HTML5
  browser.</canvas>
      <figcaption> <br/>
        Picasso Was Here</figcaption>
  </figure>
</article>
</body>
</html>
```

When you test this revision, the results are pretty close the original drawing. Compare Figure 13-10 and Figure 13-13 to see how close the program-generated image is to the original.

You can use the lines to draw anything that has no curves. In the next section, you'll see how to add curves to your artistic canvas tools.

Figure 13-13: The final drawing of the briefcase.

CURVES

Making curves, even with drawing tools, is trickier than drawing straight lines. To understand how to make curves, I'll start this section with a discussion of arcs and the canvas DOM methods for creating them. We'll look at some of the geometry, but not a lot. (You do need a little understanding of geometry, but don't worry — it's basic.)

The first thing that you need to understand is the difference between degrees and radians. Most people know that a circle has 360 degrees. On a compass rose, 360 or 0 degrees (12 o'clock) is due north. As you move clockwise to 90 degrees (3 o'clock), the compass points east; at 180 degrees (6 o'clock), south; and at 270 degrees (9 o'clock), west.

However, you have to use radians instead of degrees, so all degrees must be converted to radians. Use the following formula:

Radians = (PI ÷ 180) × degrees

So, let's say that you want to know the radians for due west (9 o'clock), 270 degrees:

Radians = (3.14159265 ÷ 180) = 0.01745329251994

Radians = 0.01745329251994 × 270

Radians = 4.71238898

A simple way to do the same thing is to just multiply degrees by 0.01745329251994 or in JavaScript write:

```
radians = (Math.PI/180)* degrees;
```

You can find plenty of calculators online to do the conversion for you.

Arcs

The canvas DOM method for drawing arcs is `context.arc()`. The method has several parameters that need to be understood in concert and individually:

- `x,y`: Circle's center
- `radius`: Radius of circle
- `startAngle`: Start point of arc expressed in radians
- `endAngle`: End point of arc expressed in radians
- `anticlockwise`: Boolean (`true` is counterclockwise and `false` is clockwise)

I find it helpful to envision either a compass rose or a clock with the four cardinal directions and time/degrees — north (12 o'clock or 0 degrees), east (3 o'clock or 90 degrees), south (6 o'clock or 180 degrees), and west (9 o'clock or 270 degrees). A full arc statement looks like the following:

```
contextNow.arc(150,100,50,six,0,true);
```

This arc has its center at x = 150 and y = 100, and it has a radius of 50. The start angle is set to 6, which is a variable that we've created to represent the 6 o'clock position of 180 degrees. The variable's value has been converted to radians. Both degrees and radians have the same value at the 12 o'clock position (0), and it is used as the ending angle. Finally, the arc is set to true — anticlockwise.

This next program is one used to experiment with different arcs. Four variables — 12, 3, 6, and 9 — are set in radians corresponding to the positions on a clock. Certain statements are commented out but will be used later.

```
<!DOCTYPE HTML>
<html>
<head>
<script type="text/javascript">
CanvasMaster=new Object();
CanvasMaster.showCanvas=function()
{
    canvasNow  = document.getElementById("beHappy");
    contextNow = canvasNow.getContext('2d');
    contextNow.beginPath();
    contextNow.moveTo(0,0);
    contextNow.lineTo(300,0);
    contextNow.lineTo(300,200);
    contextNow.lineTo(0,200);
    contextNow.closePath();
    contextNow.stroke();
```

```
        // RADCON = (Math.PI/180) ;
        RADCON=0.01745329251994;
        twelve=0;
        three = RADCON * 90;
        six = RADCON * 180;
        nine = RADCON * 270;

        contextNow.beginPath();
        contextNow.arc(125,100,50,six,twelve,true);
        //contextNow.closePath();
        //contextNow.fill()
        contextNow.stroke();
    }
</script>
<style type="text/css">
body {
        font-family:Verdana, Geneva, sans-serif;
        color:#cc0000;
}
</style>
<meta http-equiv="Content-Type" content="text/html; charset=UTF-8">
<title>Smile</title>
</head>
<body onLoad="CanvasMaster.showCanvas()">
<figure>
  <canvas id="beHappy" width="300" height="200" > You don't see a smile because you
  don't have an HTML5 browser. No smile for you!</canvas>
  <figcaption>
    <p>Rectangle represents canvas boundaries</p>
  </figcaption>
</figure>
</body>
</html>
```

The RADCON variable is a constant ($\pi \div 180$), so all degrees were set to radians by multiplying their values by RADCON. As noted, the variable names represent the positions on a clock. In addition, a rectangle around the area where the arc is drawn represents the boundaries of the <canvas> tag's width and height. Figure 13-14 shows the result.

The starting point of the arc is on the left, and it moved anticlockwise to the ending point on the right. Change the following line:

```
contextNow.arc(125,100,50,six,twelve,true);
```

to:

```
contextNow.arc(125,100,50,six,twelve,false);
```

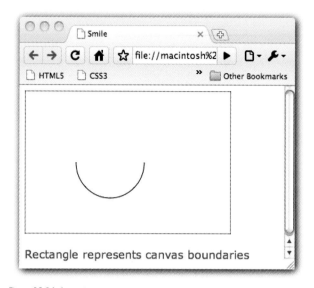

Figure 13-14: An arc in `canvas`.

That changed the drawing from anticlockwise to clockwise, but it made a major difference, as you'll see when you test it.

Next, using the same program, change the line back to:

```
contextNow.arc(125,100,50,six,twelve,true);
```

Then remove the comment lines (//) from the following line:

```
//contextNow.closePath();
```

And test it again. The final change to the program will fill the arc. Uncomment the line from the following:

```
//contextNow.fill()
```

to this:

```
contextNow.fill()
```

And add comment lines so that the stroke statement reads:

```
//contextNow.stroke()
```

When the changes are made, your arc now looks like a kettle, as shown in Figure 13-15.

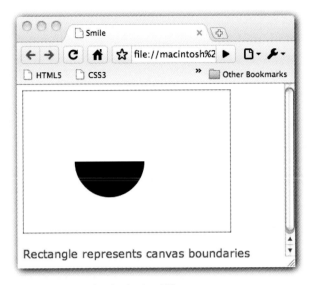

Figure 13-15: An arc with a closed path and fill.

The only way to really learn to work with arcs is to practice with them. Use the script in this section to try different things.

Circles and gradients

Thus far, only a single type of fill has been used — a solid one. In this section, you'll see how to make a circle using an arc and fill it with a gradient.

First, making circles is easy using the `context.arc()` method. The radian parameters are 0 and `Math.PI*2`. And the anticlockwise parameter is `false`. (That's the trick.) For instance, this next example uses the following line to create a big circle that will be filled with a gradient, to make it look like a sunset:

```
contextNow.arc(200,200,150,0,Math.PI*2,false);
```

To create a gradient fill, both linear and radial, is fairly straightforward. The first step is using the canvas DOM `context.createLinearGradient()` method. The method expects four parameters: `x0, y0, x1, y1`. The gradient fill moves from `x1` to `x1` and from `y0` to `y1`. A straight linear gradient from left to right would have a single value in `x1`, and the rest would be 0. A gradient from top to bottom would have value in either `y0` or `y1`, with the rest set to 0.

To set the gradient colors, use the `gradient.addColorStop()` method. It expects two parameters. The first is a zero-based number from 0 to 1 and the second is the color. Once that's completed, assign the `context.fillStyle` the gradient. The following snippet shows the steps in adding a gradient fill:

```
sunsetGradient=contextNow.createLinearGradient(0, 0, 0,379);
```

```
sunsetGradient.addColorStop(0, "yellow");
sunsetGradient.addColorStop(1, "#cc0000")
contextNow.fillStyle = sunsetGradient;
```

In this particular example, the gradient is a vertical one. The first color, yellow, is at the top, and the second color, red, is at the bottom. Putting it all together, the following script (Sun-set.html in this chapter's folder at www.wiley.com/go/smashinghtml5) creates a sunset for you.

```
<!DOCTYPE HTML>
<html>
<head>
<script type="text/javascript">
CanvasMaster=new Object();
CanvasMaster.showCanvas=function()
{
    canvasNow   = document.getElementById("sunset");
    contextNow = canvasNow.getContext('2d');
    sunsetGradient=contextNow.createLinearGradient(0, 0, 0,379);
    sunsetGradient.addColorStop(0, "yellow");
    sunsetGradient.addColorStop(1, "#cc0000")
    contextNow.fillStyle = sunsetGradient;
    contextNow.beginPath();
    contextNow.arc(200,200,150,0,Math.PI*2,false);
    contextNow.closePath();
    contextNow.fill()
}
</script>
<style type="text/css">
body {
    font-family:Verdana, Geneva, sans-serif;
    color:#cc0000;
}
</style>
<meta http-equiv="Content-Type" content="text/html; charset=UTF-8">
<title>Sunset</title>
</head>
<body onLoad="CanvasMaster.showCanvas()">
<figure>
  <canvas id="sunset" width="400" height="400" > A shame you can't see the beautiful
  sunset because you don't have an HTML5 browser. Aloha... </canvas>
   <figcaption>
      <p>Sunset</p>
   </figcaption>
</figure>
</body>
</html>
```

When you test the page, you'll see a big circle with a yellow-to-red gradient. You can use the same gradient technique with other shapes as well. Figure 13-16 is displayed in the mobile version of Safari on an iPhone.

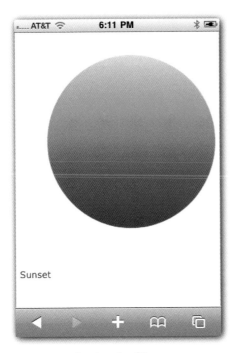

Figure 13-16: A circle with gradient fill.

281

There's far more that you can do with canvas, and one of the best features of images created using canvas DOM objects is that they aren't as expensive (they don't take as much band-width) to load as bitmapped graphic files. We've only skimmed the surface of this new powerful element in HTML5.

TAKE THE WHEEL

Working with `canvas` is so much fun and varied that it's hard to know where to begin. So, try the following little projects to test-drive this great new element in HTML5:

- In Figure 13-13, you see two line objects — a briefcase and a house. See if you can draw the house using the methods employed for creating the briefcase.

- Take an image of a picture frame, and superimpose another image that appears to be in the frame. (This project requires you to fix the frame and image sizes so that one will fit in the other.)

- Find or create a digital photo and superimpose a sunset on top of it. (Alternatively, create an image with another kind of gradient and superimpose it on a digital photo or other image. What about a gradient filter?)

14 ADDING FORMS

ONE OF THE most important features of any Web page is its ability to interact with a person. In computer science lingo, there's a subfield called human computer interface, which treats humans as another type of interface like a printer, USB drive, or Webcam. This doesn't dehumanize people using computers. Instead, it treats people like something they're not, and that's bound to get you in trouble sooner or later. This chapter shows both how to add interactive forms and treat people like people.

ADDING A FORM

Forms are really in two parts (even more in some cases). The first part is the `<form>` tag that sets up a container for different kinds of input. The typical form can be envisioned as the following:

> Begin Form
> > Input 1
> > Input 2
> > Input 3
> > Input 4
> End Form

So in discussing forms, we're really talking about the form and its attributes and input elements and their attributes. With HTML5 forms, you'll find plenty of new attributes and elements.

Just so that you don't get bored, the following (`degree2radians.html` in this chapter's folder at `www.wiley.com/go/smashinghtml5`) is an example of a simple calculator for converting degrees into radians (see Chapter 13 for a practical use for the converter). Just enter the degrees you want converted, and you'll be presented with the equivalent radians.

```
<!DOCTYPE HTML>
<html>
<head>
<script type="text/javascript">
FormMaster=new Object();
FormMaster.resolveForm=function()
{
    const RADCON=Math.PI/180;
    degreesNow=document.converter.degrees.value;
    radiansNow=degreesNow * RADCON;
    document.converter.radians.value=radiansNow;
}
</script>
<style type="text/css">
/*048ABF,049DBF,F2F2F2,595959,0D0D0D */
h3 {
    font-family:"Arial Black", Gadget, sans-serif;
    color:#595959;
}
body {
    font-family:Verdana, Geneva, sans-serif;
    color:#049DBF;
    background-color:#0D0D0D;
}
</style>
<meta http-equiv="Content-Type" content="text/html; charset=UTF-8">
```

```
<title>Convert Degrees to Radians</title>
</head>
<body >
<article>
  <header>
     <h3>Degree to Radian Converter</h3>
  </header>
  <section>
    <form name=converter>
      Enter degrees:<br>
      <input type=number name=degrees required >
      <br>
      Radians:<br>
      <input type=number name=radians>
      <br>
      <input type=submit name=submit value="Convert to Radians" onClick="FormMaster.
  resolveForm()">
    </form>
  </section>
</article>
</body>
</html>
```

If you're at all familiar with forms in HTML, you know that this form is different — it has a number input that treats the entries as real numbers instead of text that has to be converted to numbers by JavaScript. That wasn't available in older versions of HTML. Figure 14-1 shows the number "spinners" that appear in Opera when Web pages use the number input.

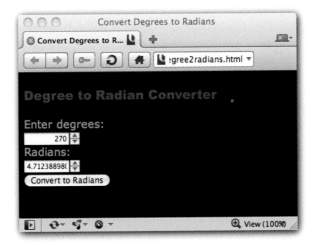

Figure 14-1: Entering numbers for calculations and conversion.

As you'll see in this chapter, much is new, and using JavaScript and (later) PHP, you can do a great deal with HTML5 forms. So, prepare to find a good deal of new features and reasons to update your browsers to HTML5.

GENERAL FORM ATTRIBUTES

The form (think the mother ship) has several attributes that impact every input element in the form container. However, the first focus is on the form itself. It has the following attributes:

- `accept-charset`
- `action`
- `autocomplete`
- `enctype`
- `method`
- `name`
- `novalidate`
- `target`

Many of these attributes are rarely used and some only make sense when you start using programs like PHP and ASP.NET where you pass data to and from a database. However, we'll examine them all.

Accept-charset, enctype, and novalidate

The `accept-charset` attribute, if specified at all, usually assigns `utf-8` as the character encoding to be used with the form data. That is, it treats all input as `utf-8` encoding. A simple statement like the following is sufficient:

```
<form name=motherShip accept-charset=utf-8>
```

If no character encoding is assigned, it is assumed to be unknown and uses the default character encoding. When using multiple encodings, each is separated by a space in HTML5 instead of by commas and semicolons as in earlier versions of HTML.

Most of the time, the `enctype` attribute is left blank and uses the default state. The `enctype` attribute has three keywords and states (keyword/state):

- `application/x-www-form-urlencoded` (default)
- `multipart/form-data`
- `text/plain`

A form may be set up to accept plain text and would be assigned the following:

```
<form enctype="text/plain">
```

For the most part, though, this is another attribute that is not included in the `<form>` tag. That's because the default (`urlencoded`) is what you want.

The `novalidate` attribute is a Boolean used in form submission; it blocks validation of the user-inputted data during submission. This can save time, but it can also lead to foul-ups. Sometimes a simple form or a wide-open (unknown submission data) form does not validate because setting up traps for validation is unknown as well. If present in the form tag, the submitted elements will not be validated:

```
<form nonvalidate>
```

That effectively blocks submission validation.

A better solution lies in the Boolean `formnovalidate` and `required` attributes that can be placed in individual input elements. For example, the following form has no validation for a cancel button and the middle name is not required, although the first and last names are.

```
<form name=motherShip accept-charset=utf-8>
  First name:
  <input type=text name=fn required>
  <br>
  Middle name:
  <input type=text name=mn >
  <br>
  Last name:
  <input type=text name=ln required>
  <br>
  <input type=submit name=submit value="Send the info!">
  <input type=submit formnovalidate name=cancel value="Cancel">
</form>
```

The `accept-charset`, `enctype`, and `novalidate` attributes aren't ones you're likely to use too much. However, the `input` element attributes for requiring data entry and nonvalidation can be quite handy.

Action and method

You're not going to need these two important attributes until Chapter 16, so this section is going to be brief and to the point. The `action` attribute is assigned a URL that's launched as soon as the Submit button is clicked. It sends the form data to the URL (a server-side program like Perl, PHP, or ASP). The method attribute is either POST or GET. When you send data from your Web page or send and retrieve data, use POST. If all you want to do is retrieve data, use GET. The following shows typical values assigned to the two attributes:

```
<form action="http://www.sandlight.com/treasures.php" method="post">
```

In Chapter 16, you'll find that both of these attributes are always used when dealing with PHP.

Autocomplete

A fairly simple but important form attribute is `autocomplete`. It has two states, `on` and `off`, and it defaults to `on`. Basically, if you do not want autocomplete, just set it to `off`. Otherwise, it's the default state of forms. Sometimes autocomplete can be a bother; if so, just add the following line:

```
<form autocomplete="off">
```

With the state set to off, a reused word will not pop up. For example, if you change your e-mail address, your old address may show up automatically in e-mail address boxes if the `autocomplete` is not set to `off`.

Name and target

The `name` attribute is one of the most important attributes of a form because it's used in the DOM to identify it. As a property of the document object, it can be referenced either as an array element, such as `forms[0]`, or by name. Organizationally, it's far easier to reference a form and its children by a name.

In addition to a `name` attribute, forms have a global attribute, `id`. Both attributes have names. In the DOM, the reference is to the `name` attribute. However, within a single Web document (page), other elements can identify the form with a reference to the form `id`. What's more, a new feature of HTML5 is that the form child can exist outside the `<form>` container and have a form attribute linking it to any form in the page. For example, the following text input element is part of the form with the `id` of `ralph`.

```
<input type=text form=ralph  name=hometown>
```

The text input element can be anywhere on the page, and that means designers don't have to put all the input in one place. Try the following script (`FormID.html` in this chapter's folder at `www.wiley.com/go/smashinghtml5`) and test it with Opera (which has implemented this new feature).

```
<!DOCTYPE HTML>
<html>
<head>
<script type="text/javascript">
FormMaster=new Object();
FormMaster.resolveForm=function()
{
    favorite = document.formName.favURL.value;
    personName=document.formName.person.value;
    message=personName + "'s favorite Web site is " +favorite;
    document.formName.output.value=message;
}
</script>
<style type="text/css">
```

```
h3 {
     font-family:"Arial Black", Gadget, sans-serif;
     color:#97CCA6;
}
body {
     font-family:Verdana, Geneva, sans-serif;
     color:#EFF09E;
     background-color:#AB1F33;
}
</style>
<meta http-equiv="Content-Type" content="text/html; charset=UTF-8">
<title>Remote Form Inputs</title>
</head>
<body >
<article>
  <header>
    <h3>IDs to Connect</h3>
  </header>
  <section> What is your very favorite Web site?<br>
    <label>Favorite Site:
      <input type=url form=formID name=favURL>
    </label>
  </section>
  <section>
    <blockquote> This section represents a break between the first input (requesting
  a URL) and the rest of the form to which the URL form belongs. This gives designers
  far more leeway in putting together an interactive site. </blockquote>
  </section>
  <section>
    <form name=formName id=formID>
      <label>What's your name?
        <input type=text name=person>
      </label>
      <br>
      Output:<br>
      <textarea name=output cols=50 rows=5></textarea>
      <br>
      <input type=submit name=submit value="Gather in the Chickens"
  onClick="FormMaster.resolveForm()">
    </form>
  </section>
</article>
</body>
</html>
```

Notice that inside the `<form>` container with the `name=formName` and `id=formID` is a single input element, a `<textarea>` tag and a Submit button. More important, though, notice that the input element with the `name=favURL` is outside of the form container. However, it assigns itself the id of the form on the page — `formID`. In HTML5, it's treated as though it were inside the `<form>` container. Figure 14-2 shows that the data entered in the url type input element (name=favURL) is picked up by the DOM in the JavaScript as part of the same form as the rest of the form input elements belonging to the form named formName.

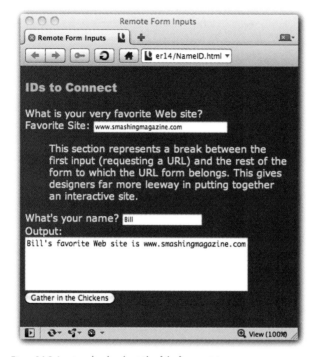

Figure 14-2: Input can be placed outside of the form container.

Now, you don't have to worry about where you put your input forms. As long as input elements are assigned the form ID of the form, they're treated as though they're inside the form container.

The target attribute refers to the browsing context of the form upon form submission. If no target value is assigned, the browsing context is the same as if _self were assigned to a target attribute. The other browsing contexts are _blank, _parent, or _top. The _blank browsing context is quite helpful where you have information from a server-side script that replaces the content on the calling page with its own content. Using _blank enables users to see both the calling page and the information from the called page.

THE FORM AS PART OF THE DOM

Although the DOM is generally discussed as an arrangement of nodes, it can also be described in terms of objects — after all object is DOM's middle name! In order to see how forms and inputs are arranged in the DOM, you can use JavaScript references to different parts of a form. The DOM references the form elements as a form array within a document. The input elements related to a form are array elements of the form with the first node being elements[0], using a zero-based counting system. Likewise, forms make up a zero-based array with the first form being forms[0]. (***Note:*** Both elements and forms are plural, even though <element> and <form> are singular.)

To help see the parts in a DOM arrangement, the following simple script (NameID.html in this chapter's folder at www.wiley.com/go/smashinghtml5) demonstrates different ways of referencing the same objects in a document with forms. The preferred manner is by object and property name. The different combinations are for demonstration only. It also uses several types of input as well.

```
<!DOCTYPE HTML>
<html>
<head>
<script type="text/javascript">
FormMaster=new Object();
FormMaster.resolveForm=function()
{
    alpha = document.motherShip.elements[0].value;
    beta = document.forms[0].secondInput.value;
    gamma = document.motherShip.thirdInput.value;
    delta = document.forms[0].elements[3].value;
    epsilon = document.motherShip.fifthInput.value;
    const cr="\n";
    message=alpha+cr+beta+cr+gamma+cr+delta+cr+epsilon;
    document.motherShip.output.value=message;
}
</script>
<style type="text/css">
h3 {
    font-family:"Arial Black", Gadget, sans-serif;
    color:#677E52;
}
body {
    font-family:Verdana, Geneva, sans-serif;
    color:#89725B;
    background-color:#B0CC99;
}
</style>
<meta http-equiv="Content-Type" content="text/html; charset=UTF-8">
<title>DOM and Forms</title>
</head>
<body >
<article>
  <header>
    <h3>DOM, the Form, and the Nodes</h3>
  </header>
  <form name=motherShip>
    <input type=number name=firstInput>
    Number<br>
    <input type=email name=secondInput>
```

```
       E-mail<br>
       <input type=text name=thirdInput>
       Text<br>
       <input type=text name=fourthInput>
       Text<br>
       <input type=url name=fifthInput>
       URL<br>
       <textarea cols="15" rows="6" name=output></textarea>
       <input type=button value="Send to DOM" onClick="FormMaster.resolveForm()">
     </form>
    </section>
  </article>
 </body>
</html>
```

When you test the program, enter the appropriate text and numbers and them click the button, Send to DOM. In the JavaScript program, notice that as long as either the element names or their proper element name (or node name) is used, the entered materials are sent to the text area that is used for an output display. Figure 14-3 shows the results you can expect to see.

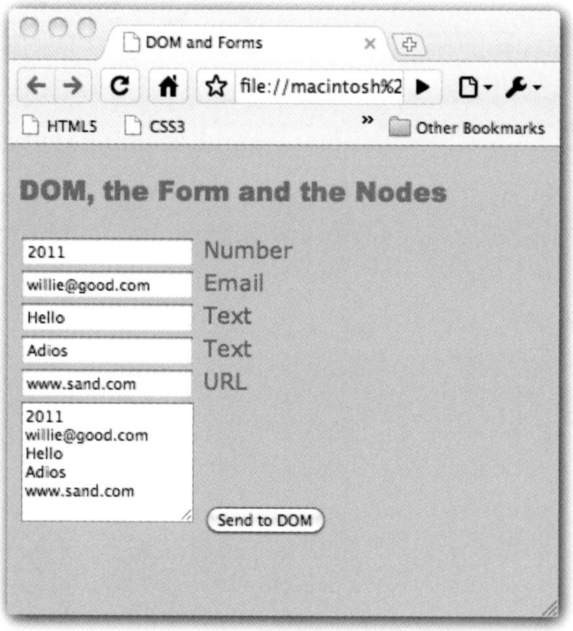

Figure 14-3: User entries displayed on the page.

The contents are retrieved through the DOM paths and placed into variables and then sent to the `<textarea>` element for display. Between the five elements a constant (`const cr="\n"`) places a control character to force a line feed.

THE MANY KINDS OF INPUT

One of the major new features of HTML5 is the addition of several different types of input attributes. Not only that, but the different input attributes work with mobile devices. For example, if you use an `email` or `url` input type, a special keyboard with dot (.) and dot-com (.com) appears when you begin to enter data into the form on some mobile devices.

Along with new types of input are additional attributes that affect how your page interacts with users. Of the 29 input attributes, 11 are new to HTML5. Like the new types of input, we want to see how to use these attributes. Because of so many types of input and other attributes, they've been gathered in two tables. Table 14.1 shows all the different type values you can use with the type attribute and Table 14.2 shows all the attributes, each with a short description.

Table 14.1   Type Values for the HTML5 Input Element

Type Value	Features	Type Value	Features
button	Action button	checkbox	Selection
color*	Color well	date*	Date picker
datetime*	Date picker	datetime-local*	Date picker
email	E-mail address	file	File upload
hidden	Not displayed	image	Image coordinates
month*	Date picker	number*	Numeric value
password	Hides password	radio	Selection
range*	Number range	reset	Clears entries
search*	Search word	submit	Send form data
tel	Telephone number	text	String value
time*	Date picker	url*	Web address
week*	Date picker		

*New to HTML5

At the time of this writing, not all these types have been implemented in the major browsers. However, because browsers keep working to fully implement the new HTML5 standards, don't be afraid to experiment on your own with different types. Now for the general input attributes (including type!) in Table 14.2.

Table 14.2   Input Element Attributes

Input Attribute	Features	Input Attribute	Features
accept	File type accepted	alt	Hint of file loading
autocomplete*	Complete typing	autofocus*	Sets focus to field
checked	Selected state	disabled	Unusable
form*	Set form id	formaction*	Form override
formenctype*	Form override	formmethod*	Form override
formnovalidate*	Form override	formtarget*	Form override
height*	Height in pixels	list*	Datalist suggest
max*	Maximum value	maxlength	Maximum length
min*	Minimum value	multiple	Multiple values
name	DOM name	pattern*	Regular expression
placeholder*	Disappears on entry	readonly	Cannot input
required*	Must fill	size	Num char visible
src	Source	step*	Number of steps
type	Input kind	value	Assigned value
width*	Width in pixels		

*New to HTML5

With all the different combinations of attributes and their values, the next several sections take a look at different groupings of form-related elements, attributes, and values in combinations. The first section covers using the datalist element with the list and form attributes. As with all the following sections, this one packs in as many features as possible while still focusing on the key features under discussion.

THE LIST ATTRIBUTE, THE URL TYPE, AND DATALISTS

One of the new attributes that can be used with forms is list. At the beginning of this chapter, I noted that Web pages should be smooth, interactive experiences for users. The less work that users have to put into an interactive form the better. The list attribute provides a list of suggested items in an input element, and users may select from the list or type in a response. However, the list attribute is actually a reference to a <datalist> tag elsewhere in the Web page. Further, if you place the <datalist> container within a <form> container, the <input> elements after the data list don't show up on the page. So, what you have to do is provide an id attribute in the <datalist> tag and assign it to the list attribute in the <input> tag. The data list is kept outside of the <form> container but is connected through the data list's id.

Displaying a choice in the alert window

A simple example sets up an input for users to type in or select a URL. After the URL is entered, the user presses a Submit button and an alert window pops up with the address. The following script (DataList.html in this chapter's folder at www.wiley.com/go/smashinghtml5) shows how to put all the parts together.

```
<!DOCTYPE HTML>
<html>
<head>
<script type="text/javascript">
FormMaster=new Object();
FormMaster.resolveForm=function()
{
    place=document.traveler.getURL.value;
    alert(place);
}
</script>
<style type="text/css">
h3 {
    font-family:"Arial Black", Gadget, sans-serif;
    color:#B9121B;
}
body {
    font-family:Verdana, Geneva, sans-serif;
    color:#4C1B1B;
    background-color:#FCFAE1;
}
</style>
<meta http-equiv="Content-Type" content="text/html; charset=UTF-8">
<title>List and Datalist</title>
</head>
<body >
<article>
  <header>
    <h3>The List and Datalist</h3>
  </header>
  <section>
    <datalist id=favoriteSites>
      <option value="http://www.smashingmagazine.com/" label="Smashing">
      <option value="http://www.sandlight.com/" label="Sandlight">
    </datalist>
  </section>
  <section>
    <form name=traveler>
      <label>Enter one of your favorite sites:</label>
      <br>
      <input type=url  list=favoriteSites name=getURL>
      <br>
      <input type=submit value="Show your URL" onClick="FormMaster.resolveForm()">
```

```
    </form>
   </section>
 </article>
</body>
</html>
```

In looking at the script, you may be wondering what the `label` attribute is doing in the `<option>` tag in the `<datalist>` container. There's no `label` attribute in either the `form` or `input` element (see Table 14.1 and Table 14.2). That's because the `label` attribute is not in the `form` or `input` elements, but in the `<option>` tag. Although that may seem obvious, when you open the page, you see not only the URLs but also the label in the URL input window. What's happening is that the `<input type=url>` tag holds a reference to the data list's options through the list attribute in the `input` element's markup.

At the time of testing, the data list shows up in Opera using either Windows 7 or Mac OS X.

In the top-left panel, you can see the selections available in the data list (along with a label for each). Once the user makes a selection, it appears in the input window as shown in the top-right panel. Finally, in the bottom panel, you can see that it's passed to the JavaScript function that displays it in an alert window. (Note that the Opera alert window also displays the domain.)

The important point about this process is that users don't have to type in URLs. Everyone who has ever typed in a URL has made a typo at some point. By using the data list to help out, not only is the suggested URL more likely to be selected, but it's easier for the user.

Datalist elements on mobile devices and URL keyboards

Tests of the application on the Mini Opera browser on an iPhone revealed that the data list did not appear. Further testing with the mobile version of the Safari browser showed that it did not work with Safari yet either.

However, during these tests, a unique keyboard for the new `url` and `email` type of input elements was revealed. The mobile Safari browser recognizes an input form typed as `url` and `email` and when used it displays a keyboard that includes both a dot (`.`) and dot-com (`.com`) key, plus some other keys commonly used with URLs and e-mail addresses. Figure 14-4 shows the Safari mobile (left) and Mini Opera (right) browsers side-by-side displaying the data list program on the same iPhone. If you look carefully, you can see the difference.

The importance of a mobile browser recognizing that the input expects a URL or e-mail address is that it considers the user. With the special keyboard, users don't have to switch between the numeric/symbol keyboard and the alphabetic one as much.

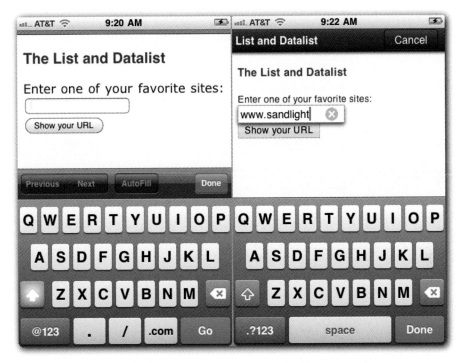

Figure 14-4: Special mobile device keyboard for URL form (left) and standard mobile keyboard (right).

RADIO BUTTONS AND CHECK BOXES: EASY-TO-SELECT INPUT ELEMENTS

If you're using radio buttons and check boxes with external programs accessing databases or doing some other kind of server-side operation, it's very easy on the HTML5 side. Just use a Submit button and everything gets sent to the server side for those programs to handle. (I show you how to do that using a version of this example in Chapter 16.)

Because this next Web script bounces the input back to a `<textarea>` object on the page, the entered data had to be checked using JavaScript with a little loop to first see whether the `checked` attribute was `true` or `false`. If the item has been checked, it then adds the value to a `FormMaster` property named `this.countVal`. (It's like a variable, but in keeping with DOM-like programming, it's assigned to an object.) Once that's finished, it sends only those checked to the output. The following (rather long) Web script (`RadioCheck.html` in this chapter's folder at `www.wiley.com/go/smashinghtml5`) does that.

```
<!DOCTYPE HTML>
<html>
<head>
<script type="text/javascript">
FormMaster=new Object();
FormMaster.resolveForm=function()
{
    this.countVal="";
```

```
        this.topCount=document.checkRadio.length-2;
         for(var count=0;count < this.topCount;count++)
        if(document.checkRadio.elements[count].checked)
        {
            this.countVal+=document.checkRadio.elements[count].value+"\n";
        }
        document.checkRadio.outNow.value=this.countVal;
    }
</script>
<style type="text/css">
/* 735840,733119,BF5D39,352D1B,C0B787 */
body {
    background-color:#C0B787;
    color:#733119;
    font-family:Verdana, Geneva, sans-serif;
    font-size:12px;
    margin-left:20px;
}
h1 {
    font-family:"Arial Black", Gadget, sans-serif;
    color:#733119;
}
h2 {
    color:#BF5D39;
}
h3 {
    color:#BF5D39;
}
#dataEntry {
    display:table;
}
#lang {
    display:table-cell;
    width:200px;
}
#out {
    display:table-cell;
    width:300px;
}
aside {
    display:table-cell;
    width:250px;
}
</style>
<meta http-equiv="Content-Type" content="text/html; charset=UTF-8">
<title>Click-2-Choose</title>
</head>
<body>
<article>
  <header>
    <h1>E-Z Selections</h1>
```

```
</header>
<div id="dataEntry">
<div id="lang">
<section>
<h2>Web Languages</h2>
<form name=checkRadio>
  <label>
     <input type=checkbox name=html value="HTML5" checked>
     HTML5</label><br>
  <label>
     <input type=checkbox name=css value="CSS3">
     CSS3</label><br>
  <label>
     <input type=checkbox name=js value="JavaScript">
     JavaScript</label><br>
  <label>
     <input type=checkbox name=php value="PHP">
     PHP5</label><br>
  <label>
     <input type=checkbox name=asp value="ASP.NET">
     ASP.NET</label><br>
  <label>
     <input type=checkbox name=action value="ActionScript 3.0">
     ActionScript 3.0</label>
  </section>
  </div>
  <section>
    <aside>
       <h2>Specialization</h2>
       <fieldset>
         <legend> Web Focus </legend>
         <label>
           <input type=radio name=work value="Graphic Design">
           Design </label><br>
         <label>
           <input type=radio name=work value="Interface Design">
           Iterface Design </label><br>
         <label>
           <input type=radio name=work value="Front End">
           Front End Development </label><br>
         <label>
           <input type=radio name=work value="Back End">
           Back End Development </label><br>
       </fieldset>
    </aside>
  </section>
  </div>
  <section>
    <div id="out">
      <fieldset>
        <legend>Output Window</legend>
```

```
            <textarea name=outNow rows=10 cols=40 ></textarea>
          </fieldset>
        </div>
      </section>
      <section>
        <div>
          <p>
            <input type=button name=getEm value="Relay your selections"
   onClick="FormMaster.resolveForm()">
          </p>
        </div>
      </section>
    </form>
    </div>
</article>
</body>
</html>
```

Although that's a bit long, most of it was formatting so that it looks halfway decent and it's easy for users. The `<fieldset>` tag was used to highlight a group of buttons and to encapsulate the output window. It's a great tag to use when you want to group elements. The `<legend>` tag allows you to place a label in the enclosing rectangle around the field set. Figure 14-5 shows what you can expect to see when you load the page.

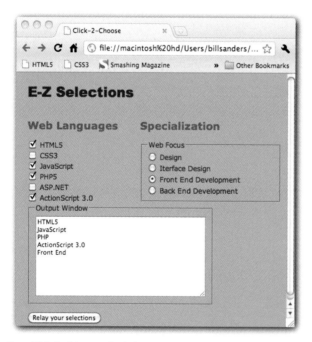

Figure 14-5: Check boxes and radio buttons.

When you first run it, you see that the HTML5 has already been selected. That's because the `checked` attribute is added to the tag. It's a Boolean, but you don't have to assign it a `true` or `false`. After the page loads, see what happens when you click it.

What you see in the output window is that all the values that were assigned to the selected radio buttons and check boxes. In more practical implementations, that same data would be passed to and stored in a database.

DATE PICKER

The last input attribute we have space to cover in this chapter is simple to implement but has impressive results. The new date attribute for the `input` element is powerful and easy to include in a form. Several new date and time attributes have been added to the input element, but only the date attribute itself is shown. The following program (`Pickers.html` in this chapter's folder at `www.wiley.com/go/smashinghtml5`) shows you how to set it up and use it to send information.

```
<!DOCTYPE HTML>
<html>
<head>
<script type="text/javascript">
FormMaster=new Object();
FormMaster.resolveForm=function()
{
     alert(document.calendar.dateNow.value);
}
</script>
<meta http-equiv="Content-Type" content="text/html; charset=UTF-8">
<title>Date</title>
</head>
<body >
<form name=calendar>
  <input name=dateNow type="date" onChange="FormMaster.resolveForm()">
</form>
</body>
</html>
```

With just that little markup in the `form` container, you're able to build a complete calendar. You can use the `onChange` event handler to capture the date selected from the calendar. Figure 14-6 shows the application in an Opera browser (the only one found to work so far with this new input attribute) in a Windows 7 environment.

In this particular implementation, as soon as the user makes a selection, the alert window opens and shows the selected date, as shown in Figure 14-7.

The purpose is to show how easy it is to pass the selected date value. Such data could be stored in a database to make online reservations.

Figure 14-6: A simple markup provides a calendar online.

Figure 14-7: Passing the date value to JavaScript.

The little window behind the alert window shows the selected date in a small window. (The little window shows the selected date with no other required programming.) The importance of this new HTML5 feature lies in the ease with which users can select a date. If you've ever worked with a similar tool in making airline or hotel reservations online, you know how valuable it is. The only problem at the time of this writing is that no other HTML5 browser other than Opera includes it.

TAKE THE WHEEL

The major takeaway from this chapter is how to use the DOM to access form information. The basic format is:

```
document.form.element.value
```

You need to use JavaScript (at this stage) to access data that would generally be passed on to a server-side program like PHP, ColdFusion, or ASP.NET. However, to simulate that, the examples in this chapter have used a button input type to fire a JavaScript program that sends the results to a <textarea> where you can see what would normally be sent to the back end for processing. Here's the challenge:

- Devise an online store that sells a line of products (at least five) or delivers services (again, at least five). Examples would be a computer store or a Web design service.
- Design an interface where users enter their name, e-mail, URL, address, city, state, zip code, and a username and password, with as little effort on their part as possible. To make it bulletproof, test it with someone who's never seen it before.
- Users then select several products or services (again with as little effort on their part as possible).
- The selected offerings are then displayed in a <textarea> with their corresponding individual prices along with appropriate tax.
- The program also generates a shipping label. It will just be displayed in the <textarea> — not printed out.

303

The more form elements and attributes that you can use that were not discussed in the chapter, the better.

15

EMBEDDING OBJECTS AND STORING INFORMATION

FOR YEARS, USERS have been able to do some pretty remarkable things on the Web thanks to different kinds of plug-ins loaded inside the browser. Generally speaking, two key plug-ins are installed with most browsers: Adobe Flash Player and Java.

Some of the new HTML5 features work best in concert with either special plug-ins directly related to the new feature or through a URL that serves the new feature. HTML5 has a number of such objects, and one of the most interesting is the geolocation object. So, it'll be the first to examine before looking at how Java and Flash work with HTML5.

GEOLOCATION

The `geolocation` object is part of the `navigation` object in the HTML5 DOM. It's a means of finding your location, more or less. In several tests, it successfully located the ballpark of my location. The most important attributes of the `geolocation` object are the `latitude` and `longitude` attributes. That's because, with those values, you can load a map of your general location.

Creating an HTML page that shows users their latitude and longitude is fine, but HTML5 browsers are also able to load a map into their Web sites using Google Maps. The URL for this capability is:

```
" http://maps.google.com/maps?hl=en&ie=UTF8&ll= " + latitude + ", " + longitude +
  "&spn=0.054166,0.110378&z=13&output=embed"
```

The `latitude` and `longitude` variables contain coordinate values. So, the trick is to locate the latitude and longitude values to insert where they're needed.

FINDING LATITUDE AND LONGITUDE

Getting these values requires pretty straight JavaScript from your browser — on your mobile device or computer. Here's the basic code:

```
navigator.geolocation.getCurrentPosition(someFunction);
```

To filter out browsers that do not recognize the `geolocation` object, use a simple trap:

```
if (navigator.geolocation)
{
navigator.geolocation.getCurrentPosition(someFunction);
}
else
{
        alert("Geolocation not recognized")
}
```

This tells users whether their browsers even recognize `geolocation`.

The function called to get the position information makes the call but is expected to include a parameter that will store the actual information about location. Following the practice of using objects and methods the call is made:

```
...
navigator.geolocation.getCurrentPosition(LocationMaster.lookUpPosition);
...
```

This, in turn, gets the method that returns the requested values:

```
LocationMaster=new Object();
LocationMaster.lookUpPosition=function(position)
{
     this.latNow=position.coords.latitude;
     this.longNow=position.coords.longitude;
...
```

Note that the `position` parameter is like a variable that will store the latitude and longitude values. It is not a property of the geolocation object — `cords.latitude` and `cords.longitude` are the properties. (The name position could be any name we wanted — Rumpelstiltskin would've worked, but position is more descriptive.)

Once the values are assigned to the parameter object, they become part of the `Location-Master` object using the `this` keyword. The property names — `latNow` and `longNow` — store the values like a variable. The only difference is that they're part of an object.

GETTING THE MAP

The only thing that the HTML5 page working with JavaScript does is to get the coordinates. Getting the map, then, is simply a matter of inserting those values into the map request. So, to finish up the method, the program uses the following line:

```
document.getElementById("mapHolder").src = "http://maps.google.com/
  maps?hl=en&ie=UTF8&ll=" + this.latNow + "," + this.longNow + "&spn=0.054166,0.11037
  8&z=13&output=embed";
```

You find a new method in the HTML5 DOM core: `getElementById`. In this case, the ID is that of an `iFrame` element. Then the map is the source object — just like an image is loaded through the source identification:

```
<img src="myImage.jpg">
```

The only difference is that the place where the map is loaded is specified by the `iFrame` ID instead of by the page by default.

Placing the map on the Web page

Any other loading after the page has loaded can't be slipped in just anywhere in the page. The `<iframe>` can be a target apart from the main document. Using the `<iframe>` without any of its attributes specified produces a relatively small viewing window. However, the idea is to see how few tags and how little JavaScript code I can use to get the map displayed on the page.

Putting it all together in a simple page

I've tested all the major browsers on both Windows 7 and Macintosh OS X, and the following (`MiniGeoLoc.html` in this chapter's folder at `www.wiley.com/go/smashinghtml5`) represents a simple starting point for a page that displays a map near the originating user.

```
<!DOCTYPE html >
<html>
    <head>
<style type="text/css">
/* BF7F6C,FFDDAE,B59D7B,40372B,E6C79C */
    body {
    font-family:Verdana, Geneva, sans-serif;
    color:#40372B;
    background-color:#FFDDAE;
}
h3 {
    font-family:Tahoma, Geneva, sans-serif;
    color:#BF7F6C;
}
</style>
<script>
    LocationMaster=new Object();
    LocationMaster.lookUpPosition=function(position)
    {
        this.latNow=position.coords.latitude;
        this.longNow=position.coords.longitude;

        document.getElementById("mapHolder").src = "http://maps.google.com/
 maps?hl=en&ie=UTF8&ll=" + this.latNow + "," + this.longNow + "&spn=0.054166,0.11037
 8&z=13&output=embed";
    }

        if (navigator.geolocation)
          {
            navigator.geolocation.getCurrentPosition(LocationMaster.lookUpPosition);
          }
          else
          {
            alert("Try a different HTML5 browser. This one is not working with
 geolocation.");
          }
    </script>
<title>Minimum Map</title>
    </head>
    <body>
    <article>
      <header>
        <h3>Your Location</h3>
      </header>
      <section>
        <iframe id="mapHolder"> </iframe>
      </section>
      <section>
        <p> This example of using geolocation and Google Maps is very simple. It has
 been tested in the major browsers and mobile browsers. </p>
      </section>
```

```
        </article>
    </body>
</html>
```

When you test this Web page, try it first using the latest Firefox browser. Then try it out with Google Chrome and Opera. With Safari, which recognizes the `geolocation` object, I was unable to load the map into the `iframe`. Ironically, when tested on the mobile Safari browser on an iPhone, it worked fine. (More about that in a second.) Figure 15-1 shows the program on all browsers except Safari and Internet Explorer running on Windows 7.

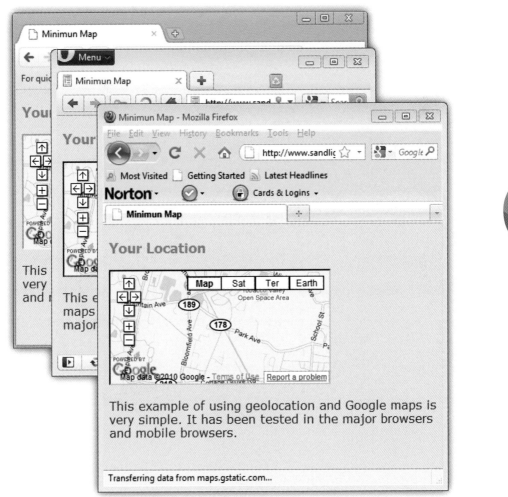

Figure 15-1: Geolocation used to find longitude and latitude for Google Maps.

Figure 15-1 shows the Web page loaded with the map in Firefox, Chrome, and Opera. You can drag the map around the `iframe` with the mouse and on Safari and Perfect browsers on an iPhone, with your fingers. However, on the mobile browsers, the `iframe` and image were extended by dragging downward.

Adapting the page for mobile viewing

To make it more practical for mobile users, I made some program adjustments to change the orientation of the map by changing the `<iframe>` to the following:

```
<section>
<iframe id="mapHolder" width="240" height="320"> </iframe>
</section>
```

Now on a vertical orientation, the map was easier to read. Figure 15-2 shows the program on an iPhone in the Perfect (left) and Safari (right) browsers. Near the bottom of the page, directions provide mobile users with instructions for enlarging the image without dragging the map out of the `iframe`.

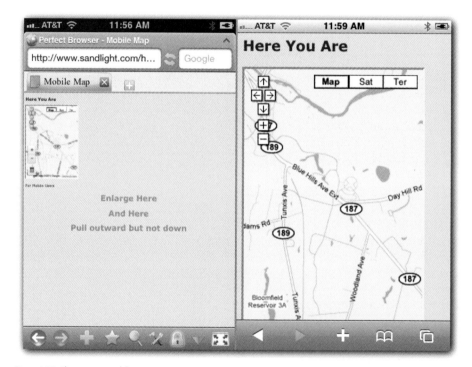

Figure 15-2: The map in a mobile environment.

Figure 15-2 illustrates that by pulling the page outward and away from the map (left panel), mobile users can adjust the map so that they can easily read it (right panel).

WORKING WITH THE GEOLOCATION PROPERTIES AND THE GOOGLE EARTH PLUG-IN

Experimenting with the geolocation object can be a lot of fun and very informative. The following is a full list of its properties:

- `latitude`: Geographic coordinates in decimal degrees
- `longitude`: Geographic coordinates in decimal degrees
- `altitude`: Height in meters
- `accuracy`: Accuracy levels of latitude and longitude coordinates in meters
- `altitudeaccuracy`: Accuracy levels of altitude in meters
- `heading`: Direction of travel of hosting device in degrees (most relevant to a mobile device)
- `speed`: Current ground speed of hosting device in meters/second (most relevant to a mobile device)

If you have a mobile device, you can experiment with different headings and speed — with someone else driving! All the `geolocation` properties can be sent to a form for display if you want. If used with a mobile device, you'll need either an open-socket server or frequent browser/page refreshing.

A final aspect of `geolocation` is the use of the Google Earth plug-in. Figure 15-3 shows a revised version of the basic Web page with the plug-in that can generate a 3-D view of the mapped area.

You can update the sample Web page to the same dimensions by giving the `<iframe>` tag the following attributes: `width=500 height=400`. Then click the Earth option at the top of the map area. If your browser has the plug-in, it will show the 3-D view. Otherwise, it'll offer you a chance to download the plug-in and install it on your browser.

STORAGE IN HTML5

Other than cookies that store data on the user's browser, when you think about storage, typically a database and other programs like PHP and ASP.NET come to mind. However, the HTML5 DOM now has a storage object that can be used in four contexts:

- Session storage
- Global storage
- Local storage
- Database storage

Not all browsers support all these storage contexts, but as browsers are continuously updated to include HTML5, they include more contexts. At the time of this writing, Safari, Chrome, and Opera supported all the contexts except global storage; Firefox supported them all except database storage.

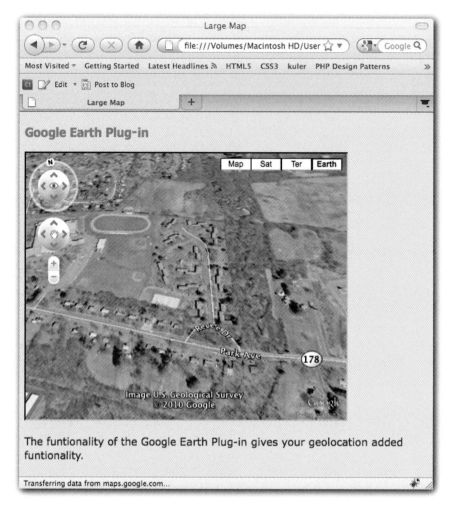

Figure 15-3: A 3-D view of the map area with the Google Earth browser plug-in.

All storage is done in key/value pairs. The key is an identifier for a given value. (The key is something like a variable with a label and an assigned value.) The next two sections explain how to work with session and local storage. Global and database storage are less universally implemented at this time, so I'm setting them aside.

SESSION STORAGE

Session storage allows users to store data for a single Web page as long as that Web page is being viewed. As soon as the user leaves the page, all stored data is lost. For interactive games, calculators, and any other kind of page that needs temporary storage while the page is viewed, you can use session storage.

To get started, you'll need to take look at the setters and getters of session storage. Here's the basic format for setting (storing) a value:

```
sessionStorage.setItem("keyName", value );
```

The `key` must be a string, while the `value` can be any acceptable data type — number, text, Boolean, object, function. The following represent some valid data assignments:

```
this.myKey="secondKey"; //Key name assigned to property
function eek()           //A function with a return value
{
     return "eeeek!";
}
jill="My name is Jill"; //A variable
//Assign values to keys
sessionStorage.setItem("firstKey",88);       //A number (numeric literal)
sessionStorage.setItem(this.myKey,true );    //Boolean
sessionStorage.setItem("thirdKey",eek() ); //Function
sessionStorage.setItem("fourthKey","My name is Jack" ); //String literal
sessionStorage.setItem("fifthKey",jill );   //Variable
```

As you can see, you can use variables for both keys and their values. As long as the variable (or property) is a string, it can be used as a `key` — you could even use a function that returns a string as a key. A value can be a string or nonstring.

Once you have stored data, you need a way to retrieve it with a getter method. The following shows the general format for getting the stored data — you have to know the `key` name for every value you want to retrieve.

```
sessionStorage.getItem("keyName");
```

You can think of the `key` name in the same way as you do a variable name. If you know the variable name, you can find its value. Key names work the same way.

This next program (`SessionStore.html` in this chapter's folder at `www.wiley.com/go/smashinghtml5`) provides a simple illustration of how to work with session storage. You'll probably be reminded of working with variables because the values are extant only as long as you don't change the page.

```
<!DOCTYPE HTML>
<html>
<head>
<script type="text/javascript">
StorageMaster=new Object();
//Set values
StorageMaster.setPositions=function()
{
     sessionStorage.setItem("firstBase",document.players.firstBase.value );
     sessionStorage.setItem("secondBase",document.players.secondBase.value );
     sessionStorage.setItem("thirdBase",document.players.thirdBase.value );
}
//Get values
```

```
StorageMaster.getFirst=function()
{
     playerName=sessionStorage.getItem("firstBase");
     alert(playerName + " is on first");
}
StorageMaster.getSecond=function()
{
     playerName=sessionStorage.getItem("secondBase");
     alert(playerName +" is playing second");
}
StorageMaster.getThird=function()
{
     playerName=sessionStorage.getItem("thirdBase");
     alert(playerName+ " is assigned to third");
}
</script>
<style type="text/css">
body {
     background-color:#EBD4B2;
     color:#273A4B;
     font-family:Verdana, Geneva, sans-serif;
}
h2 {
     background-color:#273A4B;
     color:#D49756;
     text-align:center;
}
h3 {
     color:#323F14;
}
fieldset {
     color:#790007
}
#playerTable {
     display:table;
}
#getPlayer {
     display:table-cell;
     width:250px;
}
</style>
<meta http-equiv="Content-Type" content="text/html; charset=UTF-8">
<title>Storage</title>
</head>

<body>
<article>
<header>
  <hgroup>
     <h2>Baseball Manager</h2>
     <h3>Assign Players:</h3>
```

```
    </hgroup>
  </header>
<section>
<form name=players>
  <input type=text name=firstBase placeholder="First base">
   First Base<br>
  <input type=text name=secondBase placeholder="Second base">
   Second Base<br>
  <input type=text name=thirdBase placeholder="Third base">
   Third Base<br>
  <input type=button onClick="StorageMaster.setPositions()" value="Assign
  Positions">
  </section>
  <br>
  <div ID="playerTable">
  <section ID="getPlayer">
  <fieldset>
    <legend>Who's Playing What?</legend>
    <input type=button onClick="StorageMaster.getFirst()" value="Who's on First?">
    <br>
    <input type=button onClick="StorageMaster.getSecond()" value="Who's on Second?">
    <br>
    <input type=button onClick="StorageMaster.getThird()" value="Who's on Third?">
    <br>
  </fieldset>
</form>
</section>
</div>
</body>
</html>
```

When you first load the page, you'll see a new HTML5 attribute in all the text input windows — these are place holders. In the code, they look like this:

```
<input type=text name=thirdBase placeholder="Third base">
```

As soon as the user begins to type in a value, they immediately disappear. So, go ahead and test it, filling in the three text windows, and then click the Assign Positions button. That sets the values in the session storage.

To retrieve the stored data, just click any of the three buttons in the Who's Playing What? box. Figure 15-4 shows what you can expect to see.

If you try to get the stored data back before clicking the Assign Positions button, you'll get a null value in the alert window. If you leave the page and return, you'll also get null values until you're reassigned the positions.

315

Figure 15-4: Stored data returned in an alert window.

LOCAL STORAGE

The main difference between session storage and local storage is that local storage is persistent. Users can leave the site, turn off their computers, come back the next day, and the data are still there. Local storage works very much like cookies, but there are certain differences that are important:

- Cookies allow very little storage space; local storage allows far more.
- Cookies are retransmitted automatically with every request to the server, and local storage is not — which means local storage is far less work for the server and browser. Local storage is transmitted on a request only.

You'll find that `localStorage` and `sessionStorage` use the same getter/setter methods, so once you know one, you know the other. However, you can set a value using `localStorage`, turn off your computer, go play a game of football, come home, turn on the computer, and your data is still stored on your computer. The following example (`LocalStorage.html` in this chapter's folder at `www.wiley.com/go/smashinghtml5`) shows how to store, retrieve, and clear `localStorage` data.

```
<!DOCTYPE HTML>
<html>
<head>
<script type="text/javascript">
```

```
StorageMaster=new Object();
//Set values
StorageMaster.setRegistration=function()
{
    this.hobbyNow="";
    this.topCount=document.interest.elements.length;
    for(var count=0;count < this.topCount;count++)
    {
        if(document.interest.elements[count].checked)
        {
            this.hobbyNow=document.interest.hobby[count-1].value;
        }
    }
    localStorage.setItem("uName",document.interest.userName.value);
    localStorage.setItem("uHobby",this.hobbyNow);
    localStorage.setItem("uState",document.interest.resState.value);
}
//Get values
StorageMaster.getReg=function()
{
    userProfile="User Profile:\n";
    nameNow=localStorage.getItem("uName")+"\n";
    hobbyNow=localStorage.getItem("uHobby")+"\n";
    stateNow=localStorage.getItem("uState")+"\n";
    fileLength=localStorage.length + " profile items";
    this.profile=userProfile+nameNow+hobbyNow+stateNow+fileLength;
    document.getElementById("profile").innerHTML = this.profile;
}
StorageMaster.clearReg=function()
{
    localStorage.clear();
    alert("Local storage cleared");
}
</script>
<style type="text/css">
/*962D3E,343642,979C9C,F2EBC7,348899 */
body {
    background-color:#F2EBC7;
    color:#962D3E;
    font-family:Verdana, Geneva, sans-serif;
}
h2 {
    color:#979C9C;
}
fieldset {
    color:#348899;
}
#hobbyTable {
    display:table;
}
#getHobby {
```

```
            display:table-cell;
            width:275px;
      }
      #profile {
            display:table-cell;
            background-color: #979C9C;
            padding: 3px;
            width:150px;
            font-family:"Trebuchet MS", Arial, Helvetica, sans-serif;
            font-size:14px;
      }
</style>
<meta http-equiv="Content-Type" content="text/html; charset=UTF-8">
<title>Storage</title>
</head>
<body>
<article>
<header>
  <h2>Hobby Registration</h2>
</header>
<section>
  <form name="interest">
      <input name=userName placeholder="Name please">
       Name<br>
      <div id="hobbyTable">
        <section id="getHobby">
          <fieldset>
            <legend>What's Your Favorite Hobby?</legend>
            <label>
              <input type=radio name=hobby value="travel">
              Travel</label>
            <br>
            <label>
              <input type=radio name=hobby  value="reading">
              Reading</label>
            <br>
            <label>
              <input type=radio name=hobby value="theater">
              Theater</label>
            <br>
            <label>
              <input type=radio name=hobby value="ballet">
              Ballet</label>
            <br>
            <label>
              <input type=radio name=hobby value="monster trucks">
              Monster Truck Rallies</label>
            <br>
          </fieldset>
        </section>
      </div>
      <input type=text name=resState placeholder="Your state of residence">
```

```
     State<br>
    <input type=button onClick="StorageMaster.setRegistration()" value="Register">
    <input type=button onClick="StorageMaster.getReg()" value="Find Info">
    <input type=button onClick="StorageMaster.clearReg()" value="Clear Data">
  </form>
</section>
<br>
<pre id="profile"></pre>
</body>
</html>
```

One of the features added to this example is the use of radio buttons to pass data to be stored. Radio buttons are important because they make it easy for users to make a choice. It does take a bit more work to get the correct data from radio buttons and check boxes, but it reflects the Web truism that the more work the developer does, the less work users have to do.

Another feature of local storage is that it's related to the browser. Each browser has its own storage. So, if you store the data using a Safari browser, a Chrome browser cannot access that data. Figure 15-5 shows the page loaded in a Chrome browser that has stored data using local storage. However, if the same program in a different browser (Opera, for example) attempts to retrieve the data, it shows it to be null.

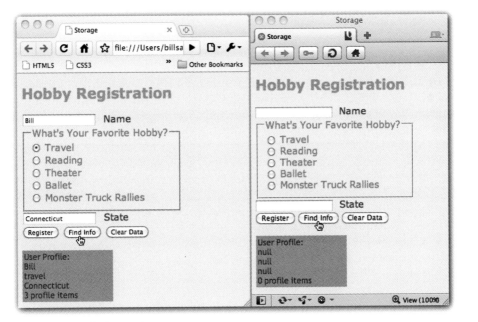

Figure 15-5: Accessing local storage data.

You may also notice that when you first load the program, you don't see the output window. Instead, you see a gray line beneath the buttons. As soon as you click the Find Info button, the information appears where the gray line was. A little CSS3 and HTML5 DOM work does the trick. First, in the CSS3, set up the ID:

```
#profile {
    display:table-cell;
    background-color: #979C9C;
    padding: 3px;
    width:150px;
    font-family:"Trebuchet MS", Arial, Helvetica, sans-serif;
    font-size:14px;
}
```

Using the JavaScript line,

```
document.getElementById("profile").innerHTML = this.profile;
```

the information stored in `this.profile` was sent to the Web page where the following tag was placed:

```
<pre id="profile"></pre>
```

Prior to HTML5, dynamically sending data to a Web page without reloading the page was far more complex. However, for certain programs like Adobe Flash CS5, it's quite easy, as the next section explains.

ADDING AND ADJUSTING OBJECTS IN HTML5 WEB PAGES

When HTML was first released, it couldn't do much, so developers began using programs like Java and Flash, which provided the functionality that HTML could not. Much of that is no longer true with HTML5, but even though HTML5 can do far more than earlier versions of HTML, later versions of Flash and Java can still do far more.

Much can be said about the relative merits of Adobe Flash CS5 (the latest version of Flash as of this writing) and HTML5, but for the foreseeable future, they'll most likely be working together, despite the fact that the Apple iPhone and iPad do not support the Flash Player. Besides the fact that Flash can do a great deal, it has also provided consistency between different platforms and browsers. So, even if different browser makers had different versions of the HTML DOM and different ideas about what was the best CSS and JavaScript implementation, the Flash plug-in was consistent across all browsers and platforms. So, when designers and developers used Flash, they were assured of a consistent presentation.

ADDING AN OBJECT

To give you an idea of how to embed an object in HTML5, I created a simple animation of a shooting star in Flash CS5. Figure 15-6 shows the little animation in the design window.

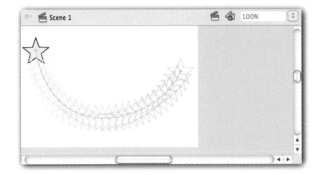

Figure 15-6: A Flash animation.

You can place the animation into a Web page in a number of different ways, but the easiest is to publish it in Flash, which automatically generates a Web page with a reference to the binary file in a `.swf` format. In browsers with Flash plug-ins, which is virtually all browsers — they ship (or download) with the Flash plug-in included — the following code (`ShootingStar.html` in this chapter's folder at `www.wiley.com/go/smashinghtml5`) shows the object in an HTML5 wrapper.

```
<!DOCTYPE HTML>
<html>
    <head>
        <title>ShootingStar</title>
        <meta http-equiv="Content-Type" content="text/html; charset=UTF-8">
        <style type="text/css" media="screen">
        html, body { height:100%; background-color: #ffffff;}
        body { margin:0; padding:0; overflow:hidden; }
        #flashContent { width:100%; height:100%; }
        </style>
    </head>
    <body>
        <div id="flashContent">
            <object classid="clsid:d27cdb6e-ae6d-11cf-96b8-444553540000"
 width="300" height="200" id="ShootingStar" align="middle">
                <param name="movie" value="ShootingStar.swf" />
                <param name="quality" value="high" />
                <param name="bgcolor" value="#ffffff" />
                <param name="play" value="true" />
                <param name="loop" value="true" />
                <param name="wmode" value="window" />
                <param name="scale" value="showall" />
                <param name="menu" value="true" />
                <param name="devicefont" value="false" />
                <param name="salign" value="" />
                <param name="allowScriptAccess" value="sameDomain" />
                <!--[if !IE]>-->
                <object type="application/x-shockwave-flash" data="ShootingStar.
```

```
swf" width="300" height="200">
                    <param name="movie" value="ShootingStar.swf" />
                    <param name="quality" value="high" />
                    <param name="bgcolor" value="#ffffff" />
                    <param name="play" value="true" />
                    <param name="loop" value="true" />
                    <param name="wmode" value="window" />
                    <param name="scale" value="showall" />
                    <param name="menu" value="true" />
                    <param name="devicefont" value="false" />
                    <param name="salign" value="" />
                    <param name="allowScriptAccess" value="sameDomain" />
            <!--<![endif]-->
                <a href="http://www.adobe.com/go/getflash">
                    <img src="http://www.adobe.com/images/shared/download_
    buttons/get_flash_player.gif" alt="Get Adobe Flash player" />
                </a>
            <!--[if !IE]>--->
            </object>
            <!--<![endif]-->
        </object>
      </div>
    </body>
</html>
```

ADJUSTING AN OBJECT

The key HTML5 element is the `<object>` tag. Several parameters have been included, but all of them can be changed to better suit your site. For example, the background color is set to white (#ffffff), and by typing in a different background color, you can match it to your site. Likewise, you can change the CSS and anything else you want.

Another program variously called Flex and Flash Builder also generates .swf files. Using a very powerful language called ActionScript 3.0, developers are able to create programs with the same depth and power as established programs like Java and C++. However, all the HTML5 developer has to do is add the .swf file with his own code or code generated automatically by Flash and Flash Builder.

TAKE THE WHEEL

I think you're going to like this challenge. It involves both the new geolocation and localStorage objects in HTML5. As you saw in this chapter, all you need to place a Google Map on your Web page is the value of the location's latitude and longitude. The geolocation object generates those values for you in HTML5 in your current position. If you have a mobile device, you can generate that information in several different locations. Alternatively, you can go to an online mapping program, enter an address, and the mapping program will do it for you. So here's the challenge:

- Get the longitude and latitude for five different locations.
- Enter the longitude and latitude values into a `localStorage` object.
- Set up five buttons that will call a JavaScript program that will load five maps when requested.

Basically, you'll be making a Web page that loads maps of anyplace you choose. You shouldn't need any more JavaScript than the little that has been covered in this chapter.

16 CATCHING INTERACTIVE DATA

ONE OF THE most powerful and practical aspects of working with Web programming is the ability to store and retrieve data. HTML5 has some capacity for such data storage and retrieval; however, as Chapter 15 showed, any data that is stored is going to be related to an individual's browser. As you saw in Chapter 15, for the time-being, all the browsers aren't exactly playing nicely together in the sandbox when it comes to data storage. Plus, the data are stored on the user's computer, and while that's useful for some things, such as recognizing a user's interests when returning to a Web site, every user has some kind of local storage. How do you store data (like a blog comment) so that *anyone* with a browser can access it?

To give you a sense of what this chapter introduces, consider something simple you can do on the Web: maintain and comment on a blog. Suppose you have a blog that discusses HTML5. Once or twice a week, you sit down and write a blog entry about HTML5. Now suppose you attract a big audience of blog readers, and these readers comment on your entries. How do you store and retrieve your comments and those made by others? One way you could do it would be to rewrite your Web site for every entry and comment. But that would be so awkward that not much blogging would take place.

Blogs are set up using different server-side languages, like PHP. Thord Daniel Hedengren's *Smashing WordPress: Beyond the Blog* (Wiley) explains how to optimize using WordPress's blog software. Much of the discussion is how to use PHP to tweak your blog. However, besides working with blogs, PHP can store and retrieve database data from servers for anything from an online store to members of a football team. Unlike local storage, when data are stored using PHP, they can be retrieved using PHP by anyone anywhere. (Those people don't have to come by your house and use your browser on your computer to retrieve data you've stored using HTML5 — and thank your lucky stars for that.) Best of all, if you want to make a change, all you have to do is to type in the information, and it's sent to a database where the changes are reflected in the Web page. In this chapter, I introduce you to one server-side language, PHP. The focus is on getting started and doing some things with HTML5 that you can't do without PHP.

SERVER-SIDE LANGUAGES AND HTML5

Using HTML5, all of the processing is done on the client — your browser on your computer. In a larger context, that's called client-side processing. Your browser parses the HTML5 tags and displays the Web page that it retrieves from a Web server. All the Web server does is serve you the HTML, and your browser does the rest.

Server-side processing is different. The server — a PHP server, in this case — processes the information it gets from different sources and sends HTML to your browser to show on your computer. The big difference is that the server can interact with other kinds of data that your browser cannot. For example, it can interact with a database that stores data that anyone can send in via the Web.

Going back to our example of rewriting your Web page every time you want to make a blog entry or comment, that's pretty much what PHP does. Imagine that PHP is a little (overcaffeinated) mouse that lives in the server and is really good at writing HTML5. Whenever you make a blog entry or someone posts a comment, the mouse quickly rewrites the HTML5 so that your Web page reflects the changes. That's how PHP works. Figure 16-1 shows an illustration of the process.

Client-side processing

Server-side processing

Figure 16-1: Client- and server-side processing.

In Figure 16-1, the real work is between storage and the server. The information in storage has to be configured in a way that it can be read by your browser. And that's what PHP does — it takes the stored information (sent in as a blog entry, for example) and sends it back as HTML5.

SETTING UP PHP ON YOUR COMPUTER (WHICH THINKS IT'S A SERVER)

You can access PHP in three ways:

- Sign up for a hosting service.
- Download and install a server and PHP on your computer.
- If you have Mac OS X, it's already on your computer — just configure it.

Two of these methods involve setting up a server on your computer, and the third depends on having a hosting service. The easiest thing to do is to sign up with a hosting service with PHP. Then you just load your PHP files as you would a Web page. A hosting service that has been tested extensively and is reasonably priced is at `www.jtl.net`. (The Linux minimum service is all you need.)

If you want to install PHP on your computer do the following:

- **Windows only:** Go to `http://windows.php.net/download` and download the latest stable version of PHP5. (You'll find "What version do I choose?" in the left column to help you choose what you need for your system.) You'll also need to install an Apache server; you can get one free from www.apache.org.
- **Macintosh only:** Go to `http://foundationphp.com/tutorials/php_leopard.php` and follow the instructions for accessing the PHP on your system. (Be *very* careful because you're going to be using the built-in Terminal in your Mac and you'll be changing some key files.) This Web site shows you how to set up both PHP and your built-in Apache server.
- **The easiest method for all users:** If you want to download and install everything at once (PHP, Apache server, and a MySQL database) for your Mac go to `www.mamp.info/en/index.html` and for Windows go to `www.wampserver.com/en`. This is the easiest way to set up an actual database on your computer.

Setting up PHP and Apache can be awkward, but once it's set up, you don't have to do it again. If you use the all-in-one method (the last one listed above), you can get the MySQL server with which you can set up a database on your computer.

TESTING PHP

Once you have your system set up, whether it's on your computer or a hosting service, enter the following program and test it:

```
<!DOCTYPE HTML>
<html>
<head>
<?php
    print phpinfo();
?>
<meta http-equiv="Content-Type" content="text/html; charset=UTF-8">
<title>Test PHP</title>
</head>
<body>
</body>
</html>
```

Save the program as `First.php` and place the file in your Apache root folder. For example, the following path is a typical one for Windows: `c:/Program File/apache Groub/apache/htdocs/php`. The added folder, php, is where to put your `First.php`. On a Mac, using the built-in PHP, the path is `Macintosh HD/Library/WebServer/Documents/php/First.php`.

Next, open a browser and type in `http://localhost/php/First.php` and press Enter or Return. Unlike a regular Web page, you have to call the file from a browser. You can't just double-click it on the desktop — `localhost` is the server's name that it runs on. Figure 16-2 shows what you'll see if everything is installed correctly.

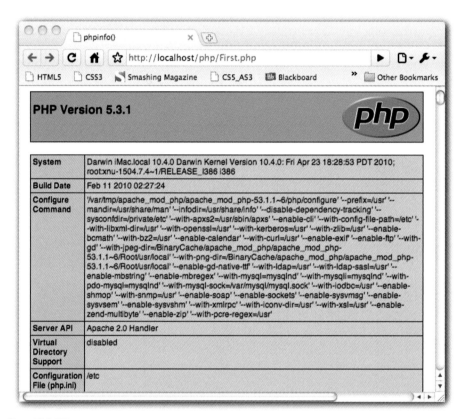

Figure 16-2: PHP test page.

Your installed version may be different, but that information tells you that PHP is installed on your system and ready to go.

PHP BASICS

Before getting to something practical, the first few steps describe some basic syntaxes and operations of PHP. PHP has many unique features, but it's very much like JavaScript with a slightly different set of symbols. The most important fundamentals begin with PHP "catching" data sent from the client. In order to emphasize the difference between client-side and server-side operations, the PHP code will be divorced from an HTML5 wrapper.

When you enter data into an HTML5 form and click the Submit button, the form data are sent to the server. In this first example, the name and e-mail will be sent from the client-side HTML5 program to the server-side PHP program, and it'll return HTML to the client. If you have a remote sever — a hosting service — be sure to include the full URL of the PHP file. This example assumes a localhost with both the HTML5 and PHP file in the same directory, but that's just to make it simpler. The following HTML5 page (SendData.html in this chapter's folder at www.wiley.com/go/smashinghtml5) will send the data.

```
<!DOCTYPE HTML>
<html>
<head>
<script type="text/javascript">
SendMaster=new Object();
SendMaster.eLert=function()
{
     alert("Oops! Seems to be a little boo-boo in the e-mail format.");
}
</script>
<style type="text/css">
body {
     font-family:Verdana, Arial, Helvetica, sans-serif;
     color:#336600;
     font-size:14px;
     background-color:#FFCC33;
}
</style>
<meta http-equiv="Content-Type" content="text/html; charset=iso-8859-1" />
<title>Data Sender</title>
</head>
<body>
<form action="formCatcher.php" method="post">
  <fieldset>
    <legend>Send Name and Email to PHP</legend>
    <input size=20 name="formName" placeholder="Enter Name">
    <p/>
    <input type=email size=32 NAME="formEmail" placeholder="Enter Name"
  onInvalid="SendMaster.eLert()" >
     <p />
  </fieldset>
  <input type="submit" name="sender" value="Send" >
</form>
</body>
</html>
```

The script includes both a text type and email type input form. (If no type of form is assigned, it defaults to a text type.) An important detail to note is that the Submit button is given a name (sender) that is used by the PHP script to determined whether the data from this form has been sent.

THE POST CATCHER

On the PHP side that catches the data, the `$_POST` array expects the name of the form. Two variables are first declared — `$name` and `$email`. Variables in PHP have a dollar-sign (`$`) prefix. However, before the PHP program attempts to assign the variable with data from the `$_POST` array, a good practice is to check the `isset()` function that checks to see if the Submit button (named `sender`) has sent the data. (The following code is in `formCatcher. php` in this chapter's folder at `www.wiley.com/go/smashinghtml5`.)

```php
<?php
//Catch HTML5 Data
$name;
$email;
if(isset($_POST['sender']))
{
    $name=$_POST["formName"];
    $email=$_POST["formEmail"];
}
print "$name's email address is $email";
?>
```

Formatting the output using the `print` statement combines the variables and text in a single set of double quotes. Within quotation marks, PHP still recognizes variables because the dollar sign (`$`) prefix tells the interpreter that, even within quotes, the word is a variable. Most other languages require concatenation when joining variables and literals. Figure 16-3 shows both the form as filled and the output generated by PHP. (Note the `localhost` address in the URL window for both the top and bottom panels.)

That's a simple program, but it does show how PHP passes data from HTML5 to PHP. You'll also find a very interesting result in the e-mail window when you type in something that's not in e-mail format. You'll find that it isn't passed to the PHP module. Instead, it uses the new HTML5 structure — the e-mail input format — and it acts like a data input validator that doesn't tell the user that she's messed up.

DATA VALIDATION

In order to help users, the HTML5 portion of the application uses an error catcher routine and informs users that they've made an error in the two parts of the Web page. First, the e-mail form includes an error handler:

```
<input type=email size=32 NAME="formEmail" placeholder="Enter Name"
  onInvalid="SendMaster.eLert()">
```

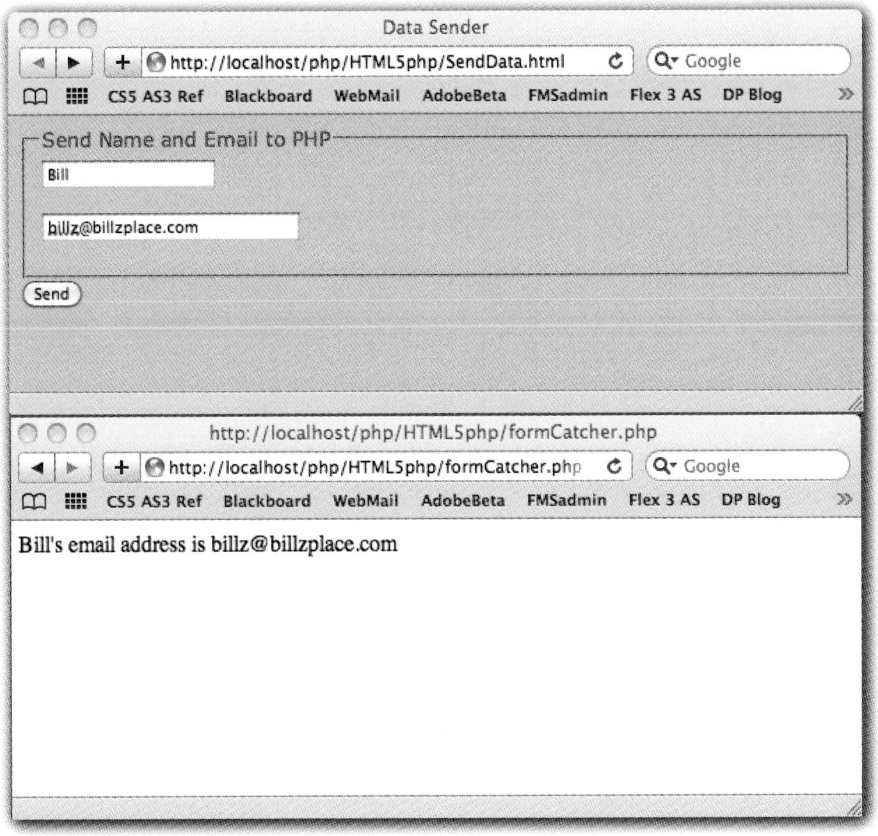

Figure 16-3: Data entry and data output.

Second, the JavaScript routine in the `<head>` of the page triggers an alert message:

```
SendMaster=new Object();
SendMaster.eLert=function()
{
    alert("Oops! Seems to be a little boo-boo in the e-mail format.");
}
```

You might want to note two important features about the coding:

- **It uses** `onInvalid` **instead of** `onError`. The `onError` event handler is so commonly used for any kind of error that you might assume it would work here as well, but only `onInvalid` works in this case.
- **The error-catching routine is in the** `<input>` *e-mail* **instead of the** `<input>` *submit* **tag.** Because the error occurs on clicking the Submit button, it would seem that the error handling would be in the Submit button tag, but it's not. Figure 16-4 shows the error message and the error that caused it — note the hand cursor on the sent (Submit) button.

Figure 16-4: Invalid entry caught in the e-mail format.

The `value` attribute of the Submit button should be named anything but "Submit" as a good interactive design practice. That's why its value is set to `Send`. (No wants to submit.) Also, the message isn't one of those hysterical gasps like "FATAL ERROR! E-mail format illegal!" Some users find such messages disconcerting. Also, they're inaccurate — no one died or was arrested. It was just a boo-boo.

BASIC PHP PROGRAM STRUCTURES

In this short introduction to PHP, you still can learn enough to make a practical application. However, first, you'll want to learn some of the basic structures of PHP. If you know JavaScript or some other scripting or programming languages, the structures will be familiar. PHP does have its idiosyncrasies, though, and many readers are unfamiliar with programming, so this discussion is basic and focused.

TEMPORARY DATA STORAGE

All languages include a certain way of storing data temporarily in containers called variables, constants, or some kind of object such as an array. Some languages are strongly typed and others are weakly typed. Java, C#, and ActionScript 3.0 are all strongly typed. That means that you have to decide on a certain data type and assign that data type to your storage. For example, an ActionScript 3.0 variable is declared as:

```
var userName:String="SoSueMe";
```

That means you only can assign string data types to the variable, `username`. If you assign it a number, Boolean, or nonstring function, it throws an error.

PHP is like JavaScript. If you assign the PHP variable,

```
$userName ="SoSueMe";
```

you can change it to any other data type or expressions such as,

```
$userName =55;
$userName =true;
$userName =(15 * 3);
```

Weakly typed languages have certain advantages and disadvantages, but they tend to be easier to learn initially.

Variables

As mentioned earlier in this chapter, all variable labels begin with a dollar sign ($). They can be placed in other strings and recognized regardless of data type. Try out the following (variableInString.php in this chapter's folder at www.wiley.com/go/smashinghtml5):

```
<?php
$ram = "dynamic random access memory";
$speed ="much GHz in";
$money= 2;
$truism ="You can't have too much $ram or too $speed a processor. (That will be
  $money cents for the advice.)";
print $truism;
?>
```

When you test that code, you'll see the following output:

```
You can't have too much dynamic random access memory or too much GHz in a processor.
  (That will be 2 cents for the advice.)
```

In most other languages, you would have to use concatenation.

Constants

Constants are like variables in PHP except they do not change in value. They're assigned values in a much different way than variables are, and they're case-sensitive. By convention (and good practice), they're in all caps (LIKE_THIS). The basic assignment format is:

```
define("CONSTANT_NAME", "value");
```

Try the following little script (constants.php in this chapter's folder at www.wiley.com/go/smashinghtml5), to get an idea of how they work:

```
<?php
define("FRED", "Fred J. Jones ");
define("MONEY", 200);
define("BUCKS", "$");
echo FRED , " donated " , BUCKS , MONEY , " to charity.";
?>
```

333

The output for that little script is:

```
Fred J. Jones donated $200 to charity.
```

As you can see by putting the dollar sign character ($) into a constant, you can use it with financial expressions and it won't be mistaken for a variable. By the way, you can use either echo or print (as well as other statements) in PHP to send output to the screen.

Arrays

An array is an object that holds several values. It's like a container on a container ship where different objects are stored — dolls from China, car parts from Detroit, computers from Japan, and corn from Iowa. They work just as arrays do in JavaScript, but they're configured a bit differently. (See Chapter 12 for more on arrays.)

Arrays are named like variables except they're assigned array objects. For setting up an array, you can use one of two basic formats. The preferred format works like an associative array. Instead of identifying an array element with a number, it's given a key with a value — a key-value pair. Here's the general format for setting up an associative array:

```
$associate = array("key1" => "value1","key2" => "value2");
```

The other kind of array has a numeric key. Most typically, it's set up by listing the array elements in the following format:

```
$numeric=array("el0","el1","el2",3, true);
```

However, it can be set up using the key=>value method as well:

```
$assoNum = array(0 => "value1",1 => "value2",1 => "value2");
```

The following little script (array.php in this chapter's folder at www.wiley.com/go/smashinghtml5), shows several different combinations you can see:

```php
<?php
$associate = array("key1" => "value1","key2" => "value2","keyEtc" => "valueEtc");
$boxCar=array("tools","oil drum","cow",7, false, "computer parts");
$mixedBag=array(1=>"first",2=>"second","third"=>3,4=>4);
echo $associate["key2"] . "<br>";
echo $associate["keyEtc"] . "<br>";
echo $boxCar[5] . "<br>";
echo $boxCar[0] . "<br>";
echo $mixedBag[2],$mixedBag["third"];
?>
```

You'll see the following output:

```
value2
valueEtc
computer parts
tools
second3
```

Arrays are important in PHP because database data are often loaded into an array for output.

Objects and properties

Objects in PHP are based on user classes — there's no `Object()` object like there is in JavaScript. Making a class is like creating an object with all the variables, arrays, constants, and functions you like in one place. Here are the basics of creating a class, adding properties, and adding methods in this example (`PropMethod.php` in this chapter's folder at www. wiley.com/go/smashinghtml5):

```php
<?php
    class PropMethod
    {
        private $propString="I work well with HTML5";
        private $propNum=2044;
        private $propBool=true;
        public function showString()
        {
            echo $this->propString, "<br>";
        }
        public function showNum()
        {
            echo $this->propNum, "<br>";
        }
        public function showBool()
        {
            echo $this->propBool;
        }
    }
$testPM=new PropMethod();
echo $testPM->showString();
echo $testPM->showNum();
echo $testPM->showBool();
?>
```

The output for that little class is:

```
I work well with HTML5
2044
1
```

335

Everything but the 1 was probably expected. Some languages will treat Booleans as either a true/false or 1/0 pairs. So true + true = 2, and true * false = 0.

The `$testPM` object is the object, and it works just like every other object in other languages. In JavaScript, though, the object and property are separated by dots (.) while in PHP, they're separated by arrows (->). The following are equivalent:

```
myObject.myProp=20; //JavaScript
myObject->myProp=20; //PHP
```

You'll find other differences, but the similarities are far more numerous between PHP and JavaScript.

KEY PHP OPERATORS

Like all Web languages, PHP has operators, and a full listing of them can be found in the official PHP manual at `http://us.php.net/manual/en/language.operators.php`. Here, just a few that will be used in the program to make an email application, and some others are unique in other ways. So while you'll have to depend on the manual for all PHP operators, the one examined in the next few sections will have you up and running.

Assignment

To assign a value to a variable or object, the equal sign (=) serves as the assignment operator. Compound PHP operators assign the value of the current variable plus, minus, multiplied by, or divided by the assigned value. The following example (`assignment.php` in this chapter's folder at `www.wiley.com/go/smashinghtml5`), shows the key uses of assignment operators:

```php
<?php
$sampleNum=20;
$sampleString="Hurricane";
$sampleNum += 50;
$sampleString .= " is coming.";
echo $sampleNum,"<br>";
$sampleNum *= 2;
echo $sampleNum,"<br>";
$sampleNum /= 4;
echo $sampleNum,"<br>";
echo $sampleString;
?>
```

Before you look at the outcome, see if you can predict what they'll be:

```
70
140
35
Hurricane is coming.
```

One of the unique operators in PHP is the use of the dot (.) for concatenation. A compound operator joins two operators into one for easier coding, and the . = compound operator takes the left value and joins it with the right value. Another way of looking at it is that it assigns its current value and the value assigned to it to make a third value, which becomes the variable's new value.

Arithmetic

The arithmetic operators are fairly standard compared to other programming languages. The main ones include

- + (addition)
- − (subtraction and negation)
- / (division)
- * (multiplication)
- % (modulo)

About the only one that anyone has problems with is modulo (%). It refers to any remainders of whole numbers after division. However, they can be handy. For example, the following little program (modulo.php in this chapter's folder at www.wiley.com/go/smashinghtml5), demonstrates how it can be used with a Boolean:

```php
<?php
for ($count = 1; $count <= 12; $count++) {
    $valid = $count % 2;
    if ($valid)
    {
        echo $count, " is odd<br>";
    }
    else
    {
        echo $count, " is even<br>";
    }
}
?>
```

The program iterates through a series of numbers divided by 2. Even numbers divided by 2 return 0 and odd numbers return 1 — the values Booleans recognize as false and true, respectively. The if() statement is looking for a true or false and will accept ones and zeros as Booleans. When sending out alternating backgrounds in table data coming from a database, the modulo operator is used to switch colors back and forth using the trick of dividing record numbers by 2 and using the remainder (modulo) as a Boolean.

MAKING AN E-MAIL APPLICATION

After all the work done with forms and different types of input in HTML5, you'll find that with a little PHP you can make e-mail forms with which users can send queries. The first form will be very simple and provide users with a comment section they can use for your Web page.

The basics of making an e-mail application center around the `mail()` function in PHP. The `mail()` function expects three or four parameters. In the first e-mail application, only the first three are used.

A SIMPLE E-MAIL APPLICATION

The first thing you want to do in an e-mail application is set up the HTML5 portion of your HTML5-PHP pair to provide a clear entry for users. Using the validation checking built into some of the input forms (`onInvalid`), you can prevent users from inadvertently sending an e-mail, phone number, or URL or other form data that are incorrectly formatted. So, this first HTML5 e-mailer will (again) use the e-mail input form and use the `onInvalid` event handler. The following program (`EZmailer.html` in this chapter's folder at `www.wiley.com/go/smashinghtml5`), should be fairly familiar.

```
<!DOCTYPE HTML>
<html>
<head>
<script type="text/javascript">
MailMaster=new Object();
MailMaster.eMess=function()
{
    alert("Hmmmm... It seems that the e-mail entry has something out of sort. . . .
 Please take a look at it and see if you can fix it up.")
}

</script>
<style type="text/css">
/*DDDCC5,958976,611427,1D2326,6A6A61 */
body {
    background-color:#DDDCC5;
    color:#1D2326;
    font-family:Verdana, Geneva, sans-serif;
}
h2 {
    background-color:#958976;
    color:#DDDCC5;
    text-align:center;
    font-family:"Arial Black", Verdana, Arial;
}
h3 {
    color:#611427;
}
fieldset {
    color:#6A6A61;
}
</style>
```

```
<meta http-equiv="Content-Type" content="text/html; charset=UTF-8">
<title>Simple E-Mail</title>
</head>
<body>
<article>
  <header>
    <h2>Mailer</h2>
  </header>
  <section>
    <header>
      <h3>Fill in the form and send us your questions, ideas, and rants.</h3>
    </header>
    <form action="mailer1.php" method="post">
      <input name=userName>
       Please enter your name.<br>
      <input name=mailNow type=email onInvalid="MailMaster.eMess()">
        Enter e-mail address to send reply.<br>
      <input name=subject>  What subject would you like to address?<br>
      <fieldset>
        <legend>Comments</legend>
        <textarea name=talk cols=70 rows=15 ></textarea>
      </fieldset>
      <input type=submit name=sender value="Send email">
    </form>
  </section>
</article>
</body>
</html>
```

One of the key lines in the HTML5 script is the action in the form that sends the information to PHP for processing:

```
<form action="mailer1.php" method="post">
```

The form was not given a name because, for this application, we didn't need one. However, adding a name to the form is generally a good practice, and if it's needed, it should be available.

All the name attributes in the input elements are crucial. Each name in the input element tags is passed to PHP as an array element in the $_POST array. The element is then passed to a variable that is used in the e-mail that is sent to a recipient — typically, the Web site owner. In this case, that's you. Figure 16-5 shows the input page and the form data that will be sent to the PHP program for server-side processing.

As soon as the user clicks the Send E-Mail button, he receives a notice:

```
Your e-mail has been sent to waz@wazooHome.net. Thank you for your interest in Wazoo
  Web Site Design and Development.
```

To see how that happened, we'll have to look at the PHP portion of the application.

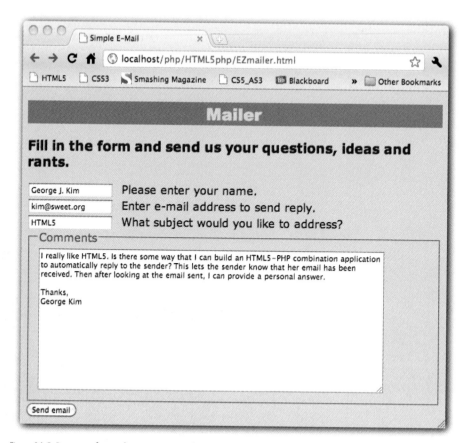

Figure 16-5: Data entry form to be sent as an e-mail.

PHP CATCH AND SEND

Next, a PHP program catches the data sent from the HTML5 and sends it to the intended recipient, the business owner. First, take a look at the PHP code in `mailer1.php` (available in this chapter's folder at `www.wiley.com/go/smashinghtml5`). Then, you can see how the e-mail is sent.

```php
<?php
$name;
$email;
$comments;
$subject;
$eBiz="waz@wazooHome.net";
if(isset($_POST['sender']))
{
    $name=$_POST["userName"];
    $email=$_POST["mailNow"];
    $comments=$_POST["talk"];
    $subject=$_POST["subject"];
```

```
}
$comments .= "\r\r\r\nFrom-> $name : Send reply to: $email";
mail($eBiz,$subject,$comments);
echo "Your e-mail has been sent to $eBiz. Thank you for your interest in Wazoo Web
  Site Design and Development.";
?>
```

In looking at the PHP code, you can see it doesn't take much. First, the four chunks of data from the HTML5 page are passed to four PHP variables:

- `$name`
- `$email`
- `$comments`
- `$subject`

Next, the `$comments` variable is concatenated with information about the sender's name and e-mail address. Then, using the `mail()` function, the program uses the following line to send everything to the Web site owner:

```
mail($eBiz,$subject,$comments);
```

Finally, a simple message is sent to the user who sent the e-mail. Figure 16-6 shows the e-mail received by Wazoo Web Site Design and Development.

Figure 16-6: E-mail generated by PHP code and HTML5.

By having an automatic e-mail page on your site, you (or your clients) can generate far more business. The key to using some kind of Web-generated e-mail is to make it easy for the user to send an e-mail and generate more business for the site.

ADDING A HEADER AND AUTO-REPLY IN PHP

As was hinted in the fictitious e-mail used in the example, it would be nice to have an automatic e-mail reply to users when they send an e-mail. Again, using the `mail()` function in PHP, all you have to do is add a second mailer. Using the `$name` variable and `$email`, you can personalize a reply. Additionally, you can add a header to the e-mail that is sent to the user and to the Web site owner.

First, the `mail()` function requires a fourth parameter. Breaking down the four parameters, you can lay out the following:

- Recipient (e-mail address)
- Subject (what is placed in the subject line)
- Content (the body of the message)
- Header (the From and Reply To addresses)

In the initial example, the From and Reply To address was concatenated to the content. However, using the header parameter, you can let the header take care of it.

This next listing (`mailer2.php` in this chapter's folder at `www.wiley.com/go/ smashinghtml5`), shows the same program with the added header and the auto-reply. Very little has been added, and much has been enhanced.

```php
<?php
$name;
$email;
$comments;
$subject;
$eBiz="waz@wazoo.net";
if(isset($_POST['sender']))
{
    $name=$_POST["userName"];
    $email=$_POST["mailNow"];
    $comments=$_POST["talk"];
    $subject=$_POST["subject"];
}
$headers = "From-> $name :\r\n Send reply to: $email";
$reply="Dear $name , \r\n Thank you for sending us your comments. We at Wazoo Web
  Site Design and Development believe that customer care is an essential of doing
  business—not an optional service.\r\n";
$reply .= "As soon as we can review your comments, one of our associates will get
  back to you.";
$reply .="\r\n Sincerely, Phillip Pickle,\r\n President, WWDD";
mail($email,"Thank you for your thoughts",$reply);
mail($eBiz,$subject,$comments,$headers);
echo "Your e-mail has been sent to $eBiz. Thank you for your interest in Wazoo Web
  Site Design and Development.";
?>
```

The $headers variable adds the header material that had been concatenated to the content. A new variable, $reply, provides the text for automatically replying to the sender. In this way, users get immediate feedback. Figure 16-7 shows what the auto-reply looks like to the recipient.

Figure 16-7: Auto-reply e-mail.

The user sees that his name is in the header, and the subject line is based on what the user just sent. Even though the user probably realizes that it's an auto-generated reply, he likes the fact that a Web development company can do that for his business.

The addition of the header makes it easier to add a header where you want it. In the first example, the header was really a footer at the end of the message. This time, it's where it belongs at the top of the e-mail, as shown in Figure 16-8.

Figure 16-8: A header added to an e-mail.

As you can see in Figure 16-8, the header is at the top of the e-mail. Also, in all the examples, PHP did an excellent job of keeping the format that was originally entered in the comment box in the HTML5 input form.

TAKE THE WHEEL

One of the points made repeatedly throughout the book is to make your page easy to use. The e-mail form used in this chapter was very simple, but what about some information that the Web site owner wanted to know? A comment form is open-ended and is a valuable tool to communicate with your users. However, sometimes you or your client needs very specific information. This challenge calls for a few changes in the e-mail program to include the following:

- Four radio buttons requesting information about user's type of business
- Four check boxes requesting information about the services the user was interested in using

That may not look like much of a challenge, but if you can make data entry easy for users and access that information in PHP, then you have some very powerful tools at your beck and call.

Index